"Rebel Spirit" is the s
wholeness. Dealing wit
weaves the stages and challenges of life into a captivating read. Inspiring and heartfelt. I couldn't put it down."   Cherlita

I love this book! It is a treat to read this journey which shares such honesty and vulnerability. It is inspiring and has motivated me to learn to live by my guides and to TRUST. I highly recommend this book for people who want to remember the magic of following their own heart and listening to their own guidance."   Rain

"My daughter and I are reading your book out loud together. We're hooked! I am sure it will touch many many people!"   Sitara

"Rebel Spirit was moving and inspiring!   Jessica

"Rebel Spirit is written with such raw honesty and vulnerability. It touches upon many faces of being human and then magically has a dose of humor just when it's needed! I couldn't put it down." Christine

"I read this in just a few days. I found I just didn't want to put it down. I could relate to the invisibility so deeply. This book gives me hope that I can have a truly much richer life. Spread my wings..."   Mari

"Loving your book! Reading it slow because I don't want it to end. But then it dawned on me that I will just read it again."   Carol

"I'm so glad this beautiful story found its way into my hands and heart. I finished it in a matter of days although it felt like years. As I was getting to the end I was pondering the beginning of the book and thinking "that was so long ago". There were so many parts I identified with and felt like it could have been written about myself. Thanks to the author for sharing this story!"   Sarah

rebel SPIRIT

RHEA MACERIS

A spiritual journey inspired by true events.

Siblings

Friends

Spirit Guides

Creativity

Girl Scouts

Camping

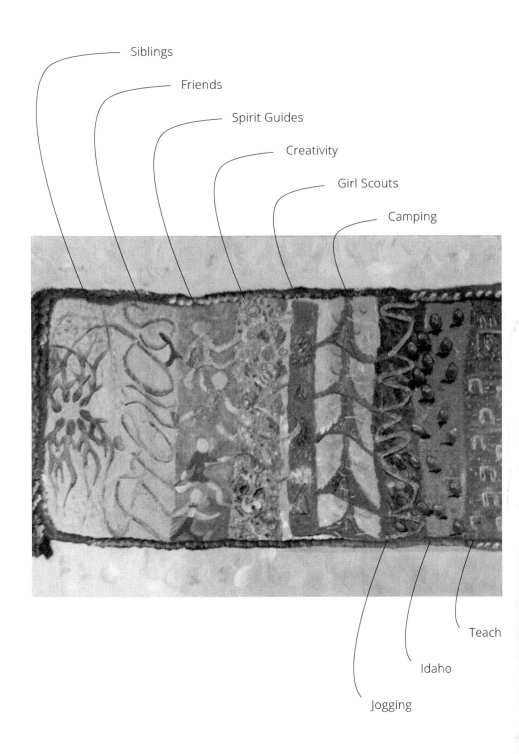

Teach

Idaho

Jogging

Sedona

California

Vashon Island

Art Classes

Seattle

Colorado

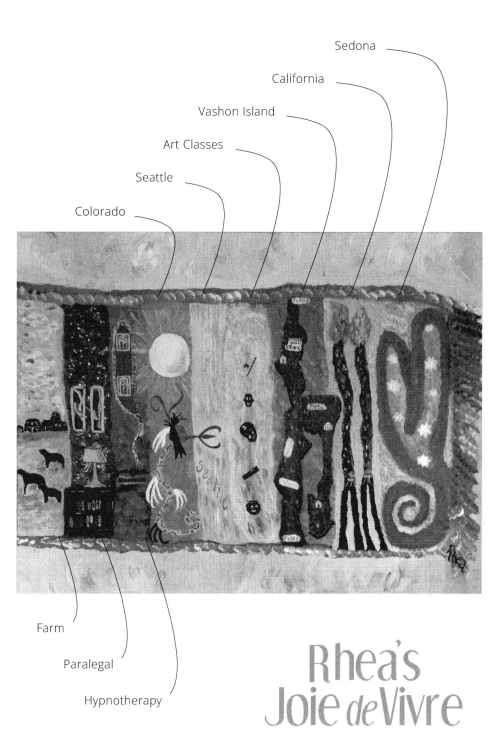

Farm

Paralegal

Hypnotherapy

Rhea's
Joie de Vivre

— *Pregnant Bed*

Dear Radiant Reader,

I wrote this abstract story much like I paint. I invite the words, ideas, and meanings to flow from deep within me, from my magical inner world. In this process, I can get lost in my creativity. Just as my abstract paintings need colors, textures and a variety of diverse strokes to embellish them and bring them into fruition, so does my story's conception. It needs the same loving patience, attention and nurturing. As I am creating from my inner place, I begin to see and feel sensations I've never experienced before, thus widening my perspective. Through my writing, I've learned my heart and soul know far more than all the information I've collected in my brain. I've learned to trust the depth and sincerity of the love I feel in my heart.

Recently I read that special motion cameras observed an energy field leaving the human body after death. This means life continues on without our physical form. This idea begs the question, could this frequency leaving our body after death, be who we truly are? And everything around us is merely an illusion?

I believe, after working with nearly a thousand clients, this energy field, call it soul, spirit, jewels or whatever you wish, is patiently awaiting our recognition of it. I have found a way to connect with my energy field and write, paint and ideally create my life from this place. Also, I have watched my clients meet and connect with their own energy field. How empowering and beautiful it is each and every time they meet their soul.

This story is my perspective of my illusion, dancing with my freedom of expression and creativity.

Enjoy my evolutionary illusion!

Why I dream is a captivating question. Is it memory consolidation, emotional regulation or a threat simulation? Is it imagination at play? It seems whatever I am exposed to during the daytime can have an impact on my dreams at night. Despite the uncertainty, I adore my dreamtime. It's as if my thoughts have a pleasant way of slipping through their collars and running free.

I am flying through the air while experiencing the ultimate freedom of my graceful movements. Cruising with the feeling of lightness and boundlessness, I am able to fly anywhere I wish. What an adventure it is to soar above the treetops, unencumbered, gliding on the wind. With grace, I maneuver through the vast array of puffy clouds as if this is my natural mode of transportation. I am somewhat aware I am dreaming and can stay entangled in my form of aerial dancing or come back. I'm choosing to remain in my stellar flying excursion, as I gaze down at the ocean's blue green depths of mystery, reflecting its stunning brilliance back at me. I hear a sound, a rhythmic noise which seems familiar, yet very far away. Swish, swish through the air, I spread my arms fully to turn right and left, as if a delicate bird at flight.

The rest of my body flowing in alignment, as exhilaration accompanies each inhalation of fresh air. Gazing across the sky, I notice a spark of bright light fly past me, as if longing for my undivided attention. What could this light be? What could move faster than I'm flying?

My curiosity about the bright light is interrupted, as I hear the sound yet again, a bit closer this time. My consciousness is being triggered, while I am becoming more aware of this vague sound. My flying body is resonating with its comforting vibration, even though the sound still seems far removed. It's musical, yes it's the cadence of rhythmic drumming. Coming into consciousness a bit, I stretch my body and notice our quirky cat, Ninja is snuggled right between my legs. Ninja stays entrenched having grown accustomed to my movements of the night. I ponder this mysterious drumming in my world. Is it trying to tell me something? Is it urging me to snap out of my dreamworld?

I choose my flying world, as I roll over in my egyptian sheets, with a smile perched on my lips. I attempt to drift back to my feel good dream, as I realize the mysterious sound is my phone. This idea has the power to awaken me a bit.

As I straighten my legs again, this time with determination to wake up, Ninja hurdles into the air, and lands on Merrick's bare torso. Between the constant sojourn of sound and this cat dance of sorts, it's becoming very apparent—it's time to take a hiatus from my flying world and my wonderment of the bright light.

Coming into consciousness, I open my left eye and see a blurry 4:00 am on the clock across the room perched on the Scandinavian dresser. Opening my other eye, I begin to take in my subtle surroundings, the full moon's reflection dancing on my otherwise dark wall, the welcoming aroma of coconut oil and the feel of my cutie's warmth next to me.

I'm wondering, who would be calling at this time of night? This question triggers my mind to awaken fully as only important calls are made in the wee hours of the morning. I stretch my right arm toward the bedside table and my finger lands perfectly on the button of my speaker phone. I perceive a shaky voice echoing in the room.

"Rhea...Rhea are you awake?" There is much panic in her voice.

"Rooney?"

"Yes, it's me."

"Are you OK?"

"Yes, uh, Rhea?"

"What?"

"What I'm about to tell you isn't easy for me."

"What is it Rooney?" says Merrick.

"Well, I have some sad news to tell you both." Pause. "Cameron was in a terrible car accident this morning."

I readily receive Merrick's comforting hand, as he reaches across the bed, embracing my shaky one, as I have just fainted inside. Gone is the light flying feeling from only a moment ago, replaced by a sudden heaviness.

"What?" I find my lips, "what happened?"

"Cameron died on his drive to work. At least it was fast and apparently, he died on impact."

My mind is fully awakened by these words and I realize I need to sit up in bed, acknowledging much adrenaline moving within me. Ninja jumps off the bed and shares his humorous cat version of talking, thinking it's time for him to eat and go outside to play.

"Died on impact." Did Roon say this sentence again or is it my mind simply echoing the potency of these three little words?

We had just seen Rooney in California, along with the rest of my family. They had been wishing for a reunion for quite some time. This is quite a request given we have many people in our immediate family, including siblings, their significant others and grandchildren.

I still don't know the exact amount as boyfriends and girlfriends of the nieces and nephews can fluctuate depending on the time of day. All of us committed to gathering in the beauty of La Jolla, California.

My friends own a resort right on the Pacific. Swimming, surfing, biking, jogging, and even a wild and crazy charades expedition graced our week-end. All the participants were required to take a shot of homemade brew before their turn. Did I mention some of the family members were getting smashed? Becoming carefree as kids again, I realize how much I missed my buddies, my family.

These are a few of the many memories I carried from our reunion. After all we've been through, I think I love them. The question remains, can I feel safe enough to actually open my heart to my big family?

"How is Naomi doing? Was she in the car?"

I remind Merrick that Naomi is Cameron's wife, realizing how difficult it is to remember everyone's names, having just met some of them for the first time at the reunion.

"Pretty much as you can imagine. Naomi has such a wise, spiritual side to her accepting his sudden passage and yet she's still in shock," Rooney comments.

"And how about Mason? Have they told her yet?" My heart skips a beat as I think about his beautifully wise daughter, my niece, who I had the pleasure of having over for sleepovers when she was young. She is very special to me and will always be in my heart. Yet the sadness seeps in again, knowing what I witnessed with her.

"Yes, she knows and is driving home as we speak."

"How are you Rooney?" Merrick asks.

I consider how tight Rooney is with Cameron. I've never been close to Cameron, but the stinging pain is still vying for my attention, mixed with an eerie sense of relief.

"I am hanging in there," she whispers.

Rooney's otherwise strong and humorous personality, has subsided temporarily.

"How's Mom? I mean her first child to die. Just, Wow."

"I haven't spoken with her yet, but I hear she's in a state of shock as well. We really aren't prepared for death in our society, are we? I thought I was until this situation. It's final, you know?"

"Or is it? Final I mean?" I need to put this idea out there.

Rooney knows the part of me that is open minded, as she and I have had many discussions on this topic. And she is aware of all the years of sessions I've shared with my Clients, including regression sessions, which reminds us there is much more than this lifetime.

"Roon, can I go off topic a bit?"

"Sure, Rhea."

"I so enjoyed seeing you and the family at the reunion. I'd been away from everyone for so long, it was great for my heart and soul. So thank you for being you."

"Aw, you're sweet."

"I told Merrick and Tatum they would love you as well."

"Thanks Rhea, it's mutual. I loved interacting with Tatum, your adorable son."

The rest of the conversation between Rooney and me, revolved around making the promise to keep in touch. It seems when one family member dies, the other ones become that much more special and important to each other.

"Take care and thanks for calling," pipes in Merrick.

"Talk soon Roon. Love You."

I appreciate Rooney and I are at the 'I love you stage' again.

I click my phone's button off, thus ending my life as I know it.

Merrick comes over to me for a hug and his embrace feels different somehow. Or is it me? Of course, my heart is hurting at the moment for what could have been. The reality of Cameron's death brings up many emotions for me. I am so full, I have trouble identifying how I'm feeling. I realize it's going to take a bit of time to process this shift in my reality, especially, when the person who passed is Cameron and the family secret is still lingering.

Reflecting back to the reunion, I was so perplexed how difficult it was for me to talk to Cameron, as I could actually feel myself emotionally becoming a little girl again. All I wanted to do was to run away, needing to protect her, wanting to protect myself.

Cameron and I tried to converse, however, I couldn't muster up the courage to speak to him about anything with any substance, as if it might lead to the inevitable. As I watched him from across the large living room, large enough to hold all of the family, I noticed how Cameron carried his stiff body. Is it guilt he is carrying around? Does he regret what he did? Now I'll never know the answer to these questions.

It's been challenging, however I have chosen to forgive him so I could remove all of the "victimhood" from my toxic system that has had the power to create numerous sleepless nights of doubting and many days of questioning myself. I have done my best to release any judgments I have been carrying from Cameron's actions.

I didn't have the opportunity to tell him I forgive him. I truly forgive you Cameron. I couldn't find the appropriate moment to tell him that I am OK, finally, I am really OK.

In the quaint neighborhood where I was birthed, all of the houses were at least three stories tall and so close to each other that I could hear my neighbor's regular progression of sneezes. Almost always a series of three, except on those rare occasions when one loud sneeze seemed to do the trick. Bless you dear neighbor, we all seemed to need some type of protection in this little ole town.

All of the cars on our narrow street were symmetrically parked on both sides of the cobblestone road like a perfect puzzle. Over time, the vehicles' size increased to match the amount of children being birthed to these proper parents who were from the world of 'we don't believe in birth control.' The many larger vehicles created a type of barrier to travelers and it became challenging to maneuver down our already narrow street. I remember when a firetruck had to carefully find its way through the haze of dim light, side swiping several of our neighbor's cars.

The cloudy skies seemed to reflect the struggling city life of Elefont, New Jersey. Downtown Elefont really wanted to be big. Oh, it so tried to be a thriving city. It was a "wanna be" city, just like I was a "wanna be" special. And as a result, Elefont never carried the comforts of home and nurturing for me, as it reflected one of my greatest fears, that I would never be someone special in the eyes of my family. It was as if I was attempting to survive in a foreign country while trying to communicate with this group of people known as my family. I didn't understand the language of this mysterious land and therefore, I never felt I truly belonged. My little self was insecure as a candle in the wind, never knowing who to trust when the rains came. And did it ever pour buckets of rain, especially in the spring and fall, as the skies seemed to favor hints of grayness for its primary clothing.

My family life was my greatest challenge and my greatest teacher. I am number three in our family of five children, coexisting with four other siblings. So being a middle child has allowed me to have many teachers, or rulers depending on how you look at it. Most of the time, I would become the observer, garnering my invisibility cloak which was created as a necessity for emotionally surviving. However, this version of hiding for protection could become lonely, as well.

My Mom carried quite a polarity bouncing back and forth between the demanding Captain who needed to try to control everything and the wounded little girl who didn't get to fulfill her dream of going to college. When she pleaded with her father over the breakfast table, all he said was, "Why do you need to go to college? All you're going to do is get married and raise kids."

This comment made my Mom pause with a spoonful of cereal halfway between the bowl and her mouth, dripping her mixture onto the porcelain kitchen table below. I do feel compassion for my Mom, for she truly can be a wise woman and also very sweet. I could only hope she would show up as my sweet Mom.

As a result of my grandpa's sexist words of wisdom, my Mom took her job of 'getting married' quite seriously. Right after my parents wedding, a tragic accident occurred. My Mom's sister and husband died suddenly in a car accident leaving their three year old son, Cameron, who was adopted by my parents. She birthed four more kids.

She later told me she had two miscarriages before I arrived. Could my soul have been the miscarriages? Was I aware of the challenges I would face and felt ill-equipped to enter this rather large, wobbly environment called "family"?

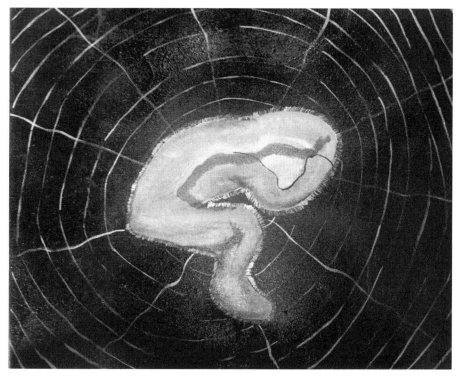

— *The Womb*

There's a tall, dark, handsome man in my life, affectionately known as my Dad, who is a complete stranger to me. He was the type of person who said very little, however, when he did speak everyone listened. He was a maritime engineer and a lover of the sea. One of his challenges, besides financially supporting a family of seven enthusiastic eaters was to return home after a long day of working to the world of "Wait Until Your Father Comes Home." He had to turn into 'the bad guy' as soon as he walked through the large, wooden door, on those days when we misbehaved. There seemed to be a lot of those type of days.

My parents' favorite form of punishment was to ground me. This type of punishment meant I could not leave our house for weeks at a time except to go to school and the necessary sojourns with them. After so much leisure time in my bedroom, the room I shared with my two sisters, Sarah and Muriel, I needed something to occupy my time by finding ways of entertaining myself. While lying in bed, starring at the cycling pattern of the ceiling fan, I began rubbing my off white, purple and pink ballerina bedspread so forcefully with my thumb and first finger that eventually my blanket, my other form of protection from the world, was whittled down to oblivion.

I found this form of movement allowed my imagination to run free of its boundaries and took me into a type of wonderland within. This became one of my favorite places, finding some form of escape from the frightening feelings within me being formed by the chaos surrounding me. Thus I would spend hours in my special trance place. Eventually, I began creating from this inner place. I took this artistic flow into my childlike world around me, in the form of awesome homemade plays, creating new rules for board games and ball games in our alley.

These plays, games and colorful adventures were created with my many neighborhood friends. Any place could become a stage; our big front porch, the sandbox allowed us to create intricate cities, or the neighbor's back yard. For our skits of choice, we designed costumes out of old material, blankets and colorful clothing, while applying any of our mom's makeup, we could find. It didn't matter where we were hanging out, my imagination found a way to get its air time through expression.

One of my favorite skits involved each of us turning into moving toys in a local department store. We were all some sort of wind up mechanical robots. Mine was of a boy and girl kissing. I was standing face to face with a boy and when they turned the key, we would project forward from our waist and touch our lips ever so lightly as if kissing without using our arms. It was laughable and fun.

This creative outlet had a way of saving me from the real world that I felt wanted to swallow me alive because I didn't know how to play the "societal" game the way I was supposed to. "You're not acting like a good Catholic girl," seemed to be my parent's favorite expression to lay on me. I never really knew what a good Catholic girl acts like however I was pretty sure I didn't want to go there. It seemed to be too rigid for me and my expressive side that wanted to explore life fully. Over time, after hearing this expression of disap-proval over and over again, it had deep ramifications and propelled me back into my dysfunctional cycle of not being good enough. This lead to my needing attention and then becoming the troublemaker, getting grounded and bringing out my imagination once again. Thank God for my alive imagination, for it truly saved me from my mind that began to believe the idea from my parents, "You're not a good Catholic girl."

Hello imagination; I can always carve out a little space for expres-sion, as I ride out the turbulence.

One cloudy day, when I was about four years old, I overheard my parents talking to our neighbors across the gray metal fence in our backyard. They were laughing as if justifying having yet another baby, "We thought our family was complete with two children and then Rhea arrived," producing more laughing. My little, sensitive mind interpreted this conversation as, "I wasn't really wanted and not a part of their ideal family." Ouch. This seemed to enhance the beginning of my sense of unworthiness.

My two younger sisters came to join our family. Muriel, wearing her cute personality like a magnet, seemed to capture my Dad's heart strings. This connection of theirs played havoc on my soul as well and, yeah, I have to admit I became a bit envious of their connection.

When Dad became the sports coach at our grade school, I became an avid runner to try and draw some of his attention. Dad and Muriel would talk and laugh together, eventually he became her personal coach, requiring them to spend even more time together. My beautiful Mom, showed irritation watching Dad's attention going to Muriel. So guess where my Mom's frustration went? I was swatted on my bum with a metal spatula for saying some 'snotty' remark, and this action left a nasty black and blue bruise. I showed it to my friend and somehow the sharing of my colorful tattoo story found its way back to my Mom. Oh boy, was she angry. She couldn't swat me again, so she just screamed and shook her arms and hands wildly in the air, "You're not a good Catholic girl," and of course, the inevitable grounding occurred.

As a spinoff of my 'so many siblings' dynamic and wanting more attention, I found the perfect solution. I became the teen rebel. I was excellent at playing the role of the troublemaker. At least then I could grab a moment of my Dad's focus by staying out all night, having large drinking parties while my parents were away, or a sleepover with friends on our large front porch, where we slipped away into the moonlight for some fun and adventure. And trust me, with my unworthiness running rampant and my need for more attention, this created the perfect storm of dysfunction. On one special occasion I had pushed my father too far. He proceeded to take me down into the basement and push me around and hit me. The topping was served with a big dose of 'grounding'. I didn't remember asking for the combo meal.

This wandering off into the cobblestone streets of Elefont served my need for diversity and provided an avenue for me to get lots of attention and support from others outside of my immediate family. Or was I truly running away from the person that was being created in this family environment, in our house of craziness? Being in the middle, I learned to fend for myself. It seemed when my invisibility cloak was on within my family dynamic, I needed to be more out there in my other life to get my need for love met and to find some kind of sense of balance, or I would shrink away to nothingness.

Imagine seven people living in one house with only one bathroom. In this open space of one loo, I can remember taking a bath with my two sisters, while my older brother was sitting on the toilet with a front row seat facing us splashing in the tub. All at the same time.

This invasion of privacy somehow became the norm, creating the perfect setup for incestuous situations lingering in the brick walls surrounding us. This was a typical night at our house until finally, a second bathroom was built when we were becoming too old to be walking in on each other while taking a bath. By then the precedence had been set.

— *Invisible*

My family lived approximately a fifteen minute drive from down-town Elefont, which had two major department stores, Rokos and Elk's Furnishings. For my seventh birthday, my mom took me on a bus ride to visit the downtown area and I was given a one dollar bill to buy anything I wanted. This was a lot of money to me, since I was never given any allowance as a child. The lack of allowance seemed to echo the idea that I wasn't worthy again. Double ouch. My parents couldn't afford the luxury of giving their children much money. I mean, having this many children is just not realistic for anyone to try and maneuver and they did their best with what they had.

The journey downtown could have been so special except I had already begun the inner questioning of what was my place in this family? Essentially, I began to wonder "who am I?" One of the most complex questions ever. As I wiggled on the seat next to my Mom, the big, electric bus echoed a void in my heart, a space that could not be filled by all the activity of the city. The movement of people, glaring lights and the general commotion and busyness of the city life, somehow inspired me to open up my heart to feel, if even for a moment. It found me wanting to pull those three little words out of my Mom's bright red shiny lips. I yearned to hear the words, "I love you" as if those words could form a life jacket around me, to save me from all the waves of confusion pounding within my little head. All of those emotional cuts, well they needed love to help them heal. Would my mom ever be able to say those words to me? My little heart wanted to hear them so desperately. Would she, could she reveal any real feelings for me? There must be something other than being judged, found guilty and punished. She couldn't listen, probably from the overwhelm of our large family. Could my Mom tell me she loved me or is her generous gift of spending one dollar on me the only gift of the day? Could this really be all there is? This girl's too young to be singing the blues.

I found the grace to keep myself from falling completely. I did manage to bring shining angel friends into my life. Their wisdom and insight reminded me to see more of myself beyond the many 'negative' labels I believed. One of these lovely souls came as a Savior for me; she arrived when we were still only children. Her name was Eva.

We became friends early in grade school. She seemed to understand me and my uniqueness, in a way that nobody else could. Once, when we were in fourth grade, we were playing a hand game, sitting knee to knee on the grass at the park and brightly colored butterflies were landing on her active shoulders. This allowed me to feel safe with Eva, just like the butterflies did.

In the fifth grade, Eva and I found ourselves looking into the bulging eyes of a bloody deer head, which was hanging in our friend, Selene's garage. It was dangling from the wooden rafters above us, spewing its remaining blood like a form of art on the dirty, oily garage floor below. I looked curiously into its deep set eyes and felt a chill go down my spine, as if the deer was looking into my soul.

Remember, we were in "huntingville" New Jersey, where every year was deer hunting season and an open invitation to hunt and kill Bambi. Apparently, Selene's dad was a hunter and the head was left after the rest of the deer's body had been butchered for venison consumption. As Selene proudly showed us the deer head, my well-oiled imagination saw it with a thick cord around its neck and hanging upside down on the door handle of a car. I shared my vivid idea and we agreed this would be a bit risky, yet fun, and after some deliberating we decided to take the deer plunge.

Discussing whose car to use for our dangling expedition, we chose one of our teachers, adoringly referred to as Mr. Krabs. Yes, I realize his name has many connotations and Mr. Krabs had a funny thing he did with his mouth: his lower lip would protrude outward when he finished saying certain words, exposing his upper teeth like a beaver. We tried imitating his facial peculiarity and it resulted in much laughter and knee-slapping delight. I have to admit, I learned how to make fun of others quite well having learned it from all my siblings. It seemed humor was a safe island to meet upon, where we could cover over any criticism with a smile.

Choosing Mr. Krabs car, which was right next to our large school, required some sneaky maneuvering because it was also across the street from the Nun's convent. These nuns enjoyed hitting our knuckles with a wooden ruler whenever we misbehaved. If their intention was to instill pain, it certainly proved beneficial.

Selene played the part of the lookout person, watching for any teachers, traffic, students, or curious nuns. When all was clear, she gave us the thumbs up and Eva and I began our masterful deed of tying the bloodied head to Mr. Krabs car. The driver's side of his car was facing the street, so we had to stand in the middle of the street to follow my vision of him arriving to put his key into the lock and seeing the deer head looking up at him.

We used a thick rope, also from Selene's garage, and attached it to the deer's neck and hung it on the door handle. The head was hovering down about a foot above the ground. Still bleeding, it produced an array of red lines tattooing his car with its primal eyes starring into the distance. As we were tying the last loop, making sure it was secure, a car was driving in our direction. Eva and I looked at each other in surprise and automatically made a barrier with our bodies in front of the head, blocking the view of our deer project from the driver. The car drove by slowly and stopped right in front of us, putting us between the bloody head and the driver's sight. It was a friend's dad and he wanted to know if we were okay. We smiled and said, yes, we are playing a game of hide-n-go-seek. Getting the hint, he winked at us and drove away without saying another word. Thank God he didn't see the trickles of blood accumulating on the ground behind our shaky feet.

An important thing I learned from being a troublemaker, was how to tell believable lies to cover my mischievous ways. Relieved we escaped this close call, we completed the last knot and then ran to wash our hands before our volleyball practice began across the street in the school's gymnasium.

Sister Gertrude, the tall, stern Principal at our school made her way into the gym with a serious look on her face. We were right in the middle of our volleyball practice with the fifth, sixth and seventh grade girls, and the volleyball almost hit her right in the head. I was laughing watching this hilarious dynamic, when all movement was halted as she walked right up to me, straightening her black and white veil.

"It was you, wasn't it?" she asked with her knowing eyes. I had quite the reputation for being a troublemaker at school. Getting in trouble worked so well at home to get some form of attention, some form of love, why not try what I had mastered at school as well.

"What?" I tried to act surprised.

"Mr. Krab's car!" she hollered.

"Yeah," I said, as my downcast eyes met the hard, shiny gym floor.

"Get to the office right now!" she yelled, "Who else was involved with this situation, Rhea?"

"No one," I said.

"Who else?" she screamed.

"Just me," I turned my back to her and slowly walked to the door closest to the office.

She followed me to the office. Silence surrounded our journey in the tall hallways, except for the echoing of our shoes on the hard tiled floor. I refused to tell her the names of any of my friends and I was prepared to take the heat. Me and my imagination joined forces again. Somehow along with my insecurities, I adopted the idea that everything is my fault. It seems once you're a troublemaker, this label penetrates to the soul.

In her large office, that reeked of bleach, Sister Gertrude wasn't too interested in hearing my story; she was more interested in punishing me, just like at home. How lovely! So I sat in the firm wooden chair across from her desk as she shook her arms and hands at me much like my mom.

"I don't understand how you could have turned out like this? I've known your older brother and sister and they have both been such perfect students. What happened to you?"

"I don't know," I mumbled avoiding eye contact.

"Rhea, look at me! You should be ashamed of yourself. Your mom and dad are such upstanding people in this community."

"I'm sorry." The words found my lips as if out of obligation.

"You will tell Mr. Krabs that you are sorry, also."

"Yep."

"What are we going to do with you?" echoed in the large office, "You're not acting like a good Catholic girl."

Oh Lord, my favorite sentiment yet again.

"I'm going to have to call your parents, you realize," she was finding more of a calm voice.

"Yes," I said, as if expecting this. Time to bring out my invisibility cloak before my parents arrived. I turned my dialogue inward as my finger began writing privately on my thigh:

OH DEAR

HERE I GO AGAIN

I'VE MESSED UP

YET AGAIN

With shaky hands, Sister Gertrude called my parents and told them to pick me up at the office. They arrived right on cue, complete with their disgusted masks I had learned to know so well. With the combination of my invisibility cloak and their masks, communication was stunted and had no chance of getting to any form of authenticity. And of course, I was grounded again. This time it was for two long weeks. An eternity.

My friends came over to our house and wanted me to go to a party with them the following week-end. They pleaded with my parents to allow me to go. My parents said "no" to my friends. I cried, as they left our house to attend the party without me.

Hey darkness my dear friend. I've come to visit with you again. I spent another long evening with my imagination, which was becoming my favorite buddy out of necessity.

In these teen-age years, when I was free, I ran the streets and went to the local parks to party with the cool kids, where the teenage girls wore their shirts oh-so-tight. It was a vicious cycle of needing attention, getting into trouble, being held captive in my bedroom, making me angry and resentful of my entire existence and eventually going within to befriend my imagination once again. When I was set free, this anger fueled my reality, thus creating this cycling process again and again. I couldn't imagine any way out of its clutches except to create. Therefore, I became the sign and greeting card maker of our family's many parties. Our family celebrated almost everything so I mass produced special abstact cards. I created anything and everything my mind could imagine.

My spirit didn't have a voice on the outside, so it began the process of finding a voice to express itself from the inside.

It seemed to be the atmosphere of this land, this particular part of Elefont, where the people were fine doing as they were told, whereas, I wished to change and become a different person since I couldn't believe this was all there is to life. This amenable mentality created a staleness in my soul, for I knew in every part of me that my life, as I knew it, was destined to change. I wanted to be different. My heart needed more than this city could offer and a part of me knew there was more adventure for me. Good-bye cobblestone road, where the dogs of society howl. I came to realize my future resided beyond this neighborhood, just as I knew by the age of seven, that there was another place beckoning for me to call home. But where was it?

Living in the city had its many advantages and disadvantages. It appeared the inner turmoil I carried was being reflected outwards as well. On the nearest street corner from our house, our sixteen year old female neighbor was kidnapped along with two other young women. After about six hours, the abductor was captured by the police and two of the women had been killed by him. Our neighbor somehow survived the ordeal. And on the exact same corner, my older sister, Rooney was returned after being kidnapped. The perpetrator had just returned from fighting in the war and wanted to replace his wife, who apparently had left him. He opened his heart to my sister, while crying and pleading his case. My wise sister talked her way out of this predicament by using psychological thinking and eventually found her way home safely. This same hard cobblestone corner, where he dropped her off, would haunt most of my dreamworld. It left its seeds planted in my life. In my perilous dream,

It is a dark night with little moonlight and I am standing under the street light, on this same corner. I am about six years old and I'm waiting for a person...a man. Not quite sure who, except I know I have to wait for him. Soon a tall thin man appears. There are no words exchanged, yet there is an eerie understanding between us, as I sense I have to walk around the street block with him. Occasionally, I touch his arm and hand as we are walking so closely. We move away from the street light as darkness envelops us except for the hint of moonlight. The stillness of the night becomes deafening. Suddenly, I realize if this mysterious man and I make it around the entire block together, he will kill me. We pass the first corner and I'm shaking and frightened, making my legs move one step at a time. The block is long as the night, yet it seems we are turning the second corner and I realize I am too young to die. I feel tears streaming down my cheeks as we turn the third corner and are about five houses from our destination, my death corner. I realize I don't want to die. I have to learn how to come out of this dream before we reach the next corner, so I can live. Somehow I do it. I successfully come out of the dream panting and sweaty. I will live and I will become someone special, I tell my little self.

I have had this dream about a dozen times; the last time was as an adult. I found a way to awaken myself every time, as I had to learn lucid dreaming in order to survive my dream. A lucid dream is any dream in which one is aware that one is dreaming. In a lucid dream, the dreamer has a greater chance to exert a degree of control over their participation within the dream or be able to manipulate their imaginary experiences in the dream environment. Lucid dreams can be realistic and vivid. There is an increased amount of activity in the parietal lobes making lucid dreaming a conscious process.

It was time for my friend Chloe's surprise birthday party. She was turning fourteen and I was so excited, as her parents and I were planning the event for her. Yes, I was being noticed for something beyond my antics and this had the power to make the wind in my chest fill up. On Saturday, Eva and I would take blond haired, blue eyed Chloe to Sherwood Park. I hadn't been to this park, yet it was the perfect place because it was only about a five minute walk from the birthday gathering. Eva and I would bring Chloe to her house and everyone would be there ready to surprise her.

We were swinging on the Park's gray, metal swing set and laughing joyfully in our exhilaration. As we propelled ourselves by the swing's constant momentum, we began kicking off our shoes into the wind and seeing whose would go the highest. I was glancing at my cheap gold wrist watch, monitoring the time so we could get the party girl back to her house. Laughing as we went to retrieve our shoes, I saw my penny loafers in some boy's hands who stood with a group of other teenagers. "Where did they come from?" I asked myself, for I had not seen anyone else at the park when we arrived. I ran up to him, still in the bliss of the moment and attempted to grab my shoes. Just as I went to take them from his outstretched hand, he moved his arm around to his back and said,

"You can have your shoes after you let me pants you."

Still not realizing he was serious, I began laughing as if this were part of our innocent game of shoe tossing. Producing my loafers in front of him again, I reached to take them and he declined yet again, swiftly moving his arm around to his backside.

"I want my shoes," I said.

It seemed I could be a bit more courageous with my friends and attempt to take off my invisibility cloak, unlike with my family. It was as if I was living a form of a schizophrenic life.

"It's time for us to leave," I said, as I was feeling responsible.

"Can we come to your party?" he snickered.

"I want my shoes," I repeated this time even louder. "Please, can I have my shoes."

"If you let me finger you......" his voice trailed off.

"In the vagina," one of the other cool boys shouted, finishing his friends' sentence as if they were working together. Suddenly, surrounding us were five teenage boys, who had joined the shoe fest. It was a game to them as well, only an adult version had swept into our naive one.

Realizing we needed to get to the party, I surrendered and agreed to play the game.

"Put my loafers on the ground and then you can do as you wish."

He looked at his other companions with a heightened air of accomplishment as he dropped my shoes, his bribing tools, on the ground next to him. The high school boy found his way down to the grassy ground beneath him while I walked up to my shoes and reached down to grab them. My ankle was just inches from his grasp. With shoes in my hand and his fingers reaching up for my thigh, I turned and ran like hell...away from the boys and their startled yells and cursing.

"Run Chloe and Eva. Run quickly!" I hollered over my right shoulder to both of them. Fortunately, they were on the track team as well, and followed my determined lead.

I ran so fast noting my track practices with my Dad were paying off. I was able to actually escape across the grassy park, the size of a football field, and out to the street. I outran the boys, with my friends close behind.

I had claimed both my loafers and my power and these guys, who thought they were so darn tough, seemed to be only chasing me. Victory for me and my penny loafers. This victory lasted only until I began to ask myself, "Why was I the one they chose to pick on? Why was it my shoes they chose to take? Why was I the one they chose to harass?"

"I am not just a gift for these boys to open," I thought. Where did that idea come from? I quickly pushed it away, as I had a reason to celebrate with my friends.

The following Monday, I was enjoying my lunch in the massive high school cafeteria, which was ablaze with the noisy display of teenagers trying to be noticed, when in walked another high school student. She came right up to my table and said,

"Tara Farrow wants to see you outside, right now."

My face must have shown my fear, as Tara Farrow was the badass of our class, actually of the entire high school of about four hundred students. She wore leather hightop work boots with metal embedded in the toes. She had quite the reputation as the toughest fighter in our school. Everyone knew you don't mess with Tara Farrow. Even the boys were afraid of her. Continually, there were stories circulating around the school about Tara and her courageous mouth and how she had beat up yet another student to the point of bloodshed. She seemed to carry the misery and angst of the world on her shoulders and enjoyed taking it out on her peers.

I noticed I had only eaten a small part of my lunch but I couldn't stomach any more, as I noted there was no escape route. I had to go outside and face the girl who I had become her personal enemy. My knees were wobbly as I ventured down the long hallway, while wondering if I could withstand her mighty blows. What did I do? I had little time to contemplate my uncertain future, as I approached the large metal doors with fingerprint-smeared windows. The doors met me too quickly, as I pushed them open to enter the terrifying fate of a steel-toed, badassed, Tara.

Slowly, I looked to my right and on the grassy mound area there was a group of about ten high school girls sitting in a large circle with Tara standing in the middle, hands on her hips and leather boots apart. Darn, I tried to make my purple converse gym shoes move with confidence but it seemed I had left any shade of trust inside the building. I was mentally trying to prepare myself to fight this young woman.

As I approached the circle, Tara said, "Well hello, Ms. Rhea. Look who has decided to compliment us with her presence. Please have a seat in the middle of our circle."

This startled me even more, to hear her say my name, for I didn't realize she knew who I was. I did as I was told, wondering if my stiff knees would crack. Fortunately my knees were behaving that day, with no cries or moaning from the sudden spiraling to the grassy ground beneath me.

Tara found her way to join the other girls in the circle, leaving me all alone with a beating heart that threatened to jump out of my chest.

I looked at her, "What do you want from me?"

"I heard you were in 'Our' park this past week-end."

"What?" I asked truly confused.

"I was told you and some of your friends were in 'Our' park?" Her voice became meaner somehow.

"What do you mean 'your' park?" as I began reflecting back to the week-end.

"Sherwood Park is OUR park," Tara said.

"Oh, it's true I was there with my friends."

She lowered her voice, "And what were you doing there?"

"We were simply swinging on the swing set."

I felt a bit relieved understanding the charges fully.

"Well I also heard you were fooling around with 'Our' guys," she said.

I began putting more of the pieces together; Sherwood park, throwing shoes up in the air, the teenage boys.

"Oh, my friends and I were just visiting your park until my

friend's birthday party began. I didn't know it was your park and we weren't doing anything with your boyfriends. They took my shoes and that's it."

As the words found their way to my lips, even I was surprised by the somewhat comfortable delivery of them. Maybe I do have a voice.

"What do you mean they took your shoes?"

"We were kicking them off while swinging and one of the boys took mine."

"Why did they take yours?"

"Now, how would I know that? Ask him," I found more of my voice along with some anger, an anger which was fueling me somehow.

"They said you were flirting with them? Is this true?" she snickered.

I had to laugh at this point, releasing some energy building within me.

"I didn't even see them until your friend was holding my shoes," I explained.

"Is that the truth?"

"Yes, ask any of your friends if you wish."

"Maybe, this is a different story then I was told," she said.

"What were you told?" I was curious.

"They said you were flirting with them in 'our' park."

I rolled my eyes, "We did nothing with your friends, we were only there for about thirty minutes and we were swinging on the swing set. Period."

"Well, my boyfriend sure liked you," Tara replied.

"I'm not really responsible for your boyfriend's feelings now, am I?" I continued picking up momentum and confidence, "I don't even know who your boyfriend is. I never met any of 'your' guys before that night and we didn't even exchange names or anything, for that matter."

"Honestly?" she asked.

I looked deeply into her eyes, "Yes, Tara, I had never met them before and quite frankly, I don't really care to see them again. Nothing personal."

"OK. Well, it looks like you're free to go. But stay out of 'our' park," she said as if rather deflated given the fact that her entire entourage was watching.

I took a deep breath and moved my body ever so quickly out of the circle of interrogation. I was free at last. What a relief, as I somehow bypassed the possibility of a nasty something.

This dynamic with Tara and her badass followers moved me up in the 'hierarchy of coolness" at my high school. I was soon being asked to ride to school with two of the coolest girls who both drove convertibles. This was the epitome of excellence in the high school realm. Oh dear, was I really special after all?

I'm recovering from a divorce. Glory be, what an experience. Imagine the process of what seems like putting everything I own on a blanket and then throwing the blanket into the air and wondering what will break and what will remain intact when it lands? This is a version of what I was feeling inside of me as my marriage is being whittled apart, one fiber at a time.

Jade and I were married for nine years, however, I knew within the first year he wasn't the love of my life. As I lay on the floor in our old farmhouse, counting the wooden rafters above me, the truth came seeping into my reality. I misread the meaning when I agreed to marry Jade. I thought marriage meant connecting and sharing our stories, desires and dreams. I stayed, I persevered, I tried to make this marriage work. I don't care what anyone says, a breakup is a breakup, even if I was the one initiating the separation. The whole process is still highly painful and exhausting.

Well, like many of us, I married someone almost exactly like my father. Typical Psychology 101. My dad was caring, honest, tall, handsome, hard-working and kind. I didn't get to really know this man but I sure wanted to.

One year, Jade even surprised me with a gift of a beautiful old Mercedes Benz, complete with real wood on the dashboard. A great catch, yes? Everyone thought we were the perfect couple. We were living the American dream after we purchased a big house on five acres of land. It was in need of lots of love and care, so we happily renovated the beautiful wooden floors, painted the walls, put in a wood burning stove, filled our world with oak antiques and called it home. It was perched perfectly on a hill with wildflower gardens covering the entire front lawn and a long curvy pine tree-lined driveway. We had Angus cows, chickens, honey bees and a little pond reflected my misery right back at me.

And here comes the big "but"; my husband didn't know how to communicate. He truly didn't know how to carry a conversation. Yes, it was that simple. While we were dating, I thought with time he would open up to me and if I loved him enough, he would share his deepest desires and dreams with me. Shortly after we met he revealed one of the things he liked about me was that I actually blew my nose in front of him! Imagine how revealing this one idea was in depicting the world he grew up in. A little, shall I say, stifled?

I mean, honestly, how does someone maneuver through life without having the skills to communicate? Jade ran his own photography business successfully. How could this be? When his dear Mom found out we were getting married, she hugged me for what felt like an eternity and cried on my shoulders, for she didn't know if he would ever find someone he liked, much less want to marry. She mentioned Jade was very picky.

We planned our small wedding to be held outdoors at my future In-law's property in the country. It was a beautifully green, peaceful setting with the smell of jasmine inviting feelings of romance. It started raining twenty minutes before our ceremony, so both of our families had to cram into the living room of their house. A friend said the rain was good 'juju' because it was cleansing our connection, so I hung onto this idea. I literally embraced this possibility that the rain was good karma, until the honest truth became as clear as the raindrops that day. My sweet husband could not hold any depth in a conversation, so I couldn't feel connected to him like I so desired. I prayed he would unpack his heart to me. It's never going to happen, I realized, as I cried myself to sleep at night, feeling more alone with him than I had ever felt in my entire life.

Getting to know Jade's parents would confirm this sense of confinement. His Dad was the Elder of their Christian Church. One of the stipulations of his position was all of the family members had to attend service every Sunday. Willing to give it a try, I attempted to go to their Church to honor my new family dynamic. I watched as all the males of the Church expressed their opinions and ran every-thing. Not once did I witness a woman speak during service.

One particular Sunday, I decided I didn't feel like watching this male dominated show called Church. Shortly after the service was over, my Father-in-Law, showed up on our front lawn with his trusty bible in his dominant hand. Surrounded by beautiful wildflowers, I was swinging in the hammock enjoying a peaceful Sunday. He walked right up to me, a bit too close for my comfort and asked,

"Rhea, why weren't you at Church today?"

"I am fine and you?"

"I'm good. Why weren't you at Church today?"

"Do you want me to answer honestly?" I ask stalling a bit for clarity.

"Well sure."

"I have noticed the woman don't have a voice, this doesn't seem fair to me. It seems the men do all the talking and make all the deci-sions. And being a woman myself, this doesn't feel comfortable."

"Well Rhea, let me show you this passage from the Bible."

He then proceeded to open his bible and said, "If a woman has a question during the service, she can ask her husband on the drive home."

If I weren't in a hammock, I might have fallen over from such an absurd answer.

"But what if she isn't married?" I wanted to know.

"Then she can ask a male in her family," he continued.

"But what if....." I decided this wasn't even worthy of my time. I find people caught in the religious loop are generally stuck in their beliefs and probably won't care to hear my ideas or even care to listen. Yes, given my childhood of not being seen and heard, this is humorous to me as I could be stepping into another dynamic like this one. Good Lord. Rather than changing my mind about attending, my Father-in Law only confirmed what I had been feeling about his church of Christ. I never attended another service.

So rather than going for the divorce directly, I met a lovely man who enjoyed the art of chatting. Yes, we had a little fling, which I realized was only a way to motivate me out of my marriage. Once the divorce was complete, this new talkative man came over to my condo and as I opened the door I said, "Sorry, this isn't going anywhere." I said my goodbye and shut the door. I had earned my freedom and I was ready for whatever life brought me but, obviously, it wasn't with him. I began to wonder if being starved of my dad's attention as a child, was I merely seeking attention from the opposite sex?

Leaving my marriage was challenging for many reasons. Jade's dad wrote me a four page letter trying to talk me into staying. His mom requested a meeting with me in a parking lot, so she could pour out her heart to me. She cried and cried wanting me to stay married to her son. Jade's younger sister found out about the affair and confronted me at the law firm where I was working. And dear Jade, he could not understand why I was leaving him. He thought he provided everything he was supposed to. Well, yes, he did provide for me as my husband, except he forgot about the heart part.

One day he asked me to write down all the things I didn't like about him, which I did. I saw this as his desire to make changes in himself and to have a better life. He then proceeded to carry this list in his jean pocket, pulling it out to show friends and my family members. As you can imagine, this went over wonderfully well with my siblings to the point where some of my family members began inviting Jade over for their celebrations and didn't include me. Just Wow.

Getting divorced also meant facing my inner demons, as there were many insecurities I carried from my childhood. I allowed myself to believe my family's ideas of me: that I was a failure, a trouble maker, and all the many names they gave me. All of this led to the infamous Catholic guilt trip.

I temporarily found a way to shift my angst away from the past or it could lead to way too much pain and anger. I've become the master at avoiding the deep pain within me that wants to swallow me like an ocean wave. Why does this deep angst keep coming back into full throttle? Yikes.

5

I am working as a proud paralegal. I am solemn about my job, as I'm living the single life and must handle all of my finances myself. I didn't even pursue the possibility of alimony for myself. We separated easily and harmoniously. In fact, after the divorce, Jade wanted to come over to my new place and cuddle (or so he called it.) I declined his offer.

Allowing my guilt to override what was equally my financial part of the divorce, I left the multi-million dollar home and property to Jade, now my ex-husband. What was I thinking? I was judged, juried, and hung for divorcing Jade. My family does not like—no, even better—they do not even believe in the process of divorce.

My intention at this moment is to move beyond allowing the guilt to affect me any longer. Or is it something deeper? I choose to remain positive, reminding myself 'when everything goes, anything goes.' Freedom, yes, I did have my freedom and there's that. A dear friend of mine, has a sign at the end of her driveway which says, "Anything is Possible." I wish for my life to be about this idea, "Anything is Possible."

Working at the law firm of Toth and Smith in downtown Elefont, I'm dating Mr. Toth, as in the first name of the law firm. Yes, it seems crazy, however, I'm feeling proud because I revealed to him when he first asked me to go out, that I wanted to wait until he was officially divorced, especially after my recent affair. Too many lives were touched by my selfish behavior and too much pain ensued.

I admire Mr. Liam Toth as he has been Attorney of the Year in New Jersey for the last five years. He is so handsome, wise and caring and he really seems to want to help those who are less fortunate. I was recently promoted to a case working directly with him and I feel empowered and motivated. Yes, I am going places! I am going big places in my career.

I'm also feeling excited and proud to be making a difference in people's lives, adult lives. You see, I graduated beyond simply being an elementary school teacher for many years. In some ways, it seems like eons. It has nothing to do with the idea of teaching or the students; I love and adore playing with children. However, what was missing was the respect I felt entitled to as a great teacher. It is so sad to witness over and over again how teachers can be treated and, of course, the obvious element of being so underpaid. Personally, I would like to hand over some of the millions Professional sports brings in and give it to the educational realm.

Therefore meeting all these very important legal people, or so I thought, seemed to give me some needed confidence and feelings of validation, for if the truth be told, I have very little confidence in how to finagle this experience called Life.

On the 16th floor, with absolutely no view of anything but gray, sat my teeny glamorous cubical. A note of sarcasm here, as my cubicle was anything but glamorous. It's designed like a large cardboard box with its four white sides reaching about five feet tall. I work in the middle of my box, ready to be shipped to who knows where?

My Paralegal position consists of doing many of the same things an Attorney does. I assist two Attorneys who both have Secretaries. I prepare court documents, interview witnesses and go to a lot of depositions. Occasionally a case does go to trial and I help to prepare all the paperwork. And my personal favorite responsibility is reviewing the entire file and summarizing the possibilities. This is where my imagination plays.

Pulling me out of my concentration of the legal case of the moment, I overhear another Paralegal talking about this psychic she had gone to the night before. I'm beyond intrigued, being a person who enjoys saying "yes" to many new adventures. At the risk of proving I was eavesdropping, I sought her out like a thirsty person looking for water, making my way over to my coworker's cubicle. I need some answers for my new singles life.

This loud talking paralegal is the kind of person everyone seems to like and I enjoy her company as well. This certainly amps my motivation to chat with her. Leaning my tall body toward her to avoid being heard, I whisper, "I overheard you talking about a psychic? Did I hear you correctly?"

"Yes," she whispers back. "My friend introduced me to her. I'm so thankful I went to see her. I'm still spinning with delight over what she revealed to me."

"Really, like what?" I ask as I lean in closer to hear. My curly red hair falls over my eyes and quickly I shove it back with my fingers.

As if considering how much to say, she pauses far too long for my comfort. I begin again,

"Did you believe her? Was there any way she could be making it up? Would you go to her again?"

"Yes, yes, and another yes," smiling broadly, she quietly says as she nods her cute smiling face. She seems to be glowing.

"She told me things about myself that she would have no way of knowing, very personal things I haven't told anyone before."

"Fascinating, do you want to share any of it?" I ask being aware of all the legal ears around us.

"Well for one, she said there was a woman I work with, who has red hair and green eyes who needs to see me also."

"What? She really said that?"

Those words thrilled me — actually brought goosebumps out on both of my arms.

She nods her head, as our eyes meet at this moment and seem to lock in time. I shake from this revelation, as she whispers,

"I guess you're the one she was talking about, Rhea. When she said it, I dismissed it until right now considering how darn large this office is and I heard they hired more attorneys yesterday. Any way, are you interested?"

Suddenly she laughs out loud, startling me and our nearest office mates. "Well, that's a silly question, I suppose, considering you are standing here with obvious enthusiasm and you certainly have green eyes and red hair!"

I've never been good at hiding my truth, even with the affair I finally had to tell my husband because I could not handle the lying and sneaking around. My friends continually tell me I have a very active face.

"Well, Rhea, are you in? This may sound far-reaching since you haven't experienced a psychic. I can assure you I told her nothing and she found this through her cards and her intuition."

"You mentioned her cards? Like playing cards?" I ask.

"No silly, you'll see. It's probably best you experience it first hand instead of me telling you about the experience," she adds.

"Sure," I respond.

"I have her phone number right here for you. Go visit her and then we can share our stories."

"Thanks," I say as I take the piece of yellow sticky note paper with the number of my future on it.

Meandering back to my desk, I'm thinking to myself, would this be my first psychic experience? I recall I have had bouts of intuition throughout my life. For example going into a room of people and being drawn to a certain person, or thinking of someone and I hear from them, or feeling the gentle tug to go to a certain place and watching the magic appear. I so appreciate this flowing part of myself.

This reminds me of the time when I was kicked out of my parent's house as soon as I turned eighteen years old. The bewildered part of my dad packed my bags preflight. I was truly shocked and surprised as it hurt my heart to the core. Apparently, my parents had enough of me and my disrespect of the family. At least my dad had set up a place for me to live with my older sister, Rooney. She agreed even though she was clearly aware of my reputation in our family. Will I ever recover from this life-long negative image? I do not know.

Another symptom of being the middle child of the family, the Rebel of the family, is they are the family member who will always tell the truth, no matter how disturbing. That would be me. My body hurt just thinking about this lingering possibility of always being known in this negative light.

Still pondering the idea of intuition, one time while living in this set up arrangement with Roon, things seemed to be flowing quite well and we were establishing a bit of a friendship. One sunny day in March, Rooney comes home with a typical brown lunch bag in her hand and says, "Let's play a game, this is your birthday present, see if you can guess what it is?"

She hands me the bag and I hold it for a moment or two. It's surprisingly light.

"It's Brazilian agates," I didn't know I was going to speak until the words were out of my mouth. Why those words in particular? I had no idea.

I open the paper bag and pulled out a beautiful earthy looking wind chime. The top portion was made of a dark wood and attached with clear fishing line and hanging symmetrically together were four beautiful Brazilian agates. I was correct! Even though I didn't know what Brazilian agates were at the time, I surprised myself how easily I found these two mysterious words.

My sister's eyes seemed to double in size, "What? How did you know? Rhea, you're totally amazing that way."

I made a note of "that way" remembering so many memories of my childhood that were not "amazing." Given my history with our family, I wanted to impress her and felt very proud of this display of some kind of worthiness. Feeling good about this memory, I realize I am ready to learn more about this intuitive world through my new adventure of meeting the psychic. I am jazzed.

That night I venture into the Google world, for more understanding of Brazilian agates.

I read, *'This is the stone everyone should have for protection. This group of stones are variegated chalcedony. The agate is one of the oldest stones in recorded history. Agates attract strength. Agate is a protection from bad dreams. It also protects from stress and energy drains. Agates have been used in jewelry since Biblical Babylonian times. The agates with banded colors were placed at the head of a sleeper to give rich and varied dreams.'*

Thanks Roon for a wonderful gift! Did she intuitively realize I would need a lot of protection?

Within a few days, I am at the Psychic's doorstep ready to ring her door bell, when I realize how incredibly anxious I'm feeling. Not that it would have enough power to take me anywhere else in the world at this moment. I bring my left hand to the doorbell and push as if my life depends upon it. A tall lady answers the door immediately. Kellye is dressed in a light blue summer dress with a simple belt highlighting her figure, flat shoes and a smile to melt anyone's heart. Her piercing green eyes seem to shine as she greets me.

"Hello, you must be Rhea."

Her radiant smile becomes contagious as we shake hands. Does she notice my sweaty palms? If so, she doesn't seem to care, or perhaps she is familiar with this human quirk. Her genuine smile seems to be just the medicine I'm needing at the moment. I'm noting a hint of something move through my body. Is it called a little bit of trust?

As I appreciate her simple silver jewelry, I find her presence to be inviting. Her demeanor has a light sense of kindness that helps me feel welcome in her home.

Wondering what I may find inside, I'm pleasantly surprised how normal her home looks, I take a deep breath and relax my shoulders a bit more.

"How long have you been doing this kind of work?" I attempt a half smile.

"Oh, for many life times," Kellye giggles while sweeping her long brown hair back from her face.

"What do you call yourself? Am I correct in calling you a Psychic?" I notice the investigative part of my personality has arrived, which serves me well while interviewing potential witnesses for trial.

"I am what is referred to as a Seer, Rhea. One of the most painful discoveries for me personally about this gift is accepting the Seer's burden. I notice that as I move into mystical realms, the struggles of my mundane life become more difficult the further I advance. It seems I openly invite chaos into my life, in order to stand in this place of being a periscope for the soul."

"Wow, I hadn't thought of it that way!"

"Well yes, I want my clients to see the reality of doing this kind of work, for it truly is a commitment to do my own personal work as well."

"Your own work?" I ask innocently.

"Yes, my inner work. As I was meditating before you arrived, I was seeing us talking about this idea of doing your own inner work, my dear."

As Kellye leads me through her living room and dining room toward the den area, I scan her furniture, which is artfully eclectic including her numerous tchotchkes from around the world, decorating each corner perfectly. I gaze into her backyard and notice a large rectangular purple picnic table demanding all of the space, as it seems to have quite a presence. It's as if it is big enough to hold thirty people, sitting fifteen on each side.

I'm guided by her outstretched hand to sit on the couch opposite of her, a coffee table centered perfectly between us. "Now what?" my excited heart wants to know.

"Have you been to a Seer before?"

"No," I shake my head.

"I'm being asked to tell you to pay attention for you are meant to be here."

"OK? I'm not really sure how you know that but I'm thrilled to be here and to learn more about how you access your intuition, for it has been a part of my…"

Kellye jumps in, "Rhea, the less you tell me about yourself, the more authentic my information can be, does that make sense?"

"Of course. Thanks for the reality check."

Kellye stretches her left hand across the table to my hand as if to reassure me and says, "We'll start with the cards and then you can ask questions afterwards if you wish, OK?" She pauses to look at me, as I nod my head.

"Please take this deck of Tarot cards and feel free to put your energy into them as you shuffle them."

"What does Tarot mean?" I asked innocently.

"The tarot is a deck of cards, used from the mid-15th century in various parts of Europe to play a group of card games such as Italian and French tarot. From the late 18th century until the present time the tarot has also been used by mystics, like me, to use as a map of mental and spiritual pathways."

"OK," I say as I take the cards from her. I wonder what the heck my energy has to do with any of this. I did as I was told imagining my energy going into the cards. I have no idea if I'm doing it correctly, however, I am more curious about what she is going to tell me. I make a note to myself to explore this "energy" idea later as well. So many new ideas already. My head feels as if it is swimming in a kaleidoscope of new possibilities and we haven't even begun yet or have we?

"Choose any ten cards you feel drawn to and place them on the table face down."

Kellye proceeds to spread my cards in a circular pattern on the wooden table. Some cards were face down while others were facing upwards. After closing her eyes and taking a deep breathe, she begins to explain what each of the cards means, adding her intuitive twist. The first card was the Tower card.

Kellye explains, "This card means: Disruption, conflict, change and sudden loss. Overthrow of an existing way of life, major changes of well worn routines. Ruin, disturbance and dramatic upheaval. Change of residence or job sometimes both at once. Widespread repercussions of actions. In the end, freedom and enlightenment."

I'm trying to digest all these possibilities she is reciting. She leans into me and smiles,

"You are a wise spiritual being. Do you realize this?"

I'm thinking to myself, spiritual being? I only know myself as inadequate; of being the rebel of the family, the black sheep. But spiritual? That sounds way too religious for me. My parents tried to instill some, as you call it, "spiritual," into my bones but it wouldn't take. I couldn't relate to the stand up, sit down, fight, fight, fight!

"You'll be finding out more about spirituality as you allow yourself to follow your truth and your passions. And you clearly have many passions, it's a genuine part of your personality."

"But what does it mean? What is spiritual?"

Kellye pauses for a moment then says, "Simply put, spirituality is a life path focused on reaching your Authentic Self. It can involve free expression and meditation among many other things. For your purpose just imagine it means finding more of your truth, beyond what your childhood told you."

"Yeah right, you won't catch me meditating. That sounds so boring," I laugh out loud.

Despite my defensive words, I can feel parts of myself open up as she refers to the idea of more of my truth, as if this part of me has been waiting for my attention or anyone's attention. I'm truly curious to hear more.

"But Rhea, you have some shadows within you that must be found and dealt with first. You must face your inner boogies."

"What does that mean "face my inner boogies?" I ask curiously.

"Ah, yes, this must be related to what I'm sensing, why you had to become invisible as a child. What were you hiding?"

"How did you know I was invisible as a child?" This word "invisible" has fully captured my attention. I'm spinning inside as I look around her room in search of something to write on, as if reading my mind, she hands me a piece of paper and a purple pen.

I write:

Why became invisible as a child? This idea pierces my heart and soul deeply. But why?

Find Inner boogies? (sounds painful)

Spiritual? Authentic Self?

Meditation (I don't think so.)

Not missing a beat, Kellye continues, "This next lovely card reveals, you are a creator of sorts. Are you an Artist? If not yet, creativity and art expression will be an integral part of your life."

I write:

Artist...yes!

Kellye turns over the next card, moving in a circular pattern on the table, "You will meet the love of your life, your soul mate, oh but, this card tells me it won't be until much later in your life."
I write:

Love...later...darn!

My face must be showing my disappointment, for she adds, "Sorry to have to tell you that part. However, realize when you do meet your beloved, it will be a lovely coming together again. Complete with the white picket fence."
I write:

Together again?

I have secretly been hoping my current love interest was going to be something more than a boyfriend and ask,
"What about Liam, the attorney I'm currently seeing? I thought he could be a possible partner?"
"Yes, I see he is a lovely man, except he's not quite available yet unless he can do some spiritual growing and changing. But enjoy the time you have with him, for you can still learn from him, yes, I see he has something to teach you for other relationships."
I write:

Learn from this relationship with Liam?
Future relationships?

I'm very curious about this response "he will teach me?"
As I'm beginning to entertain this idea, Kellye pipes in, "Yes you must begin to see your life as your greatest teacher! This is one of your lessons for today."

"Oh so you're the teacher now?" I joke with her.

She smiles as I write:

My life: My greatest teacher?

"Explain please," I ask.

"Just imagine it's like having new eyes, new lenses and you are looking at your life for understanding as to where you get stuck. Look for answers. How are your relationships? What triggers you? What angers you?"

"Funny you say new eyes as my green eyes are one of the only things I really like about myself."

"Rhea, that is one of your boogies talking right there."

"What?" I need to think about this one a bit more.

I write:

New eyes, related to boogies?

"New topic, new card. Well Rhea, you are definitely from another planet."

I pause, this statement has more impact than I can fathom. "What do you mean?"

"Do you feel, different at times?" Kellye inquires.

"Well yeah, but doesn't everyone?" I ask.

"I suppose, to a degree."

"From another planet?" Even the words feel funny yet familiar as I say them out loud.

I'm remembering a conversation with a friend. It was a lovely summer night and we were standing on my back deck talking about the beautiful starry sky. He was adamantly opposing the idea of there being life on other planets. I was quite surprised and found myself wanting to prove to him there are other planets with life forms. To me it's not even a question if there are beings from other planets, it's as obvious as the sun rising. If we are the only planet with beings, that seems to be a lot of wasted space. Coming back to Kellye's house, she is looking at me with wondering eyes.

"Rhea, are you OK?"

"Yes, just remembering something."

"Can you relate to this idea of being from another planet? You know, many of us are."

"It's understandable, I'm just trying to understand," I say.

There's my dyslexic wording I so enjoy, as we laugh together. This is good, the laughing is allowing me to release some of my wonderments about this reading. Ain't humor great?

I write:

From another planet? Amusing!

Kellye moves to the next card.

"Your career, yes this card is powerful. What do you do for a living?

"Well, I'm currently working as a paralegal," I say.

"Not for long," she blurts out very quickly.

This. is. crazy.

I do embrace change in my life, however, I'm needing some sense of stability right now. I thought I had found an environment at the law firm to supply both my financial needs and some status proving I am somebody. Also, I realize at this moment how much I have been relying on the idea of Liam being my Savior! I'm wanting him to take care of me. Oh dear! My head is swimming with so many questions about my reality. Then she asks me, again as if reading my mind.

"Do you have any specific questions for me?

"Well, ah, yes I do. What are you sensing about my family dynamic? I've never really fit in. I feel lost with them."

"Well, I was sensing before you arrived that you would ask me about your family dynamic. I was wondering if I wanted to tell you this, so please know I have been guided to share this information so you can begin preparing yourself emotionally, for this big change."

"What?" My hands have begun sweating again.

"I'm sensing you must make a decision about how to be with your family and play the game with them or find your true self by being courageous enough to go on your own."

My heart feels sad as my short lived excitement seems to fly out the window and land on the purple picnic table tempting me to engage and stay there. Does she really know the ramifications of this idea of leaving my family?

"Really?" is all I can form with my mouth.

Seeing my perplexed face, Kellye adds "I'm not necessarily what you would call a religious type of person either, but I do resonate with Jesus, so imagine his life! He had to leave his family as a carpenter and find his own path."

"Worth noting," I say.

"I also want to ask you about the tower card again? I want to write the ideas on my paper."

She says as I write:

'Disruption, conflict, change and sudden loss. Overthrow of an existing way of life, major changes of well worn routines. Ruin, disturbance and dramatic upheaval. Change of residence or job sometimes both at once. Widespread repercussions of actions. In the end, freedom and enlightenment.'

Feeling full and needing to take the attention away from myself and do something with this uncomfortable energy brewing within me, I move my new eyes to the purple picnic table outside the large window. Somehow the mystery of it gives my mind a place to focus for a moment. I really don't want to entertain the idea of leaving my family. First my marriage, then my job and Liam and now this. How will I survive?

I fumble with the purple pen, searching for something to say, as I write:

Jesus...find MY own path?
Leave family or conform to be the good girl?

"So, Kellye, I guess you like purple, yes?"
"What?"
"The purple pen, the purple picnic table, what's with the purple table any way?

"Well purple represents spirituality. I'll tell you about the picnic table next time, you're not quite ready for that yet."

"Ready? For a purple picnic table? And how do you know I'll be coming back?"

"We'll see," she smiles.

Her approach continues to be so matter of fact that I don't even question her words. Nearing the end of our session, she tells me she wants to check in with her Higher Guidance. Higher Guidance? OK, I surrender. I will just trust what she has to say at this point.

Casually, Kellye closes her eyes and then lets me know when she is ready to answer my questions. I ask her about leaving my family, for this concerns my heart the most. I notice her demeanor and voice both change a bit as she speaks from this mysterious place within her.

"Rhea, you are ready to find yourself and it would be much easier if you move emotionally from their grasp. Yes, you must realize how strong your mother is so decide when you are ready for this to happen. Trust Yourself! You will be delighted beyond your greatest imagination to find your truth. It's quite a beautiful process from our perspective."

I write:

• *Higher Guidance?*

• *Leave family? Really?*

Kellye comes out of her inner world and I notice her looking at the clock and somehow the hour is over. I thank her as I give her a hug and find my way to the door. I'm digesting one other comment she made that is still unsettling. "Rhea, you won't meet your soul mate for many years." This seems to sting in my heart and soul as well as excite me equally that my soul mate is awaiting our reunion. As I'm approaching the door, I turn to hear her parting words, "Rhea, remember people who have never suffered aren't very deep."

As I'm driving home, I'm realizing this confirms an idea I've held as long as I can remember, that there is much more to life than what I experience with the five senses.

Later that evening, I've been invited over for dinner, along with the rest of my family. My mom's house is matchy matchy. Everything has hints of green, way over the top for my taste. It smells of the meal of the moment, as my Mom seems to be continually cooking something.

At the circular dinner table, my sister Sarah asks about my Psychic Reading. I'm questioning if I want to share it, as the information is still fresh and raw for me. I know I want to keep it to myself however, the part of me who still yearns for validation, steps in and I say,

"She told me I was from another planet."

As soon as this sentence was out of my mouth, I knew this was not going to be pretty. As if rehearsed, my family members all burst out laughing.

"Was your psychic friend wearing garlic around her neck?"

"Did she look deeply into her crystal ball?"

"How can you trust that crap Rhea?"

My brother says, "Gulp."

"Double Gulp," laughs the family.

You see, when comments are said as jokes, everyone can laugh them off without considering the ramifications of the emotional impact inside. I'm not laughing now. Why am I the only one who sees this emotional dysfunction? My exciting world of opportunities turns into a feeling as deep as a crack in the Earth. These comments cut me like a knife. The familiar pain imbues my entire body once again. I could feel myself needing to become invisible. Even as an adult with a promising career, or so I thought, I am still being treated like a child. I feel hurt and ashamed and this leads to feeling pissed at my world and most importantly, pissed at myself. Wanting some kind of connection with my family, I slipped again. I want to cry out, "hear me that I might teach you. Feel my arms that I might reach you."

Suddenly the passage, 'Don't caste pearls before swine' comes to mind. Why would I try to explain myself to my family? I should know better by now. I should keep my personal stories to myself. I really don't even like that I'm using the word "should." My friend's definition of "should" is the plural of "shit."

As I'm sitting at this table of familiar jabs designed as humor, I am taken back to my special time with Kellye. She seemed to get me. This is what I crave in my life, people who can understand and inspire me.

This frustrating situation had turned into one big joke. It was only one of many, nudging me to leave my home town of Elefont and my family. Oh wow, that's exactly what Kellye had said.

6

Yes, Kellye was absolutely right, I came back to see her many more times. Not once during my visits with her, did I ever question the authenticity of her words. She was so accurate and convincing. I began to really look at life through my new eyes and I could see situations wrapped as lovely presents begin to unwrap themselves, exposing the places I get stuck.

Delightfully, I began to watch things manifest which she had mentioned. For example, I learned from dating Liam, I preferred to be with someone who understands the spiritual part of myself. As I am befriending this part of me, I wish to be able to share and talk about it. It's like I've entered into a new country rich with heritage and possibilities. I'm loving being the observer of my new country as I learn its new language, flavors and idiosyncrasies. I realize having a partner to share this with is vital for my spiritual growth and understanding. Liam tried. He certainly did try to understand this part, however, he was way too enthralled in his law firm reality of right and wrong and black and white, Liam didn't see the need for all the colors of spirituality.

Watching Kellye channel her higher guidance, not once did I ever consider connecting with my own Higher Guidance. That was for those 'other people' like Fortune tellers or Psychics, not me.

Plus I had an image to keep within my family. I still try to fit into their world somehow, some way, despite my vague agreement to move on. Habits die hard, so to speak. Somehow I thought being a Paralegal, a very noble career, would capture their respect. It wasn't quite doing the trick as I had hoped. I'm still the rebel in their eyes. In fact, my sister told me the only way working as a paralegal changed me was when I started wearing makeup.

During one poignant session, Kellye asks me,

"Do you have any experience with Hypnosis?"

"Just this silly joke: I used to be an arrogant, self-important know it all, so I went to a Hypnotist to see if she could help me. Now I am perfect."

"Cute. Seriously, I'm sensing learning about Hypnotherapy could be a wonderful asset for you."

"I really don't think so; it's not for me," I say reluctantly.

"Why?" she asks.

"Just the idea that someone can control your mind; I am not comfortable with anyone controlling any part of my life."

"See Rhea, that is a misconception right there. A Hypnotherapist with integrity doesn't control anyone or anything, they're merely serving as a guide to the unconscious world." She continues, "Just think about it."

"Why do you imagine this would be good for me?" I ask rather defensively. I haven't begun to explore the inner boogies yet, per her constant loving request. It seems much easier to have her tell me the way. Am I relying too much on her words?

"Remember I am just the messenger. Do you want me to tell you a bit more about hypnosis?"

"Sure," I say to pacify her.

Kellye pauses to check my interest level as she pulls out a piece of paper and begins to read:

"Hypnosis is a state of deep physical and mental relaxation that helps you bypass the conscious mind to access your subconscious mind. Healing occurs as you access and release the subconscious beliefs that are still stuck in their early, childlike state. You may even know the subconscious beliefs but have been unable to release them through regular talk therapy. If they are strongly held beliefs, they need to be released from the subconscious level, not the conscious."

Kellye glances up at me with her caring eyes,

"Does that make sense, Rhea? Given your need for reflection into your childhood, this could really shed some light for you personally and possibly professionally as well."

"Hmm, I suppose."

"I'm sensing with your level of depth, intuition and spirituality, this could be a perfect match for who you are becoming," she adds.

"Who am I becoming?" I joke.

"That's the fun and the mystery of life, finding more of your true self. I believe we are all receptacles of buried treasure. This is one way to access your jewels. Our job is to find and honor our treasures."

"OK, interesting!" I respond.

"Rhea, there's a hypnotherapy training in Darwin, New Jersey which is only about twenty minutes from here."

"So hypnosis can bring my boogies out from the closet?" I snicker.

Sometimes when things get too serious for me or I'm feeling a bit uncomfortable, I summon my humor to cover the inner scars. This was one of those days. Maybe I am protecting myself with armor on the exterior, so that nothing is able to pierce my soft vulnerable interior?

All joking aside, my curious part is listening attentively.

"By using hypnosis, a person can tap into the unconscious

where all of their beliefs reside. This is the rub. Since they are in the subconscious, you may not be aware of them, so you need to go there directly for understanding and changing them. It's like putting the light on your old beliefs from your childhood; the light takes away the power of them."

"So, are you saying we are run by our beliefs?" I ask.

"Yes, most definitely! An emphasis on our unconscious beliefs," she continues,

"And speaking of beliefs, I believe one day you will be able to sit around a large table like the purple picnic table and feel at ease within yourself. This is my wish for you."

Kellye takes my hand, "Let's go practice right now, come on."

She guides me to her back yard. Even the thought of sitting at this large table has a profound affect on me. I notice my hands are sweating, my breathing has changed and I am only considering doing this, not really acting on it. It's just like a reenactment for OCD patients.

"Take a seat, my dear," she says calmly.

"OK, it seems odd how much power this simple maneuver has over me," I mention. I remember sitting at many large tables as a child and becoming invisible, unable to speak.

"I've been guided to take you here, I use this table often for situations like yours. Please know this can help you begin to heal and change your situation."

I sit at the huge table on the right side closest to the house. Somehow it seems safer. I am able to sit there for several minutes and calm my breathing, while visualizing my family sitting there with me. It's a baby step, but it's a step.

"Rhea, imagine throwing your invisibility cloak up into the air and a sublime goddess emerges!"

I love Kellye in this moment, for she knows how deep the boogies go and yet she is willing to support me with her genuine 'purpleness.'

I'm starting to put the pieces together, while realizing, yes indeed, I'm considering opening to learn more of this world of hypnosis for my own personal growth and understanding of why I had to become invisible as a child.

Later that evening, I do some further research and find this,

> *"Therapeutic hypnosis is not what Hollywood or hypnosis stage shows make it out to be. Rather, you are wide-awake, alert, conscious, clear and talking throughout the entire session. You are never out of control, rather you are often more clear than usual, and at all times you know what you're saying and thinking. You are simply in a relaxed state."*

OK, I am ready to change my life, where do I sign? I agree to a ten month Hypnotherapy program.

— *Elephant in the Room*

I've always enjoyed standing on my head. For some reason, I like the feeling of blood flowing down my body into my active mind of ideas. Even as a child, my mom would kid with me when I forgot to hang the photos back up on the wall, where I had taken them down so my feet wouldn't disturb them while doing my upside down maneuver. This training is giving me the same vibrational feeling, I so enjoy.

My hypnosis training is being taught by a husband and wife team. There are twelve students like myself. This intensive program provides intellectual learning about Jung, Freud, Pavlov and Milton Erickson, to name a few, but primarily it's hands-on. I love the learning aspect and I'm intrigued by the possibilities and mysteries of the mind.

We watch a movie about neuroplasticity showing the miraculous discovery revealing how we can actually change the neurons in our minds to form new pathways, developing new beliefs and ideas. They remind us that one of the avenues to change buried unconscious beliefs is through the process of hypnosis.

The participants work with each other while learning the hypnosis modalities. Several times, I'm experiencing a block in my inner world where I only see black. When I ask my teachers about this process of witnessing only darkness, they suggest I see a trained hypnotherapist for some deeper exploration. The Institute refers me to Devon, who comes highly recommended.

In spite of my inability to go into trance, finally I am able to with Devon. Having twenty years of experience, she certainly knows how to provide the perfect scenario for me to feel safe and receptive. This is my third visit to experience this mysterious world with her. The first two attempts took me to several scenes with seemingly little significance. Finally, I am opening to see and feel my inner world fully.

"I am a little child."

"About how old are you?" Devon asks.

"About four or five."

"Where are you?"

"I am in my adopted brothers' bedroom."

"What are you doing?"

"Sitting on the floor, like I'm waiting for something?"

"Is anyone else there?"

"No, but Cameron said he will be back...he went somewhere."

"Who is Cameron?

"My stepbrother."

"Do you like Cameron?"

"Hmm, sometimes."

"What are you wearing?

"I am wearing pj's with feet. I like the feet part."

"Why do you like the feet part?"

"Because he can't pull up my pant legs."

"Who can't pull up your pant legs?"

"Cameron," I say slowly, as tears find my adult eyes.

"Why are you crying?"

"I am not sure, I'm excited that I get to be in my big brother's room."

"Why are you sad?"

"Because I don't want to play the game any more," I say glancing over at the bed.

"What game?"

"The game that makes me squirm."

"Why does it make you squirm?"

"It just does," I continue, "My body is flooded with funny feelings. Can I say no this time? My brother will never like me. Would he play with me if I say no?"

"Say no to what?"

"The game. I am OK to play just one more time, just one more game. My area down there is getting funny, I grab my pink elephant for comfort."

"What did you say?" Devon asks inquisitively, for my little girl voice has become a whisper.

"I grab my pink elephant, my friend, for protection," I answer a bit louder.

Realizing what my adult lips are saying brings me out of trance a bit. Devon gracefully and gently brings me back to the office, back to my adult body. What did a pink elephant have to do with any of this? Being fairly new to the process of hypnosis, I found my adult mind questioning the process. I want some understanding of this scenario.

As I am opening my adult eyes, I feel the need to move my arms and legs for they have become very heavy and tingly.

"Could I have some water please?"

Devon hands me a glass of water.

Finally, I find the nerve to ask the obvious question, "What do you think of this pink elephant?"

"It'll show its meaning in time. It always does."

"But what does it all mean?"

"What do you think?"

"Well something happened to me as a child, that is pretty

obvious, could it be, uh, sexual?"

"Let's explore this before making any conclusions, shall we?"

"Sure."

"Who is Cameron?"

"My adopted brother."

"Do you have times in your childhood you don't remember?"

"Absolutely, it feels strange to have blocked out so much."

"Yes and we'll need to go in again for more information," Devon reminds me.

"More? Why would I want to know this? If IT did happen," I ask.

"Rhea, you would be surprised if you knew how common sexual abuse is in this world. Wouldn't you want to know for your own understanding of yourself?"

I hesitate.

"Possibly. Could this really have been locked away within me all these years?"

"Yes, absolutely this could be in your unconscious. Let's explore some more pertinent questions. Did you have sex at an early age?"

"Well yes, I went looking for sex at age thirteen," I admit shamefully.

"This sheds some light, for you see, most victims have their first sexual encounter at an early age or they shy away completely from sexual encounters." Devon continues, "And we're referring to a person who has experienced any kind of sexual play not necessarily sexual intercourse. Please understand the difference."

"So it may have been playing around?"

"Possibly."

"Oh dear," I respond.

"And one very important reason to explore this further is that IF this did happen, I mean sexual, then you have the power to stop this dysfunctional pattern in your own family. Do you plan on having children?"

"Well, I have felt a child around me for many years, so probably yes I plan on having at least one child."

"Then you will want to explore what truly happened so you can stop the dysfunction. And hypnosis is the best way I know to find the truth. Does that make sense?"

"Yes," I say slowly realizing the ramifications on a deep level.

I look over at the clock and we have gone over time.

"Remember Rhea, people who haven't suffered aren't very deep. I'll see you next time," Devon responds with a big hug, which I truly need right about now!

After my hypnotherapy session, my first stop is my Mom's house, for she may be able to shed some light about this pink elephant mystery. Perhaps she remembers this perplexing stuffed animal which I had found in my inner world. I begin thinking about my brother again, not wanting to believe this.

"Let's look at my baby photos together," I inquire as I enter her home.

"Sure Rhea, I like that idea. You know raising you kids has been the most pleasurable time of my life. I just wish I would have taken more time to play with you. I was way too concerned about cleaning the house. Yeah, my best times were when you kids were little."

Yes, we are very different in this regard, I thought sadly to myself, for my experiences with our large family have been confusing and strange.

"Great, Mom. So where are you keeping the photos these days? I'll get them."

"Under the stereo, you'll see many of them. I believe your baby photos are in a maroon photo album."

I find the maroon book and open its stiff binders; apparently it has been in this same position for quite some time. A variety of memories flood my mind, while the aroma of old photos fill my nostrils.

A strange feeling emerges in my body as I sit on the couch next to my mom, as we look at these black and white photos together. Soon, my heart seems to flutter as I notice a colored photo, one of the few colored ones, and it is of my young self sitting in a gray chair big enough to swallow me. I'm holding the infamous pink elephant next to my heart and it looks exactly as I had seen it during my hypnosis session less than an hour ago. A pink stuffed elephant with a very limp body, looking as if it had been held tightly night and day.

This photo is reflecting so much light, sunlight seems to actually fill the room. Pondering the relevance of this photo, my memories of this little pink buddy begin to fill my heart and soul. This sweet, cuddly pink guy was my Savior, I remember as tears find my eyes. I feel somehow stronger as this little animal provided assistance to me when I needed it. It was as if an old friend was found again.

"Mom, do you remember this pink elephant?"

"Oh Rhea, you carried that little elephant around with you every-where you went. He was your buddy. I guess you were too young to remember it."

"I really didn't remember it, until earlier today as I..." my voice trails off as I consider the ramifications of this conversation about my brother, her adopted son.

"Do you remember what happened to it? The elephant?" I ask.

"No, not really," she continues, "Do you remember Aunt Marna's neighbor's sister? I think there is a picture of her someplace... " as her voice trails off as she flips the pages.

Saved by the inability of my Mom to hold a conversation about anything deep or real. She prefers the safe route of talking about others and what they are doing around her. For once, I am very thankful for her Captain, as I silently salute her. I'm wondering if I will ever be able to tell her the truth as she rattles on about another distant relative's photo.

My Mom was a lovely woman when younger. She made her own

stylish clothes and even wore high heels, until it proved to be too impractical. In the mornings, all of the food for preparing our school lunch was perfectly aligned on the kitchen counter; the bread, cheese, meat, mustard, lettuce, etc. Our house was always clean, and we enjoyed large home cooked meals, which were ready exactly at 5:30 each and every night.

I long for a "Mom" I can talk honestly to at this moment.

I left her house with many more questions than when I arrived. Do I really want to know the truth? Honestly, do I want to know the truth about my stepbrother? It seems the "sexual" situation, as devastating as it is, is all being presented to me on a pretty silver platter. I keep the idea Devon shared with me near my heart, to find comfort with this dynamic, so I can heal and stop the dysfunction.

Many more Hypnosis sessions took me back to my brother's room with the bed. Over time, I'm being ripped open to my vulnerability, releasing old feelings that have haunted me since childhood and crying so many tears as I recognize this reality and wonder what I will do with this secret information.

Oh God, it looks like Cameron must be the dark clouds in my world. Cameron, my brother, do you still feel the scars that won't heal? Or am I the only one carrying this ghost around?

The more I dive into my mysterious past through the inner world of hypnosis, the more that is being revealed both in my hypnotherapy training and in my personal regressions with Devon. Eventually the time comes to learn a new regression technique: Past Life recall.

A Past-life regression recalls scenes, feelings and memories from another lifetime one has lived as though it were happening now. Discovering your past lives is a fascinating way to understand who you are as an immortal soul living a human life. It enables you to heal the present through the past and can bring more inner peace.

In our training we have chosen partners and each of us will

experience giving and receiving a session. We need to have a personal issue to focus on, something we can't resolve simply by logic. For me, I have the constant and mysterious feeling of a child being around me. Sitting next to my partner in a reclining lounge chair, I am gently guided within. By now, I'm becoming a pro at going to the inner place as my partner's soothing, monotonous voice counts me backward, step-by-step, 5...4...3...2...1...

'I see myself as a large African American woman standing in an elegant kitchen. The feeling of an expansive mansion surrounds her. She is facing a tiled island which sits perfectly in the middle of the kitchen. She is looking at a large wooden bowl with the remains of something having been made recently, utensils with some type of baking mixture on them, an open jar of flour and other ingredients.

She smells the welcoming aroma of homemade bread, as she reaches forward to get some plates out of the wooden cupboards above her. Her fleshy belly hits the counter in front of her before she can reach the dishes. She is halted by her lack of ability to reach the cupboard yet her hands strain to reach the dishes.

Oh my, I'm now feeling the difference of being a heavy black woman rather my thin self. I find this humorous and curious at the same time. The scene fades...

I'm now sitting in a very large, dimly lit dining room. The Master and I are sitting at opposite ends of this long table with about ten feet between us, emphasizing my sadness. As we are eating dinner, I can sense we have been lovers and we had to give our two mulatto children away because of the stigma attached to a master sleeping with his slave.

As my perception gently rises above her, I look down to see her heart is broken and yet she has developed a certain strength from the situation. It is clear they truly love each other, but they had found a place of comfortable silence to distill their connection and ultimately deal with the pain of losing their children.'

I come out of this regression completely amazed at the avenue of insights I have within me. No wonder Kellye suggested hypnotherapy for me. It is as if I have opened Pandora's box and I am truly being guided to look at my life through new eyes. This entire dynamic of exploring hypnosis has created a majestic life of its own.

I am so thankful to be able to talk to my Hypnotherapist, who feels quite sure something significant happened to me when I was a child. Twenty years of experience working with clients has Devon trusting what I'm seeing and experiencing in my inner world.

After all of this information is being revealed, I feel even more uncomfortable with my family gatherings. I can not even look into Cameron's eyes. I continue becoming invisible as a safety precaution. Plus, everyone loves Cameron and thinks he's the best. This adds to my angst.

This dynamic is giving me more impetus to leave New Jersey and my family, just like Kellye had said. How can I be myself with all of this surfacing? I need time to reflect, I need time to think. Does this really mean leaving Elefont? How? Where will I go?

I know in my heart I have to get out of here. I cry myself to sleep many nights with this idea looming in my awareness. I feel caught in a spiraling downward movement and I don't know how to get out of it. I have to find more ways to comfort myself. But what are they? What can I do? Do I talk to Cameron? I'm going a little crazy inside. I can't continue becoming invisible, I must find a better way.

— *Spirit Guides*

With all of my reflecting back to my childhood, I'm remembering one night when I was about seven years old. Our family's ritual each evening, after eating dinner, consisted of doing the dishes with the entire family. On special nights, my older siblings would use their wet dish towels to try to whip us as a fun game but mainly to get our attention. On rare occasions, they would actually hit us, the wetter the better, the more sting.

When my grandparents were visiting, we would pray together while bumping bums in the kitchen. On this particular night, I was washing the dishes and there was a broken glass in the soapy dish water. Not being able to see it, I dove right into the sharp edge piercing my first finger drawing blood, sweat and tears.

"Holy shit," came out of my little mouth before I could stop it.

"Rhea Marie!" came hurling from across the room. I knew I was in trouble when my middle name was attached to my first name. This would be my mom, doubly embarrassed because her parents were interrupted during their praying session.

"I cut my finger," I cried from the pain, "It hurts."

I showed my finger for evidence as the blood dribbled down my hand.

"You're not to talk like that in this house young lady," my dad chimed in.

"Well at least it was holy," I added.

I heard snickering from my siblings in the background.

"That's not a bit funny," he said to me. The praying had come to a complete halt and all eyes were on me.

"To your room," my dad hollered.

"My finger hurts. That's not fair," as I began crying even more. More tears flowed, from humiliation more than pain, as all eyes found their way to me, while I was trying to put on my invisibility cloak. Oh my, all these eyes felt intense on my little body.

One of my siblings shouted, "Look at Rhea's upper lip as she cries, it's quivering in a weird way."

Oh God, my fears are manifesting, as everyone is laughing and pointing fingers at me.

"Stop it," I cried even more. All this humiliating attention affected my sensitive side deeply.

With no support or comfort in this room, I left the dirty dishes and went upstairs by myself. My bedroom, seemed to provide some form of comfort by hiding me from the ridicule. I cried myself to sleep, rubbing my favorite quilt. No one came to check on me or my sore finger and I knew at that point, I was entirely on my own. It was as if the cruel treatment had backed up into my system and blocked me like a toxin.

Later that night, I awoke briefly and as I was remembering the painful dynamic from the evening, I hear a subtle noise coming from the closet. I look out of the corner of my left eye and see a tall man emerging and coming toward me, as I lay on the top portion of the trundle bed I share with my sisters. I'm terrified. I try to be still and keep quiet, my heart is pounding so loudly it's adding to the fear racing through my body. I sense reality is thin at this point; I try to swallow and I close my eyes as if by dismissing this reality, it will disappear along with my vision. What could I do? Should I scream?

This is when it really became scary for me. I tried to scream and nothing seemed to want to come out of my mouth. I could hear the sound of my heart in my chest, and the beating of blood against the back of my eyes. I was way too frightened to even make a sound, so I tried to hold my breath so he wouldn't hear me breathing. I feared he would hear me and know I have awakened and then what?

He stopped in the middle of the room and seemed to be still for a moment. I saw through the corner of my eye, he had something in his hand. Finally, fear completely took over me and I had to scream! A wail came hurling out of me unlike anything I'd ever heard before. It seemed to rock the entire bed. An eternity passed and finally, I saw the man float back into the closet, as my dad emerged in the doorway. He was staggering still half asleep while rubbing his eyes trying to make some sense of this scene,

"What is it Rhea? What is it?" Dad stammered as he turned on the bedroom light.

I cover my tear-filled eyes to protect them from the glare, "There was a man, a tall man right here in the room," I try to whisper while pointing to the closet.

"What?" still trying to fully wake up, my Dad asks.

"A man, here in the room," I repeat again pointing to the closet.

Slowly, he moved toward the closet and turned on the closet light. He moved through our clothes separating them to get a better view to the back of the closet.

"Nothing there," he assured me.

"Is that the last place you saw him?" he asked naturally surprised.

"He, uh, he seemed to go into the closet," I add.

"I'll check around the house."

I am left to lie in my bed all alone. Why am I the only one awake right now as my two sisters lay within a few feet of me? I'm trying to make sense of all of this, while doing my best to calm myself.

Of course, my dad was alarmed and now very awake, as he

proceeded to check all four levels of our house, including the attic with assorted decorations and the huge basement complete with ping pong table and foosball. We were a game playing family. Not finding anyone or anything unusual, he reported back to me.

"It was probably just a dream," he said exhausted and wanting to go back to bed. "Try to get some sleep and sweet dreams."

Where's my reassuring hug or something? I wondered. I was convinced I had seen this man, but without any evidence, I couldn't press the issue. Knowing sleep was far away, I laid in bed pondering this horrendous experience. Finally daybreak appeared as the dark became a hint of gray and I knew I had survived. I found the strength to move my paralyzed body and walked to the middle of the room where this "man" had been standing just a few hours earlier.

This nighttime adventure happened again about a month later. This time, a thin lady with long hair appeared and walked into our room from the hallway, she stopped at the end of our bed. I'm thinking how could she be in the hallway and why didn't anybody else see her or hear her? She stood facing me with her strange hat covering her eyes. Then she lifted her head to look at me. She seemed innocent enough, but the question remained, what was she doing here? She stood looking at me with her twinkling eyes, which I will always remember. Soon, the reality of the situation seemed to emerge into my consciousness and I bellowed out yet another scream of the night. She turned toward the hallway and I heard this rumbling in the hall. Oh no, I'm wondering if my dad has found her and has tackled her to the floor?

Soon, it was revealed that my poor Dad had tripped over the vacuum cleaner left in the hallway and he fell face first to the floor, making all the commotion. I guess it's pretty funny looking back at it but I'm sure my Dad didn't think so at 3:00 in the morning, as he was meeting the hard floor face first!

The third and fourth visits appeared to be different men each time, although I'm not sure where they came from, the closet or the hallway. I do know these men, with little hats, were suddenly there as I was again listening to my loud breathing heart and pondering what to do. The fourth time, my dad had enough of these morning excursions by his screaming daughter, and so he went to the attic and produced his hunting rifle, which I had never seen before. What a way to meet it! He was so convinced there was a mysterious person in our house that he once again searched the entire house, with gun in hand, looking for any evidence. Of course, I was relieved there was no scary person, but a part of me wanted him to find someone to put an end to this nighttime debacle. And put an end to my surreal reputation, which was only making my case of being unusual even more concrete.

My parent's upbringing didn't allow any conversation about this unusual occurrence or to even explore anything about these mysterious night beings. Life simply continued as if nothing happened.

As an adult exploring my spirituality, I look at these visitors in a whole new way. Could these have been my Guides? My soul family? Perhaps, with my feelings of being completely alone, were they reminding me I am never really alone? If so, what did they want from me? And why was it me? And why didn't any of the other family members see or hear anything? Perhaps my Guides wanted to be friends and I was too afraid to engage with them?

9

My two-story, condo is fresh, clean and complete with a little private patio facing a yard with large pine trees. The swimming pool serves my need for exercise. I used to be an avid runner until I ripped my right hamstring on a boating trip, right after my divorce. My friends and I were enjoying our sweet connection, as we've known each other through high school, college and beyond. We've come together for the first time in many years, to enjoy each other's company once again. We were having a joyful day boating and sunning in the refreshing water. As the full moon arose, we docked each of our houseboats side by side in a mysterious cove. With no other people within range, the freedom of fun began. We were drinking some wine as we sank into the evening feel. Four of us woman began floating in big tire size inner tubes in the luke-warm water. We would glide up to the back of our houseboat, and the fun guys poured tequila into our mouths and we would circle around and do it again. Was this like the best way ever of ignoring the pain of my divorce? Oh my God, could I really be a failure? Again? I couldn't let myself entertain this possibility for it scared the bejesus out of me. I was a master at avoiding my pain.

Big doobies were being passed around and I took several big tokes. I was feeling really good. One of my friends said, "Who is ready to go water skiing?" Without any thought, my hand flew up into the lovely evening air. I jumped into the little boat with three other skiers and off we went.

I elected to go first, having taken lots of vacations around water and feeling I was comfortable with my water skiing abilities. Well, lesson of the day, do not mix drinking, smoking and skiing. No matter what strategy I tried, I could not get up on my water skis; my body was like mush. After the third attempt, I surrendered as they pulled me back into the boat.

"I ripped my hamstring," I said, while feeling excruciating pain. I wasn't sure if I could lift the dead weight of my leg out of the water and into the boat. My right leg felt disconnected from the rest of my body. "I really doubt you ripped your hamstring, that's a serious injury," said one of my friends who was a Chiropractor.

Well, it appears my intuition was intact despite my party mode. I wasn't even sure what a hamstring was at the time but sure enough, I had ripped my hamstring in three places. By the end of the week-end the back of my leg was completely black and blue and I had to crawl around the boat, as it was impossible to walk. Fortunately, another person on the boat had pain pills to ease my discomfort. I had to use crutches for several weeks and was told I would never be able to run again. This changed my life dramatically, as running was my way to "run" away from all this craziness within me.

In the process of looking at my past, I make a commitment to forget about the sexual incident from my childhood. I see no other way to be free of its grasp on me and my life, except to let it all go and act like nothing happened. I need to find some peace of mind.

I begin feeling freer than I have in a long time and I am actually entertaining the idea of letting some happiness back in through the slightly ajar door to my life. I am ready to let it all go, including any questions about what happened to me as a child. Besides, children sexually explore each other, right? I choose to let it all go. It's a colossal relief!

I am having a sleepover. Cameron's daughter, Mason is spending the night with me. Mason is a sweet and bright ten year old child. We dance to loud music and act like we are movie stars practicing our scenes. We put post-it notes with positive sayings all around my condo. It is so enjoyable spending time with her. I truly love her and this adds to my deep burning question: Do I approach her dad with this information?

No, I'm letting it all go, it's the past, as I am learning to compartmentalize my thoughts. All these ideas about my brother have to be absent to maintain my focus for this slumber party. My main objective is having fun with Mason. After some snacks and a movie, we fall to sleep on the carpeted floor in the living room making it an officially cool slumber party.

In the wee hours of the morning, I am bolted out of a deep sleep to witness Mason's arms and legs flailing about. Mason is lying on her back, as she is throwing off the covers with her legs while screaming in a harrowing voice,

"No, Dad, no!"

"No, Dad, No!!"

All her covers fall to the carpeted floor around her, exposing her night gown and little panties. Her legs are moving so quickly I can feel the frantic air movement on my own body.

What the fuck? I jump up with a jolt, rubbing my eyes trying to take in what is happening. Unsure if this is a dream, I attempt to move to her and to bring some blood through my body.

"Noooo, Daaaaad, Noooooo!" echoes in the space,

"Noooo, Daaaaad, Noooooo!"

I move my sleepy body to her and attempt to calm her, as I can see she is breathing deeply. Uncertain what to do, I reach for her hand

and hold it. This subtle touch seems to be providing what she needs, as I see her legs and arms slowing down. I can't help but wonder had my brother, her dad, carried this sexual energy onward? Holy crap is all my mind can entertain.

I cannot let myself absorb this reality fully, as I watch Mason fall back to a peaceful sound sleep. All I want is to return to my dream world, which no matter how scary, has to be better than what thoughts are wanting to enter my current world. I want to get away from the many questions swirling in my throbbing head which are enhanced by the wee hours of the morning. Finally, with persistence, I did sleep for a few more hours.

As I awoke the next morning, thoughts of the night emerged into my consciousness. Oh darn, I thought, now what do I do? I really hoped this was a nightmare. A nightmare! My intention is to swish the ugly thoughts out and enjoy my sweet niece. I can do this I tell myself.

"Good morning lovely one."

"Good morning."

"Mason, did you sleep OK last night?" I slowly inquire.

"Fine. And you?" she asks, seeming much older than her ten year old body appears.

"I slept great, I did have a funny dream about a quilt that I kept shaking out until all the colors on the quilt were balanced," prodding her a bit.

She giggles.

"Did you have any dreams?"

"No, not really. What's for breakfast?"

The day flows into fun and pleasure. That evening, dinner is a celebration at one of our favorite Italian restaurants. My friend is moving overseas to France. I am so excited for her. A group of us are all joining to wish her Bon Voyage.

There were eight of us sitting around a dark wood table that matches the atmosphere which is very mysterious and dark, as well. As most of the tables around us are filling with hungry customers, I notice the table cloth's checkered pattern of red and white being enhanced by the rather large candle's flame burning in the middle of the table. We order some wine and appetizers while waiting for my brother, Cameron to arrive. He is running a bit late.

Finally he rushes in and spots us at our table. His shiny blonde hair is matted with sweat. His plump short body plops into the chair and it creaks under his weight. He orders a beer and begins rambling,

"The Catholic Church, do you believe those nasty priests, how could they take advantage of a child's innocence? How can they show their faces in society? I hope they are hanged by their balls. How could they do this? They need to be locked up and throw away the keys," he sputters.

I'm perplexed, as I watch my adopted brother begin speaking about the delicate topic of sexual abuse. He had heard something on the news and he couldn't let it go. It was uncomfortably long and agonizing for me. Am I the only one being so deeply affected by his sermon of sorts?

"Do you believe those nasty old Catholic men? How can they take advantage of young children?"

"No, Cameron, No," I want to scream at him.

In all honesty, I had not seen him so stirred by anything like this. He seems to be in a deep whirlwind of anguish and needs to vent. Do you believe this? Especially after witnessing his daughter's flailing the night before? I find myself fumbling for my old invisibility cloak, feeling paralyzed and drifting up to that familiar place which I found early in life.

Usually, I can go within and find some comfort from the crazy world around me. This had become my coping mechanism, my great escape. However, this is beyond my capabilities. I have to listen to his rambling voice and angered disposition. I can't speak, I can barely breathe as I am brought back to the realization of the night before, "No, Dad, No!" echoes in my head, "No, Dad, No!" as I listen to the "Dad" speak of this daunting scenario directly. I can't shake the haunting feelings from the night before. I so want to deny them.

After a long and painful dinner, even drinking my wine doesn't help me change the feelings that want to explode inside of me. Uncertain I am able to walk, I make it outside. I'm standing in the parking lot with my friend hugging her and telling her to take good care in France when she innocently asks,

"Are you OK, Rhea? You became so quiet while we were eating?" I do not wish to go there, I do not want to answer her question, instead I began to cry.

"What?" she asks again.

"I can't tell you, I'm afraid to tell you!"

Then, of course she insists, as a friend has the right to do. I reveal the previous night's events as clearly as I could through my concern of what this could mean. Her eyes grew in size, yet she is speechless and visibly shaking as well. What a send off for her. I really did not intend to tell anyone. Not yet, I promised myself. I need to think about it and ask for some form of understanding and hope-fully with some time, to find some clarity.

"I need to go," is all she can find to fill the space with the lingering possibility.

Don't kill the messenger, please! I think to myself. Not only am I alone in this, she won't even talk about it. I've come to wonder if having cancer would be easier than this? At least I could talk about the cancer and perhaps receive some empathy and support.

— *Flying Naked*

A few weeks pass by, life goes on, I'm working as a Paralegal by day and doing hypnosis by night, having completed my hypnotherapy training. I am a busy woman, understandably so, I'm trying to keep occupied to prevent me from thinking about the night with my niece. As time goes by, it makes it easier for me to come up with justifications and ways of denying this dynamic. I have become great at running away from things. Where's the pool? I need to swim swim swim. It has become medicine for my soul and a part of my survival.

Still, try as I may, I cannot get beyond the question, what if this is true, what if my brother really did do something to his daughter? My niece? I can't entertain the idea for long. What do I do? Do I talk to him directly? Suddenly I have more ammunition than I care to have. For so long I've wanted to feel connected to my family but this would only alienate me even more.

I decide to receive another Hypnosis session, for I find this deep process of looking within is beginning to make more sense than my real life. I find I enjoy a deeper conversation about what inspires me over the shallow talk of the weather or the latest fad. Let's get right to the good stuff, the real juicy part of life.

Lying in the relaxing chair, in my hypnotic state, I went to the bed yet again. I'm shaking and frightened. I can't breathe even though I'm becoming a bit more used to this place. Once again, with my pink elephant next to me, I am asked to play the game.

Why am I going here again and again? I know the answer whether or not I want to know it.

Later that day, as I'm considering this question, my coworker and friend of the family, Anya calls me. Anya married into lots of money which seems to suit her taste for the best of the best. She lives in a beautiful home with her husband and children. Her skinny body is perfectly tan and adorned with beautiful jewelry. I admire her observant eye and her ability to see life through her creativity. We've seen lots together as we hung out when we were kids. We seem to have a relationship of love and acceptance.

She's in a playful mood and asks,

"How are you, Ms. Rhea?"

I wonder when people ask this, are they really wanting to know how I'm doing or are these just words for connection. I went for the latter.

"I am fine," I reveal as my voice cracks.

'Why did I answer the phone right now?' Is the question ringing in my ears.

"What is it Rhea? Your voice sounds different?"

Darn, she knows me too well.

I had not spoken of this dynamic with anyone, except Devon, the Hypnotherapist, and my friend, at the restaurant send off party and that didn't go well. So I have become reluctant to tell anyone. I don't know if I can talk about it without crying again.

"You really don't want to know."

This only increases her silly mood and she playfully continues.

"Aw, come on, I can handle it. I'm a big girl."

"Anya, trust me, you do not want to hear this."

I thought to myself how much she admires and loves Cameron.

"It can rock your world."

A certainty about human nature, the more you dangle the carrot, the more they want it! Too late now, I tell myself. Knowing Anya's determination as a Taurus, my friend is not going to let me out of this dynamic easily. Although easy going and respectful, a Taurus can be unbelievably stubborn and inflexible in their approach. So much so, that when the logical arguments don't suit them, they will just refuse to listen.

Quick, quick, Rhea, think of something else to tell her. I am not what you call a good liar, although I used to be as a child so I could do what I wanted to do. However, that skill was long gone as I attempt to live my life with more integrity. And it just doesn't feel good to lie to anyone, much less a friend.

Just as I suspect, she insists, "Come on, we share everything."

I guess good friends have some entitlement rights of information. We do share everything.

I tell her about my ongoing hypnosis sessions and the repeated trips to Cameron's bedroom. As if being forced to read a script, I continue to share the sleepover with Mason and her screaming in the middle of the night. I pause, feeling the space, as I realize how much Anya loves Mason as well.

There was dead silence.

Moments felt like an eternity.

Then she finally spoke in a very panicked voice,

"That's weird because last summer, I noticed Cameron walk up to Mason from behind and when he touched her back she jumped a mile. I didn't understand it and thought it was very odd at the time."

I'm feeling something stir within, is it hope? What a relief, someone is willing to talk about the 'elephant in the room.'

Well, then as if someone else had taken the phone from her, Anya came back to her logical ego mind and said,

"No, I can't go there. Cameron is my epitome of a perfect man.

This would crush my reality if I let myself believe this!"

Yes, it does have the potential to rock her world and she chose denial. It's no fun being the victim. I do understand why a "victim" doesn't say anything, it's so bloody confusing.

Just when I think I can't be shocked any further. Crash, my world came tumbling down.

A few days later, I receive a letter from my friend:

Dear Rhea,

I want you to know I have thought about this situation regarding Cameron. He is an upstanding man and I respect him. I know this can't be true.

Hypnosis is all bullshit. You need to go to a Harvard Psychiatrist and stop fooling around with hypnosis.

I do not agree with nor believe any of your story.

— Anya

Reading this letter is like the sun going down on me. The pain and sadness in my heart churns into anger. I'm sad and devastated. What's more important here? I want to plead with her, don't discard me just because you think I mean you harm. Instead, I had to delve into this devastating dynamic all alone! I cried myself to sleep that night realizing no one was willing to disturb this silence.

I have heard this unfortunate idea from many of my clients and this dynamic is very common. As the "victim" nobody wants to believe me or my story. So in addition to being victimized, now I'm being blamed for accusing the perpetrator of doing this. How bizarre and so very sad.

I did surrender to my friends' idea in the letter; maybe I do need to see a "real" therapist? I made an appointment after some research. The Psychiatrist I chose came highly recommended.

During my first meeting with this real therapist, the first questions he ask me are about my home, my career and my life in general and he merely nods his head at my responses.

I told him about my childhood of possible sexual abuse and how I found this information while in trance with a Hypnotherapist. Then the real questions begin.

"Do you often feel anxious or depressed?" he asks.

"Yes, doesn't everyone?" I respond easily.

"Did you have reoccurring nightmares as a child?"

"Yes, one in particular. Do you want to hear it?"

"Yes," he replies.

I tell him of the dream of meeting the strange man on the corner at night and we have to walk around the block together without talking, knowing fully well he will kill me if we make it all the way around the block.

"Was there any significance to this particular corner that exists in your waking world?" he wonders.

"Well yes, my neighbor was kidnapped on this corner and my older sister was dropped off near this same corner after being kidnapped."

"Did you have any 'positive' dreams?"

"Yes, many and I've seen what appears to be Jesus in my dreams."

"Worth noting, were you rebellious as a child?"

"Oh heavens yes, I was always in trouble and I didn't want anyone telling me what to do. In fact, my dad kicked me out of the house as soon as I turned eighteen."

"How old were you the first time you had sex?

"I was only thirteen years old."

"Continue please," he encourages.

"Even as I share this story it scares me thinking what could have happened to me," I say noticing my body is shaking.

"My friend and I loved the night time and we would tell our parents we were staying at each other's house and then roam the streets. We would go to the local park where all the "fun" people went. There was always something exciting happening, including drinking and sometimes smoking marijuana. On this particular night, I told my friend, "I'm going to have sex tonight," ever so casually. Even though we are still friends today, I don't remember what she said, except she has always supported me in my decisions.

I hung out at a gas station, of all places, until this car of two twenty year old men drove into the station to buy some gasoline. As they were filling up their gas tank, I walked over to them with seeming confidence.

"I want to have sex tonight," I said to these two strange young men.

"Get on in," they said smiling like they had just won the lottery. I hopped in the back seat of their car and off we went to their house.

The younger man and I went directly to the bed and had sex. It was not fun nor was it pleasurable at all. I was disappointed. I had hoped for the fairy tale type of sex that is portrayed in the movies. And there wasn't any blood like I had heard about. Where was my blood? They took me back to the same gas station and I met with my friend again. As I was getting out of the car, one of the young men asked me why I was so quiet.

"Why don't you talk?"

"I don't know. Thanks, was all I said."

Looking at the therapist, I asked, "Why would I associate being silent with sex?"

"Think about it. Perhaps it was because you, as a little girl, were asked to be quiet so nobody would hear you."

The pieces were coming together and I was feeling the familiar goosebumps indicating I was onto something.

"Why would you as a child of 13, make this declaration of wanting to have sex? And be so fearless about it? Even to the point of finding comfort with the entire adult process of a first sexual encounter. Or was it your first?" He continues, "Were you ever reluctant to be alone with anyone as a child? Male or female?"

"Yes, well, with my brother Cameron, as I told you and my neighbor—he gave me the creeps."

"Please explain?" he inquires.

"I remember being at my neighbor's house, I guess around the age of eight. I was spending the night with his daughters and I remember waking up in the middle of the night feeling very upset and crying. I don't remember exactly what happened except that I wanted to go home. I cried and cried and they would not let me leave. My neighbors talked me into staying the rest of the night. And to embellish it a bit more, his wife came to me in a dream a few years ago. She was literally within two inches of my face screaming at me with accusatory eyes, "What did you do with my husband? What did you do with my husband?"

"Do you have any connection with this man today?"

"No, he's passed," I sigh.

"Do you often feel anger for no apparent reason?"

"Hmm, yes."

"Have you taken it out on anyone or anything?"

"I bullied some girls in grade school, which I deeply regret and what also comes to mind is when I was young, I remember pulling the antennas out of little ants, just to be mean. That's pretty sick isn't it?"

"Well, possibly and I am here to support you, not judge you. Did you have unexplained headaches or stomach aches as a child?"

"Yes, I had stomach aches quite often. In fact, one time my mom became so concerned, she drove me across town to visit the doctor and there was nothing wrong with me, physically anyway."

"Do you find you talk about sex and sexual encounters easily?" the interrogation continues.

"Yes, in fact in my world, everything can be related to sex as I see it. That's what she said," is my attempt at humor as it's getting really hot in this room. I am wise enough to realize all of these Yes's are leading to something.

"Do you feel you are controlling at times?"

"Yes, I have to admit I feel I need to control my environment to feel safe. I do not want anyone controlling me...ever!"

"Well, do you see the correlation? When you have been controlled and feel out of control, generally the victim, in this case your little girl, makes a promise to herself to never let anyone or anything ever control her again."

"Do you often feel challenging situations are all your fault?"

"Oh God, yes, it's so painful and then the guilt seeps in and I want to hurt someone like I've been hurt," I respond easily, "I am starting to feel like the 'Yes' woman," I smirk.

He sat up in his chair with a caring look and he says,

"Rhea, it seems you have many of the possible symptoms of sexual abuse. I suggest you continue with your journey of exploration using hypnosis. I mean how can you deny the authenticity of your pink elephant's visitation?"

"But what do I do with this information? Do I talk to my brother?"

"That's for you to decide."

"It feels as if I've been given a loaded gun," I feel tears welling again.

"I understand it must be challenging."

Silence ensues as I'm crying now. I look to him for some support.

"My business partner implements hypnosis in his practice and insists it's powerful and authentic. He gave me the book, *Many Lives, Many Masters* by Brian Weiss and I must say I read it over the course of a weekend. I could not put it down. It's all about the lives between lives and how all wisdom is within us. Are you familiar with it?" the Psychiatrist asks.

"Yes, I have read it and I resonate with it as well. I gave a copy to my friend after her husband passed away. It seemed to give her hope she will see him again,"

His parting words are,

"Rhea, as I mentioned, you seem to be finding the insight you need through hypnosis. I suggest you continue using this modality for it seems to be working quite well for you. I concur the big question seems to be, do you talk to your brother? I wish I could say there is an easy answer to this question. I suggest you follow your path and you'll know one day if you need to confront him. I wish you the best."

I walk out of his office into the much needed sunlight and think to myself, well, if that ain't confirmation, what is!

Now what?

I Google "some of the possible effects of child abuse?":

> Once you are sexually abused, your evolution is arrested at that point. Your maturity level is fixed at that early age. The stress changes your brain. The hippocampus doesn't function as it should and can be greatly limited. The hippocampus is a small organ located within the brain's medial temporal lobe and forms an important part of the limbic system, the region that regulates emotions. Associated mainly with long term memory. Sexual abuse also affects spatial navigation. Commonly, the victims don't know what's happening until "it" happens. If the perpetrator is really good, the victim believes it is their fault this is happening. There is a sense of control over the victim.

As I read, I am beginning to put together more of the pieces of how this sexual situation has affected my life.

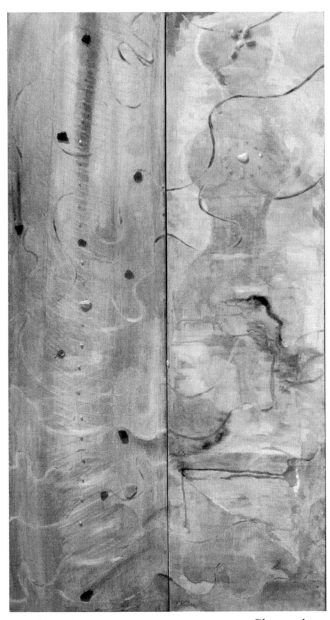

— *Choose Love*

It's a lovely morning, as I'm stepping out the door of my condo. I hear the familiar sound of my phone ringing inside and I feel something tingle in my belly. I'm learning to trust my body messages, take them seriously and listen to their advice, therefore, I turn back inside and answer my phone without hesitation.

It's Jorge, one of the instructors from the Hypnotherapy Institute, "Hello Rhea. How are you?"

"I'm great thanks!"

"The reason I've called is because my wife and I have a booth at a metaphysical fair this weekend. Um, because of some personal issues, we are unable to attend so we thought you would be perfect to fill in for us. Would you be willing?"

"Is everything OK?" I ask.

"Oh yeah, we're fine but my mother-in-law needs some help moving. You know, when family beckons?" he laughs.

Except I'm not laughing. It amazes me how even the word 'family' affects my insides.

"Well...OK, I would love to help you. Besides it may give me an opportunity to learn more about my new friend, hypnosis."

Relishing in the freedom of my divorce, I can easily respond without having to consider anyone else.

"We would like you to answer any questions about the Institute and hypnosis in general."

After the necessary details are shared, Jorge says, "Remember to trust yourself and thanks."

The remainder of the week, I prepare for the event both emotionally and mentally. I do my yoga several times, to find my centered place within and it seems to bring forth such a wonderful relaxed feeling with the added bonus of bringing in more of my confidence. Running the booth by myself is sounding exciting. As Saturday pops its sunny head into my bedroom window, I feel ready and willing.

The large Convention Hall is swarming with curious presenters from all walks of life. I enjoy people watching and notice some business people as well as the hippie-looking type. This typical metaphysical environment comes complete with patchouli aroma, sage and many colorful booths offering an array of alternative ways of healing and transformation.

As I'm setting up my table of brochures, business cards and personal items, I notice an engaging woman from across the room. With mysterious eyes, she stares right at me. Eventually, I move over to this woman's booth, or let's say her eyes pull me over to her. As I approach her brightly decorated table, I read her sign and it says "Soul Psychic Readings."

"I have one spot left and it's for you."

Her purple and blue outfit, adorned with lots of silver jewelry, compliments her gypsy look.

"You sound convinced," I say.

"You know you want a reading and what a reading it will be."

"Really?"

"Yes, what is your name?"

"My name is Rhea," I say as I present my hand to shake hers, "and yours?"

"Sonya. Yeah, I'm sensing it's time for a big change for you.

You must return so we can explore what this change is, yes?"

She keeps her deep set grey eyes on me.

With a whirl of delight, I respond, "Yes, I surrender. What time is my appointment?"

Looking at her calendar for confirmation, she reveals, "One o'clock it is."

"OK, Nice to meet you Sonya. I'll be back soon," I say smiling from ear to ear.

Many people are curious about hypnosis and I find myself enjoying 'the process of' sharing this mysterious journey within. One of the many misconceptions of hypnosis is that they will be controlled by their therapist. I explain that this trance place is as common as driving from one familiar place to another when you don't remember driving it. Your mind has gone into the memories in your brain, just like in hypnosis.

Time flies quickly, as I answer questions from a wide variety of curious attendees. I notice it's time for my 1:00 appointment, so after closing my booth temporarily, I find my way to visit Sonya while also noticing the amount of people present at the entire event. I am guessing at least 200. I sink into the chair opposite her, as I look into her enchanting eyes.

"Hi Rhea."

I shake Sonya's hand as she closes her eyes and asks for this time be for my highest good. After a brief pause she begins speaking,

"OK. Wow, I see you moving out west. You will grow spiritually and blossom into a real women. You will find your real home and probably won't return. This reading is going to be a bit different, as all the information is coming in quickly."

"A lot of realness," I giggle buying time to digest all of this.

"Do you sense where out west?" I ask.

Swishing an annoying fly from her downcast eyes she continues,

"I'm seeing the California area, do you have any connections to California?"

"Yes, my friend lives in La Jolla."

I reflect back, "When I was a teenager, reluctantly I went on a trip with my family out west. The minute I stepped onto California's soil, I told my mom I would live there one day."

My body is reacting now, I have goosebumps all over my arms.

"There's your answer, isn't it?" she quips.

"Well yes," I'm grasping the idea slowly and yet somehow I know it's true.

"You will meet your soul mate and I believe there's a child awaiting you as their mommy. You will find a spiritual family and will find a new way of being."

"How soon do you see me moving?"

"It will happen rather quickly. Are you planning a trip to California?"

This is feeling like magical dust to my ears.

"I guess after this I am," I say laughing gleefully.

After a long pause, she whispers as though too sacred to say any louder, "In your reflection you will find what you seek."

"What?"

"In your reflection you will find what you seek."

I remind myself to breath as I take in all this "moving" information. My mind is grasping this idea the best I can, as this enchanting woman continues to speak in greater detail about moving out west. To move away from the family secret and its many ramifications. Sensing the overwhelming look on my face, Sonya finds a comfortable place to bring the reading to a halt.

"I want you to know, Rhea, I do readings for a living and this is one of the most powerful and clearest readings I have ever done. You must fulfill your prophecy out west!"

"Thank you and bless you," I say between hugging her and

making an honest attempt to go back to my other reality. I can move away from all the craziness! I couldn't be more relieved.

Sonya smiles at me as I'm walking away. She then calls out, "Rhea, trust it and most importantly, trust yourself! I am very excited for you and your journey."

The words "trust yourself" linger in my ears, as I'm spinning with so many ideas. The tall, beaming woman next in line, overhearing the end of our conversation says, "I want what she's having!"

We all giggle like little girls.

Finding my way back to my booth, I digest this psychic reading which was said with such conviction, as if written in stone. No wonder my entire body wanted me to answer the phone call from Jorge earlier in the week.

A few days later, after settling into the potency of my Reading, I call my friend Kellye, the psychic. Miraculously, she lives out west in California. As carefully as I could, I told her about my reading. I ask Kellye if she would be open to a visit and if I could stay in her home with her. She happily agreed. That's one more needed piece to the puzzle.

Two weeks later, all the plans are made and I'm on my way out west. I promise myself if I am received by this lovely town within the ten days I'm visiting, I will move as soon as possible. To get a feel for La Jolla, I explore food markets, coffee shops, yoga centers and health spas. Also, in my planning, I've been able to set up a meeting with the owners of the Transpersonal Hypnotherapy Institute for a possible position assisting in the office, helping at trainings and building my Hypnotherapy practice.

Old town is a delight. No cars are allowed on this well traversed street and I explore it while admiring all the artsy shops. I spoke with many of the local people who would openly listen as I explain my situation. I feel comfortable and am received almost everywhere I venture.

This is bliss, for my soul clearly needed to be accepted here to make the big move. I wander into a random health spa and within 15 minutes, I'm on a massage table getting "rolfed" for free. They were looking for students to practice their massaging. I sign up to be a volunteer with the understanding I will return in two weeks. What am I doing, I wonder? Quickly, I remind myself of the reoccurring insights from the reading I had received and my body's positive reaction to it.

Driving up the curvy road leading to the Transpersonal Hypnotherapy Institute, it is a sight for my eyes, hungry for change. It is a lovely large house perched on the top of a hill with a deck that goes all around the house. The eight bedrooms, eight bathrooms and large basement are ready for attracting more hypnosis students.

I'm excited to meet with the owners, Andi and Troy. We talk for a few hours and it is sweet and relaxing. Hummingbirds make their presence known as we sit on the deck overlooking the ocean. Salty air fills my nostrils. I'm in heaven. They say they will let me know about the position, which appears to be perfect for me. As I drive down their driveway, glancing back to their smiling faces, I feel confident I have landed this position.

After the eighth day of staying at Kellye's, she mentions, "My phone is ringing more for you than it is for me." She adds with a smile, "La Jolla is welcoming you like a true friend."

As the end of my visit is approaching, I feel the need to go within and ask for a sign of confirmation. Getting comfortable on the sofa with cushions all around me, I close my eyes in meditation and soon find that deep place within me. The feeling is the same familiar source I experience under hypnosis. I ask that source, "Is it for my highest good to move to La Jolla?"

Pause, nothing. Pause.

Several minutes pass and just about the time I begin questioning if anything is going to happen, I begin to notice a vague figure standing with an azure glow that seems to emanate from its body.

As the figure steps forward into the moonlight, I catch my breath. I've been given glimpses of this face in childhood dreams, fleeting moments of recognition that were over in an instant. He now graced the full force of his attention on me. Frozen in this state, I stare at the man in front of me. He is the most beautiful man I have ever seen. To the modern world, he is Jesus. He smiles at me, an expression of such grace and warmth that I am suffused with it, as if the sun itself radiates from his simple expression.

I remain motionless, unable to do anything but stare at his beauty and divinity. Yes, complete with his white robe, bare feet and beard, he glides gracefully towards me. Jesus holds my gaze for an eternal moment 'standing' directly in front of me. We connect in a loving unearthly way. No words are spoken yet I had a sense of him, speaking to my heart and soul. Jesus rewards me by leaning forward and placing a single, sweet kiss on the top of my forehead. Feeling his message is received by me, he smiles and glides away. Connecting with Jesus in this fashion is both surreal and breathtaking.

Enticed by his presence and the feelings of peace and unconditional love I encountered while engaging with him, I could not deny the power of his simple message. I smile deeply to myself realizing what a perfect and undeniable sign. I'm moving to Cal-i-for-nia.

Later, appreciating the moonlight from her comfortable leather couch, Kellye asks, "What do you think Jesus was telling you?"

"I believe he was letting me know he is there for me and he blesses my journey to move here."

"Interesting," she says, "I so agree."

"The Institute called today and offered me a position. I accepted and I told them I would be right back."

She smiles and says, "You are certainly on a roll, Rhea. I feel honored to have been a part of your opening to your spirituality."

I took this as a perfect time to exit, saying,

"Sweet dreams and thanks for sharing your lovely home with me. I love you Kellye, I'll see you in a few weeks to swim with the wild dolphins."

Returning back home to Elefont is bitter sweet, I have to say good-bye to my friends of many years and my family. Quitting my paralegal job is easy as I know I probably wouldn't venture into the legal world ever again. I find there is too much right and wrong, black and white for my journey of wanting to experience and see all the colorful spectrums of life. My new passion, my new focus is on learning more about hypnosis and the mysteries of this "trance" world.

Essentially, I'm getting support from every direction, even the law firm has offered me unemployment to get me established out west. What is really underneath this charitable offering is that one of the Attorneys had made a big mistake. After investigating a case, this man took me to his home and then tried to get me into bed, to put it bluntly. So, this was the law firm's attempt to keep my mouth shut.

Nothing personal to New Jersey, for it has some down-to-earth genuine people, I just happen to be a Sun Goddess at heart. So Good-bye Grayness and Hello Sunshine with adventure and whatever else awaits me. I am ready for anything and little did I know what an exhilarating ride it would be.

While driving, I'm so relieved to actually be leaving this town I called home. I'm traveling with my forever dear friend, Eva.

She is a sweet blonde with a heart of gold. She works as an Art Director and is married to a wonderful man and they are raising their five children. When she met her husband, she referred to him as 'That Guy,' I still call him 'That Guy' to this day. She has always been supportive of me and my individual journey. She carries her heart on her sleeve and seems to intuit what's needed in her surrounding world. This can be both a curse and a blessing, as she gives so much of herself. In fact, sometimes it is at the detriment of taking care of herself. We've had many friendly conversations about the need to nurture ourselves first. It's like the description of the plane scenario. While flying in a plane with your child, if God forbid, the plane should start to go down, you must put on your oxygen mask first before putting on your child's mask, so you are available for them. I kindly remind Eva of this scenario and she says,

"I know Rhea, it must be embedded in my blood to help people first and I'm really trying to say Yes to me," she says as she winks at me. I have used this idea with her, instead of looking at it as saying no to others, it's saying yes to herself.

"Thanks for your support," she continues.

Perhaps this is why we have come together, to teach each other. For you see, I have no problem thinking of myself first. In fact, I had to learn this modality to survive in this world. Selfish? Perhaps a bit. However, I've come to learn that a bit of healthy selfishness is a "good" thing, for if I'm taking care of myself, I'm much more available for others and my friends. On the other hand, Eva supports me in listening to my many ideas and my many failed attempts to maneuver this crazy world. I have so many ideas, and so many passions I can get pulled in many directions. She seems to know what to say when I need to hear something. Yes, I get to love her. Recently, I heard that love isn't an emotion, it's an ability.

As I pick up Eva at her house, several of my high school friends are standing on the lawn at this early hour, to say good-bye and wish me well. One of my friends, is a bit upset that I only gave her two weeks notice before my move. This would be the beginning of my gypsy lifestyle, as I'm creating a new way of exploring my country.

Five days later, we arrive on California's doorsteps and its spectacular ocean views, I am ready to call you my new home. We pull up with the moving van not far behind. I'm thrilled I will be working at the Institute. I've agreed to do office work, while assisting trainings and creating my own practice.

I also arrive in La Jolla feeling a bit rudderless. I realize my money had not been transferred to my new bank account, and the movers would not haul any of my furniture out of the truck until they had money in their hands. Holy crap, my very first day in La Jolla and I'm driving around town looking for some type of establishment that will receive wired money.

Did I also mention I'm one of those people who came into this life without a compass installed in my brain? Getting from point A to point B can be very challenging for me. I'm a wreck trying to maneuver this town to find a place to perform my money transaction. Mind you, this was before the good ole invention of the GPS. I'm convinced this device was created just for me. It is one crazy welcome, I can assure you, not the peacefulness I had hoped for. Plus the apartment I had agreed to unseen from New Jersey, was so little and the view from the living room was of a gray cement wall. Really? I thought I had left the gray behind. So, reality was a little different than my optimistic mind had predicted. Finally, the bank is found, the movers are paid and all my furniture is moved into my new little space. There's barely enough room for my things, so I gift Eva with an antique desk she really likes. This feels good to me as I know it will be in a loving home.

Still adjusting to all the newness and having said good bye to my dear friend, I felt quite alone even though Kellye lives nearby. I feel a bit ungrounded at times adjusting to my new reality.

I also want to believe by making a move this far from home, I would have left a chunk of the family baggage behind me. Not quite so. It seems it had slipped into one of my bags and came crawling out ever so mysteriously to emerge into my life again. Darn!

My second week in my new little apartment, I'm invited to assist at the Transpersonal Hypnotherapy Institute in Boulder, Colorado, which is also run by Andi and Troy. Apparently, one of the other trainers at the Institute was unable to attend, therefore, I willingly accept the invitation. All the plans are made and I will be staying at Troy and Andie's mountain house during the training.

I arrive a few minutes late to the training. I am just in time to join a group event. We are to pick a partner and sit on the floor across from this person and gaze into their eyes for ten minutes without any words being exchanged. This man picks me for his partner. He is a cute, blonde, typical California type guy. Finding a comfortable sitting position is challenging as I'm still unwinding from my long drive.

While starring into this man's eyes, my body becomes still. It seems as if I know him. It is unlike anything I have ever experienced as I remind myself to breathe. This process seems to be opening doors within me, doors to my emotional world. I'm feeling sad one moment, then happiness finds its way through the window. It's as though we're communicating without our usual attempt to find words awakening new lines of exchange. Our energy is somehow dancing together creating an open heart space. So many times, I want to look away from the intensity of his penetrating eyes and these feelings moving through me reminding to hold my gaze. I would float back to my Ego, wondering how I look, as I didn't even have time to refresh my lipstick or brush my hair before coming into the resort's lovely room. The new emotions flood over my body again, rescuing me from my own thinking mind. This process moves back and forth within me many times. I find it to be very invigorating as

I attempt to understand how I seem to know this man.

Do we have some kind of a connection or is this the purpose of the process? When the ten minutes are up, I happen to glance at him further with my "regular" eyes. I notice his left hand has a gold band, perhaps a wedding ring? I'm actually relieved to see this, as I am still spinning from my recent move. Relaxing my shoulders, I tell myself at least this isn't a romantic connection. This could be way too much for me at the moment.

"What an interesting way to meet, my name is Rhea," I break the intense energy building between us, as I reach out my hand to shake hands with him.

"Yep, thanks for sharing so much with me, even on our first date," he laughs.

Oh my goodness, what a beautiful smile with lovely white straight teeth. I am a teeth sucker. I mean, I'm a sucker for a big smile with healthy white teeth.

"Sharing so much?" I repeat, "What do you mean? What did you see? Is "see" the verb I'm looking for?"

"See? I suppose it's one way to explain what we did. Yes, I was able to see you, I mean really see you."

"My name is Eli, by the way," he reaches his hand out to me. We shake hands again which seems almost humorous given what we just experienced together.

"What were you seeing in my eyes? What an experience? What is this process called?" I ask him wanting to understand. "Why am I talking so much?" I secretly ask myself.

"It's called Gazing. You missed the introduction," Eli quips.

I like that he noticed when I arrived.

We are interrupted by the Instructor who wants us to rejoin the large circle of participants sitting on pillows on the wooden floor.

"We'll talk more later," he says as he passes me a handout. I fumble to find a seat in the circle and begin reading,

'The Soul Gazing exercise is a method of communicating that is completely nonverbal. As such, it may open new doors to intimacy that were previously unexplored. Use this exercise to communicate on a deeper level and to awaken new lines of exchange. Soul Gazing harmonizes the energy of both partners, creating an open heart space. Soul Gazing can be difficult for some, because people are usually shy about looking directly into another person's eyes for any length of time. Glances are exchanged for only a few moments. When another person looks at us intently for any period of time, it may feel like an intrusion, and we may label it a "stare" rather than a friendly "gaze." The eyes are often called 'the windows of the soul.' Through the eyes you may see your partner's hidden emotions, perhaps even thoughts or emotions that remain hidden from your partner. In this exercise, you may feel uncomfortable, confronted, exposed and even afraid. You may judge yourself or your partner in your thoughts. You may feel difficult emotions. Resist the urge to look away when confronted with these thoughts and emotions. Observe these thoughts and emotions if they arise. Feel your feelings during the exercise. Allow your thoughts and emotions to pass, as they certainly will, until they give way to an inner peacefulness and calm.'

During our break, I spot Eli in the hallway.

"I went so many places in one second," I reveal.

"Yeah, I was seeing into you so deeply, as if I know you," Eli adds.

"Sounds like a pickup line to me," I kid, "Seriously, have you done anything like this before?"

"No, you're my first and Rhea, would you stop looking at me like that."

"Like what? I'm just, you know, looking at you," I respond.

"It's like you're gazing again, with such intensity," Eli adds.

"I guess we've started this way and thus we must continue. And you're looking at me the same way."

"Busted and while we're in the flirting zone, I love your green eyes," Eli offers.

"Aw, you're sweet AND I see you're married," I remind him and perhaps myself.

"Yes and we're planning on getting pregnant soon. I keep dreaming about a baby."

"Aw, the amazing dreamworld. My dreamworld is quite active and revealing as well."

"I see we'll have plenty to talk about."

I assist Troy during this powerful Training. The first part of the training is two weeks long and covers many modalities in hypnotherapy. There will be a three day break followed by another week focusing on NLP (Neuro-linguistic Programming.) NLP is an approach to psychotherapy and change based on a model of interpersonal communication. It seeks to educate people in self-awareness and effective communication, and to change their patterns of mental and emotional behavior.

One morning, prior to the three day break, while awaking in the mountain house set up by the Institute, I hear a little voice saying to me,

"Ask Eli to visit the mountain house with you."

What? This is bizarre.

The voice repeated the same message again,

"Ask Eli to go to the mountain house with you during your break," as loudly as if someone were talking right next to my ear. Why is this voice suggesting I connect with Eli? He's married and planning a baby.

The voice was so clear but who was doing the speaking? I need to think about this, however, a part of me already knows the answer. Ever since they first walked out of my closet in the middle of the night—absolutely terrifying me—my Guides have been around me. I'm in appreciation of them now and realize I need to listen when they speak in my ear like this. Ask Eli to visit me? OK, whatever you say.

What a bravura, as I ask Mr. Married blonde California guy to join me on our three day break. He says, Yes. We'll go for fun and I'm still curious why my Guides want me to connect with him?

Excitedly, we leave to go on our three day journey, cruising in my Saab through the mountain roads of Colorado. Being lost in our pleasure, we end up in the quaint little town known as Nederland. Dancing along the worn sidewalks are shiny colorful gems embedded in the concrete. Our time in Nederland is truly magical, easy and delightful, as we sip iced tea on a deck overlooking the expansion of green mountains that seem to go on forever.

Eli calls and talks to his wife often and tells her all about our time together. Even though, we are sharing our worlds, we honor their marriage vows. However, we are also aware of our karmic connection. It is becoming apparent we have met for some reason.

Having only one bedroom in this home, we chose to sleep in this room together. After driving most of the day, I am exhausted and crash as soon as my head finds the pillow. At night my thoughts have a pleasant way of slipping through their collars and running free into dream world. Clearly, this is one of those dream nights as I am captivated by this inspiring world once again.

The next morning, as we are waking up, I turn to Eli, covering my morning breath with the sheet, "I had the most fascinating and interesting dream. I dreamt we, as in you and me, were lying in a tepee together and it felt vaguely familiar."

"What? Where was it?" he says while rubbing his eyes from sleep.

"I'm not really sure, except we both were inside this brownish leather tepee and I could smell something familiar?"

"What? You could smell something in the dream?" Eli wants to know.

"Well yes, I could smell the aroma of the Earth but the primary smell was of a fire, I remember looking into the fire circle and it appeared to have glowing embers."

"Really? Tell me more?" Eli is sitting up in bed looking at me with his deep blue eyes, as his hand found my arm to rest on it gently. I felt a surge of energy go through my body.

"What I found peculiar was how familiar the tepee and the surroundings felt. The bedding, even though rough, seemed to be what my skin was used to. I felt so deeply connected to you as our hearts seemed to be as one. We were together, not only cuddling, we were connected emotionally as well," I continue, "Oh my, Eli this sounds like the best come-on line ever. Perhaps it's time to change channels, get some coffee and visit the great outdoors."

"No wait, Rhea, you won't believe this? I think I had the exact SAME dream?" Eli's voice raises at the end with a questioning sound.

"What? Is that even possible?" I'm sitting up in bed, rearranging my pajamas from their twirled position around my body. I am charged by this revelation.

"I don't know, I haven't experienced this before, yet we seem to be having a lot of firsts."

"Now you truly have my attention. Did you notice if it was day or night time in your dream?"

Eli responds, "I seem to remember seeing the stars through the hole at the top where the tepee poles meet and create a star formation and then the lighting changed."

"Do you remember sensing we were mourning something? I felt as if our children had just left or a close family member had just passed?"

"I remember it being deeply moving?" Eli responds while jumping out of bed. He begins using his entire body to make his point as his arms and hands seem to be doing some kind of jazzy dance as he speaks,

"Did you notice how the flap on the tepee door was open in the beginning and then magically seemed to be shut? I felt as if we had lost our children. Oh My!"

We both stop talking and look at each other with the realization of 'our' dream. My tears want to be seen as I say, "I do remember feeling my heart was absolutely broken."

Eli chimes in, "Now that you mention it, yes, I did notice the flap on the tepee! It seems someone from outside closed it for us, as we were facing it. I remember wondering if it was closed because the fire was out? Or was it to keep the other tribe members out as we were in mourning?"

"Wow, yes, it did seem to be very deep as if we lost our children?" I offer.

I notice he seems to be getting tears in his eyes as he says, "It was a deep pain for me, unlike anything I've felt this lifetime. And I'm also remembering it was important I cut my long hair, isn't that interesting?"

The tears run down my cheeks easily now.

Noticing my tears, Eli finds his way back to my bed and we cuddle just like in the dream.

What is happening? He is married, I keep reminding myself. Yet, I can't deny something is stirring.

Later as we are hiking in the foothills,

"How exciting, to be dreaming the same dream! Have you experienced this before?" I want to know.

"I am laughing because you already asked me this question. Not quite like this, I certainly dream about many people, but not while they are in the same room with me," Eli says.

"Sorry for the repeat, I'm digesting lots, having just moved all the way across the country and then this workshop and then You!"

There I go, needing to justify my every move. Why must I do this? As if sensing my insecurities, Eli hugs me.

I continue,

"And I too seem to have a very active dream world. It's to the point I want to document my dreams somehow."

I laugh, wanting to lighten the mood a bit, especially after our deep dreamworld of emotions. Comedy is tragedy plus time.

"I so enjoy talking to you Rhea. You're so wise and yet I'm sensing there is something holding you back as well?"

"Shit, I'm busted," I laugh nervously. Is he referring to my uncertainty...my insecurities...oh God, my boogies?! I make a note to ask more later.

"No seriously. I feel something, not sure what it is?" He looks directly into my eyes.

I'm so full at this moment and more than a bit afraid to hear about my issues. Do they ever end? Instead, I blurt out,

"I'll race you to the car!"

Eli and I are spinning in the reality of what is happening between us. We seem to know each other very comfortably. Continuously, we say things the other is thinking and actually finish each other's sentences. It's rather bizarre until eventually, I just expect it.

We return to the training. Yes, it was a hypnosis training, however I seem to be in a whole other world of trance myself wondering about my desires for Eli. I want to push them away, yet as I look at him across the room in our circle of fellow participants, my heart wants to share more with him. Oh dear! I feel excitement and wonderment dancing together.

Also, I'm looking at the pattern of bringing men into my life. What do they give me that perhaps, I need to give to myself? It's funny, not haha funny, but humorous how having the validation of a man seems to make me think I am fine. I'm making a commitment to myself to honor the fact that Eli is married. Been there, done that!

The rest of the training passes quickly, as I am assisting Troy and we seem to have a nice flow and make a good team together. It's as if I can sense his needs before he can voice them. I am so pleased I took this spontaneous job and feel good about its results. Was I guided to this event? It sure feels like my Guides wanted me to come to this training.

We've covered Dreamtime, past life regression and NLP. We have volunteers come up to the front of the room and we show the class how to put the clients into trance. It's a natural and powerful process of learning hypnotherapy modalities.

As the training is coming to an end, Eli and I part sweetly with the intention to keep in touch. Eli returns home to Northern California and his wife. I drive back home alone, often looking over at the empty seat where Eli sat just a week earlier. Did we really dream the same dream? I want to believe it, yet if I let myself go there, I also want more of this kind of a connection in my life; I want him. Do I dare let myself go there fully? I must let him go, my wiser self tells me.

I'm happy to return to my little apartment. I'm still waffling in the idea I'm living in California. I enjoy the Institute's support and guidance to be the best hypnotherapist. Things are going well as I've befriended the bike paths that have turn lanes and the designated bike lanes which flow all around. One of the bike paths begins only a block from my place, now called home. What a freedom to jump on my ten speed and find my way to the many parts of town within minutes.

Eli and I communicate regularly and the spark continues to grow even stronger. My connection with Eli seems to have a power over me beyond my conscious understanding. After a lot of conversations, contemplation and realizations, Eli calls me with some dramatic, but not surprising news. He and his wife have agreed it's best for them to separate and get a divorce.

Within a month, Eli moves in with me. The timing is amazing, as I have been asked to care for the Institute's house on the water for two months. I'm working there already so it's perfect.

This mansion is complete with timers on the shutters in the main rooms. I so love this feature as we are greeted with the beauty of the California sun each morning, reminding us to bring the light to ourselves in this lovely house. We settle into our mansion groove together quite easily.

Slowly, I'm creating a private practice with the students of the Institute. I found the perfect office space in town for doing my specialty work, which is past life regression. Looking at my past lives has been helpful to me personally, as I made a connection to other lives I've lived. Therefore, I want to share this powerful process of looking within with others. Regression work is a compassionate and effective therapy. The focus on patterns is balanced with gifts such as skills and talents that are the bonuses brought forth from the past.

Past-life regression work is largely focused on forgiveness. It doesn't mean you have to play out the situation again in this life but recognizing the wounding and challenges of a previous life will bring our attention to it and allow it to be released. In this way, the hurts of the past can be healed. It is important the hurts are forgiven and the lessons are retained. Thus, the past holds the keys to unlock the future. Regressions produce sacred stories representing gifts from the vast unconscious mind. Such sacred stories help us to redefine the purpose and meaning of life. Conducting and experiencing regressions has enabled me to grow spiritually beyond measure. And it takes the pressure off of me trying to do everything this lifetime.

Several months later, Eli began having insightful dreams about a woman he knew in Seattle. After our tepee experience, I have learned to honor our dream world and listen carefully when I hear this five letter word...D-R-E-A-M. After the fourth Seattle woman dream, he calls her.

Returning from my office later that day, Eli tells me he talked to Darcy. This is the dream woman and she is still teaching her art program of 17 years but she is also looking for someone to train as she is retiring soon.

"Are you suggesting what I think you are suggesting?" My intuitive ears are burning.

"Well, it's a possibility," he says to me.

"What? Is she willing to come here?" I ask.

"Well, that would be one way, however, she wants the person to learn "hands-on" in the classroom, in addition to the training."

"Wait, you want to visit Seattle?!"

I'm a bit nervous about the ramifications of this question. I certainly know he will move anywhere pretty quickly based on how fast he transitioned to live with me in La Jolla.

"I'm just saying, think about it."

"But Eli, you know how I love my hypnosis sessions and working here and in Boulder. I love my work."

"Honey, this doesn't mean you can't do both."

"I want to continue my past life regression work with my clients and my work with Alicia, one of my favorite clients."

I think of Alicia and Leif, whom we have just met. We were having such a good time with them, we were actually kicked out of the coffee shop for being too loud. They are a lovely couple, whom I would like to get to know a bit more. I've been doing regression sessions with Alicia and they are proving quite beneficial to her as well.

"It would be an adventure, that's all."

I'm not giving in easily, "Look Eli, I've only been here a few months. I need to honor my commitment to Andi and Troy."

"Of course, just think about it, or better yet, let's dream about it."

I began to open my mouth to defend my position and stop myself. This is a new approach for me, defending myself has become a way of life, a way of survival. I'm proud I can stop this habitual flow somewhat.

That night I dreamt I was in a lovely house and a voice said with much excitement, "You are now at the thrift store level!" The voice continued, "Look at recycling as a way of life. Metaphorically, it is time to be conscious of recycling and thinking green. Seattle is awaiting you and it has lots of thrift stores for you to explore."

Both of our dream worlds seem to be giving hints to move to Seattle. My dreams continually included bodies of water, tall trees and the most revealing dream is seeing myself teaching again, however, it's different as I'm teaching art and creativity. Eli's dreams seem to dance around having a baby. I have stopped taking the pill, per our agreement, and trust if we are meant to have a child, we will get pregnant.

— *Reflection*

The thought provoking dreams about Seattle continue. OK I get it, give me a break as I really like California. After more ideas and nudging from my dreamworld, I surrender to moving to Seattle.

I realize I can continue my hypnosis sessions as well as learn more about this art program. Darcy said she had been praying to God for someone who could carry on her art program and she felt it was me. Is it true or not? It doesn't really matter because it worked. I am sold on the idea of creating a new business using my creativity, while working with adults doing my hypnosis. And that feels like the best of both worlds.

So off we go to Seattle. We find a sweet home from a friend of Eli, who is moving out at the same time we are moving to Seattle. We sign a six month lease and it is perfect for our landing in the northwest. We set up our new digs, noticing the timing is set up like a fairy tale.

One particular day, as I am crossing our new living room to go to the deck, I look into a mirror hanging on the wall and I stop myself completely. For the first time in my life, I actually see "Myself" looking back at me in the mirror. It's truly me, although in the past I've searched my image and there was always someone else I would see. In my reflection, I've seen my mom and my sisters faces looking back at me and reflecting parts of myself.

Now. I. See. Myself.

I am so moved by this.

"Hi Rhea, so nice to meet you finally." I murmur, realizing this "looking within" stuff is really opening me and my life. I'm remembering what Kellye said to me and I share this with Eli; "In your reflection you will find what you seek," and he says, "Hmm, I like that. I'm changing also, I'm finding new heights to my width."

"Aw, you're as cute as ever to me," I say as I hug him.

He does seem to be gaining some weight lately, mainly around the middle section. He has one of those bodies that likes to hang onto extra weight...or is he protecting something?

I am learning about the art program as I find my groove in Seattle. I am loving my new life here but our six month lease is coming up much too quickly. Across the water is Vashon Island and it seems to be beckoning us. Its call of beautiful private beaches, talented artists, quaint shops and plenty of adventurous fun makes its short fifteen minute ferry ride an easy escape. From downtown Market Place, the huge, white ferry, carries up to two hundred cars across Puget Sound to the island. With three decks, we are called to the upper level to feel the breeze and smell the saltwater air. It's totally magical as it provides the best view of Mount Rainer standing upright as if watching our every move.

The ferry drops us into a little piece of paradise, an island of tall trees, as if a widespread park. In the summer time, it is covered with wild blackberry bushes surrounding the numerous secluded swimming spots, while salmon dance in the Puget Sound waters. I think I've found a touch of heaven.

One day at the beach on Vashon, two eagles were flying overhead. In one of my favorite reference books, Animal Speak, an eagle showing up in one's life represents 'Illumination of Spirit, Healing and Creation.' Eagles carry an immediate air of beauty and hold great symbology for our union. We'r~ splashing in Puget Sound, in about knee deep water when we began noticing the two eagles are imitating our movements in the water. When we move close to each other, they fly next to each other. When we separate, they separate. It's incredibly magical, watching this amazing flying dance as it continues for almost forty-five minutes. I happened to be wearing a watch this day because I have my afternoon art class. Rarely, do I even wear watches, so I could calculate the timing of playful bliss of this eagle dance. And it confirms I want to live with Eli on Vashon Island.

Our little cottage space, which we found quickly on Vashon is quaint, indeed. It's cozy with a fireplace and a little deck which overlooks Puget Sound and off to our immediate right is a forty foot waterfall. Yes, seriously, a forty foot waterfall in our backyard.

All of this beauty allows me to push away the underlying insecurities and fears that want to come in as naturally as the wind. Uprooting my life is fun and magical yet I'm becoming aware of the part of myself that needs a home to feel more grounded; to feel more in touch with myself and my desires. So settling on Vashon, I hope, will provide for this need.

Constantly, we can hear the mighty cries of the magnificent waterfall from our bedroom window. We hung a hammock right next to our waterfall, comfortably surrounded by the numerous pine and fur trees. Parked nicely on our private beach is our kayak for use whenever we feel the urge. Usually, this occurs around sunset with a glass of wine, as we watch the magic of the northwest come alive with its beautiful cloud formations reflecting multiple shades of grayish purples and pinks on the surrounding water. Allowing the flow of the water to bring out our romantic side, Eli proposes to me in our sweet little kayak, as we watch the sunset. It is a perfect setting as the pink mirrors my loving pink feeling inside.

"Rhea, we're living together, we're dreaming about a child, let's take the next step and get married? What do you think?"

"I already feel married to you, so yes, of course."

"Since we've both done the traditional type of marriage, how about we make our marriage uniquely special and different?"

"You have my attention, what are you suggesting?" I wonder.

"Well, what is a favorite place we visit since we've landed in Seattle?"

"Well, the water?"

"Close," Eli says.

"Hmm, where are you going with this?" I ask curiously.

"How about we get married on the ferry's top deck, overlooking the whales, the water and Mount Rainier in the distance?"

"I like that idea and you know my nose will be happy smelling the lovely salt air," I say smiling.

"I like you Rhea," he says while hugging me for a special moment. He looks into my eyes with such intensity, as I feel tears reaching my eyes and finding their way down my suntanned cheeks.

So that's exactly what we decided to do, get married on the upper deck of the ferry. We found rings at a local jewelry store. My ring is a silver band with a beautiful amethyst stone and Eli's ring is a plain version with the same silver band. We enjoy buying special clothing and we set our date for the ferry ride, a ride that could change our lives.

The ferry wedding could have been like any other day except as we were standing on the upper deck with our friend who was also a minister, a three piece band, which just happened to be on the upper deck, joins us and begins playing 'My Favorite Things' from one of my all time favorite movies, "The Sound of Music." This band with its flutist, guitarist and african drummer was the perfect addition to our little wedding. The music combined with the wind and our personal readings to each other, making it a perfect day. Thanks my friends, my Spirit Guides for bringing the sound of music to our special day afloat on the water.

16

Vashon Island is magnificent and the perfect place to begin our family. Our connection seems to have deepened and a mutual respect ignites our passion for each other. The dreams about having a baby continue, as both Eli and I have had reoccurring dreams describing a little child playing and we feel a deep connection with him or her. Could this be the same child from our tepee dream we shared together in Boulder? Could our dreams be about the same children who died and we mourned so deeply? I still carry the ache from this dream and believe somehow having a child can help us both to heal this pain. The dreams and conversations of a child are becoming as common as brushing our teeth.

Speaking of teeth, one particular sunny day, I return from the dentist to find my husband with a female client sitting on the steps of our back deck. They had just returned from a session and are bathing in each other's presence. They also seemed to be just a little bit too close for my comfort. Are their energies merging together as they laugh and chat with each other? Is this more than a session or just my insecurities? My heart and gut seem to be giving me a red flag. I'm afraid to listen too closely, for my body parts have been trying to tell me, if envy were acid there would be nothing left of me but my belt buckle and a few shiny teeth.

"Hi Guys," I find words, any words. I've never like being referred to as a guy so why did I say this? Clearly, I'm affected by this mysterious woman on my deck.

"Rhea, this is Logan. Logan, this is my wife, Rhea."

The mysterious woman turns her head to look at me. Is that guilt I see in her eyes?

I shake hands with her and make small talk about my trip to the dentist. Exciting stuff, let me tell you, as I want away from this sunny deck which is bringing up old cloudy feelings.

I find my way back to the familiar door handle and turn it just in time to catch my breathe. I don't like this woman and I don't even know her. What's happening? Why does her presence affect me so deeply? It's like an energy has consumed my body and I no longer know myself. Her face, the "other woman's" face seems to be sketched in my brain. Her beautiful long curly golden hair and deep, turquoise eyes have captured my attention. This visual is trapped and I can't help but compare her to myself. I realize this is so unhealthy but I can't seem to get their closeness out of my head. I feel myself going somewhere deep within me, a place I despise. I truly loathe this part of myself, it is so gut wrenchingly uncomfortable. This feeling has way too much power over me. In the past, I would jog to "run" away from it. Ah, the glory of the adrenaline rush.

I suppose in retrospect, this has been a blessing because it means I must face this feeling I have run from my entire life. But am I ready? No way! I must find an outlet for these rising feelings. I'm putting on my hiking boots to escape, when my attempt to leave is interrupted by Eli's voice saying good-bye to his new friend. Are they hugging? Crap, I am so in "it." I try to find some composure as Eli comes into my space. I know this feeling of being out of control way too well.

"So, how was your session with Logan?" I ask as calmly as I can muster.

"Great, she's such a good per......."

"I can tell!" I interrupt.

"What do you mean?" He looks at me inquisitively.

Here "it" comes, I try to hold back my insecurities, but they already have a tight grasp on me, demanding a voice.

"What were you doing out there for almost three hours?"

"We had a session and then we walked down to the beach," still clueless to my agitation.

Then seeing me more clearly, "Are you OK, Rhea?" He attempts to come to me.

My tone changes his pace, "You two were sitting way too close for my comfort."

"What?" Eli asks innocently.

"You know. You and Logan were really close on our deck."

"Oh dear," Eli sighs.

"And I could see your energies connecting. What's her story? Is she married?" My mean voice has found my vocal cords and wants some air time.

"Yes, she's married, she's been married for 20 some years and they have two wonderful children."

"Did you see how she was looking at you?" I say a bit louder.

"Rhea, truly, we're just friends," Eli chimes in.

"Friends? Get a grip Eli, she is so into you, surely you can feel this?"

"We are just friends. Be nice."

"This IS me being nice," I squeal.

"Really Rhea, I know her husband, we're friends as well."

"This doesn't change what I saw."

"And what was that?" Eli jumps in getting triggered as well.

"I saw how she was looking at you and you couldn't have been any closer on the deck! What kind of session was it any way?"

"We talked about her life and her challenges. You know...a session. Then we walked to the beach and talked more. It was innocent."

"I saw what I saw, Eli!" I'm close to the screaming range.

"It seems nothing I say is going to change your mind."

"Get real, Eli!"

"You've built a case Ms. Attorney, Paralegal, or whatever the hell you were! I'm sick of this. I'm out of here. I need the freedom to see who I want and when I want."

He storms toward the door.

"Eli, wait. I saw the way she was looking at you. Certainly you could see this also?" My voice has gone up a notch, "you're being way too trusting."

"Rhea...I'm not..."

"Do you want to be with her!!"

"Rhea? please..."

"WELL? Do you!"

"Look, I'm not going to listen to you any longer. I'm going to take a walk and perhaps we can talk more later."

There is a brief icy silence as we look at each other. Eli turns and marches to the back door.

"I really do want to believe you!" I implore.

"Rhea, we are just friends," Eli says over his shoulder as the back door slams behind him. Was he talking about Logan as just being friends? Or us? This question haunts me the entire night.

Eli never came home that night! Tossing and turning, finally finding sleep, only to be brought back sweating from a disturbing dream.

In my dream, Eli and his "new friend" Logan were in a hot tub at one of the local spas. They were all over each other. She was actually giving him a blow job. And I'm not talking about the kind you get after a hair cut.

Yes, I had to witness this on top of all of my concerns. I wonder if this is the beginning of the end of our relationship? I feel sick and completely confused. Eli has taken the car so there is no direct escape route and I barely know anyone on the island. I am scared.

I try to find some comfort in this situation, some balance. I attempt to take my thoughts to the art training which has been incredible. I really appreciate Darcy and her way of teaching, as it's all hands-on learning. We've met in her art studio, at the coffee shop and in her classroom working with her art students. She clearly knows her world of creating quite well. She taught me how to apply many different brush strokes with acrylic paint, to smudge pastels for a fine finish, to sculpt plaster masks, to create amazing clay pieces and the simple art of using charcoal. She reveals to me the training is comparable to a Masters in Art. I'm thrilled, I'm excited. Yet, I don't want to leave in the middle of it because of my conflict with Eli. Maybe I am just making excuses. I really do love Eli, don't I? I am so confused.

Eli returns late in the morning, and he seems different. His eyes are colder and his smile seems forced and I'm concerned what our next conversation will bring?

"I'm home," I hear as the front door closes.

"Eli, I'm so sorry," comes out of my mouth before I could think.

Am I really sorry or is this required for our relationship to move forward?

"I'm sorry also," Eli says as he hugs me, "I really don't have any feelings for Logan," he says shifting his eyes.

"I want to believe you..." I say, wondering if I want to share the dream I had about them in the hot tub together. I decide to keep it to myself.

"Rhea, I know her and her husband, they are having problems, but I'm with you now. Can we forgive and move on?"

I'm wondering why he has dismissed this so easily, however, I agree.

Adoring the lovely dusk sky, Eli and I have settled back into our groove, as if nothing has changed between us. We are picking blackberries together, probably eating more than we are keeping, and I look up into the sky and I am intrigued by some type of bird which is about fifteen yards off in the distance. I am mesmerized and I can't seem to take my eyes off of its movements, as I watch it flying directly towards me at a very fast pace. As it gets closer, my eyes adjust, and when I can focus clearly, I see it is a large barn owl. What I also notice is that its movements are completely silent, which adds to the surreal feeling of this connection. When it is about two feet in front of me, it stops as if hovering in mid air for another sixty seconds and then looks at me right in the eyes and the owl lets out a loud piercing shriek. I jump with the impact of its message, as it's clearly communicating with me, as it holds this impossible position in the air for an additional thirty seconds or so. I am filled with astonishment, as I gaze into the beautiful eyes of this owl. My body is lined with goosebumps as we interact in such a surreal way.

After his message has been received by me, he flies off and circles around my head two times and then leaves as quickly as he arrived. I'm spinning in this moment of euphoria. My eye to eye contact with this beautiful white owl felt like liquid magic.

Eli pops his head up from the blackberry bush and notices my dazed look.

"What is it, Rhea?"

"It's a sign, I am sure of it."

"What's a sign?"

"Did you see the beautiful white owl that came to greet me?"

"What owl?"

"Wow, I guess the owl's message was for me? Did you hear its shriek?"

"All I heard was my gurgling happy stomach filling with fat blackberries," he laughs.

Back at home, I Google the symbology of the owl and it says:

'The Owl is at home in the night. It has great awareness of all that is around it at all times. It has predator vision, which means it sees clearly what it looks at. It has great intuition. It has the courage to follow its instincts. Owl's medicine includes seeing behind masks. Owls symbolize wisdom, the ability to see things that are hidden.'

I consider the owl's message.

After two years of living on Vashon Island, we decide it's time to move to the city life of Seattle, as the art classes are doing well and the children seem to love creating with us. This will provide more access to more students in our classes. Oh yeah, Eli is teaching the classes with me, adding yet another hook for us to become even more dependent upon each other. However, the art students clearly love him and his playful side.

This new arrangement can also enhance our money flow. I've owned the idea of thrift store hunting and I love the art of manifesting anything I want with little money. It's become quite an adventurous game for us. I do wonder if this move is an excuse to get away from Logan as she and Eli are still getting together on a regular basis. It's so painful for me. But why? He insists they are "just" friends.

The idea of becoming a mom has enough power to keep me hooked in a bit longer. I remind myself every woman is an expert in her own case. I feel we have some more growing and learning to do together.

17

Looking out over the valley in North Bend, Washington, Eli whispers, as if his next words are significantly sacred,

"I want to live in that house on the river with you."

From this high mountain view where we rest from our day hike, he is pointing to an unrecognizable house in a plethora of greenness.

"My friend's house has sixteen acres of forest on a river that sits right up against the mountain. It's beautiful and magical."

"Sure," I reply, as we float to another topic.

The very next day, Eli receives a call from his friends, the ones who live on the river. They asked us if we wanted to rent their house. Our answer is a resounding, Yes! This whole process is teaching me how to relax, trust and let go of the ideas or restraints of society's ways of the 'right' way to live.

Our move to Eli's dream house on the river is memorable in many ways. The house is stocked with amazing gourmet food, Persian rugs line the floors and a hint of "the good life" runs rampant throughout the house. At least we can act like we're wealthy! There is enough room to dance easily, which we feel the desire to do.

That night, Eli and I chose to sleep in their camper next to the raging river. It is here I have a dream of a happy-colorful Dancing Bed. The next morning, after having slept wonderfully, I begin sharing my vivid dream. Eli, sensing my excitement, casually looks at me and says,

"Just paint it. Paint your dream."

These three simple words start my painting career. Even though I'm teaching art classes to many children and doodling during the classes, up to that point I hadn't actually painted my own personal art pieces.

During my first Art Show, a man is looking deeply into my bed painting. He took his glaze away from the dancing bed and slowly turned to look into my eyes,

"Did you paint this?" he uttered with misty eyes.

I nod my head yes, smiling with pride.

"Can I share my story with you?"

"Sure, please do," I respond.

"While in the hospital, with the birth of our first child, I actually saw our child's spirit come in through the window and go right into my wife's womb, just like your painting portrays."

Tears form in both of our eyes.

"I haven't told anyone except my wife of this experience. Thank you for allowing me this moment of reflection."

We are both so moved by this sharing, we hug each other.

This moment in time solidified one of the many reasons I continue to paint today. I wish to move myself and anyone who chooses to really look.

I continue to adore Seattle's many treasures! Ocean breezes, scrumptious salmon feasts, wine vineyards, artists galore and a wide array of cultural diversity make this part of Washington, an ideal place to call home. This city has the power to awaken my adventurous spirit and my creativity. In our home, its previously blank white walls are now adorned with my many art pieces. This seems to be the perfect place to call home but I still hear another destination calling me. This pulsating idea nags at me despite my focus to shake it off and come back to reality.

It's day three of our two week long workshop entitled "Finding your Magic from Within." Witnessing the power of using my imagination to support my life, and combining our learning from the Hypnotherapy Training, this workshop was created by Eli and myself over the past many months. It involves many modalities guiding our participants to their inner wisdom.

Leif and Alicia are attending. We met this sweet couple in La Jolla and they have agreed to participate and give us honest feedback on our creation. We have eleven more days of exploring, learning and sharing together. Waking up in the same home and practicing the art of "looking within" has great opportunities for all of us.

Leaning back and enjoying the comfort of the corduroy couch,

Leif says, "This workshop has been so rewarding in many ways. How about we amp it a bit? I have an idea, let's experience the rest of the workshop in Sedona!" He says with an air of innocent excitement.

"What's a Sedona?" I ask. I haven't even heard of it.

Snuggled next to him, Alicia sits up with a full smile, "I like that idea, it would be so fun." Alicia carries a natural beauty that emphasizes her smile.

"Hmm, this really could enhance the depth of your experience," Eli chimes in, really considering this possibility.

All eyes turn my way as their minds catch up to what I have just said. "Wow, you haven't heard of Sedona?" Eli asks.

I shake my head, "No, what is it? What's so special about this Sedona experience? It sounds like an exotic drug."

"I suppose it could be considered a type of drug. It's a town in Arizona...it is difficult to explain," Eli wrinkles his brow in thought.

"Try me. Eli, if you want me to completely shift gears, I'd like to at least have an idea of our destination. Are you suggesting driving all the way to Arizona?"

Eli stares at me, not saying anything. Then he takes a deep breath, "Sedona's real meaning is too deep, too elusive, too mysterious to be conveyed by our language. I'm wondering if any words can describe its meaning fully."

Turning to Leif, Eli says, "I believe you are on to something, my friend."

The admission of a lack of words spurs my curiosity. Notoriously, Eli is a man of too many words and opinions.

"Right now? You want us to drive there today? I ask. "How long would it take?"

"Rhea, my dear. Let's just do it! We can leave early tomorrow morning and be there the next day."

Alicia and Leif are nodding their heads simultaneously.

"We're going to Sedona," they sing a bit off key.

I tease them, "Ohhkaaay, I'll be the first one packed and ready to go."

The next morning, we drive off to this mysterious town in Arizona. I find it amusing to pickup and leave like this but I'm definitely appreciating my adventurous rebel spirit.

Driving into Sedona, I am immediately intrigued by its womb-like beauty. High red rock mountains and orange buttes surround this small hamlet with a motherly protection. My eyes feast on the red earth and all my senses seem to come alive simultaneously. Is this place for real? It literally looks and feels like some other planet; its red earth dusted with pockets of green trees and shrubs. This is truly invigorating and breathtakingly beautiful, a clever array of red and green diversity dancing together, complimenting the bright blue sky.

We have two rooms booked at L'auberge, nestled by a flowing creek. Our adjourning rooms are beautiful with an outdoor shower and hot tub to soak away all of the emotional baggage we are releasing during our traveling workshop.

Our first day in Sedona, Eli meets a man at the local gas station and he invites us over to his house for the evening. It is in "uptown" where all the tourists congregate. If Sedona were a beach town, uptown is comparable to the popular boardwalk area complete with shops, art galleries and restaurants with lots of tourists.

We arrive at his driveway by nightfall and it is unusually dark compared to Seattle's night sky. We can actually see falling stars streak across the sky, begging me to remember all the magic around us. Entering into his little birdhouse of a place, I feel right at home as he introduces his wife.

In no more than two seconds after shaking her hand, I say very innocently, "I'm moving here!" This sentiment flows easily out of my mouth.

She says, "Yeeeesss!" while giggling.

"I mean here...in this house!"

She says again, "Yeeeesss!"

I must have looked completely shocked because she followed up with, "My dear, I see you moving into this house and ironically, we are moving to Seattle!"

Much later in the evening, it is brought to my attention she is one of the most renown Psychics in Sedona. The entire evening was wonderful exchange of magic and conversation. Eli and I left feeling both exhilarated and completely exhausted.

During one of our off-times from the workshop, I decide to see if my art program, Creationship, will be accepted at one of the elementary schools. Without an appointment, I confidently walk into the school office with my many art samples and ask if I could speak to someone about my after school art program.

The secretary looks at me curiously and says,

"Just one minute, I'll see if anyone is available."

I enjoy the idea of children exploring nearby, while feeling unusually certain about last night's proclamation to move here.

"The Principal can see you right now."

Excited, I walk into a large office with windows all along the left side overlooking the red rocks. She is studying me as she reaches out her hand.

"Hello, my name is Rhea," as we shake, "Beautiful view. Do you ever get tired of looking at it?" I ask.

"Not so far," she answers.

"I'd like to try to get tired of it," I'm grinning.

"May I show you some examples of the artwork my students have done in the past?" I ask; I love when things flow so easily.

"Of course," she says while moving papers from her desk to provide more space for my presentation.

Proudly, I lay copies of the many art pieces my past students had created; a pastel dragon, an abstract Picasso face painting, a dancing bowl drawn with pen and ink, cross-hatching and stippling lines, a plaster mask and a few clay pieces.

"I believe the universe buries personal jewels deep within all of us. Creativity provides an avenue to access these jewels," I say.

She picks up each of the pieces, examining them like they are priceless.

"This is the easiest decision I've made all day. A big YES to your art program, Ms. Dalton."

We agree to three days a week for my art classes and then see how it unfolds.

Upon returning to the hotel room, I confront Eli, "I'm moving to Sedona. The elementary school wants my Creationship program. I just know I'm supposed to move to this lovely town! Eli, if you wish to join me, it's up to you but I know this is what I have to do."

"Well, of course, I will move with you, Sweetie."

Our friends from the workshop also decide to move here and I'm so glad I followed my buddies' intuition to follow them here.

After moving to Sedona and settling into our little birdhouse in Uptown, I begin watching Eli, as someone watches a frightening mystery movie. Eli cannot resonate with Sedona as it seems to bring out his worst, his shadow side. Suddenly, we can't seem to communicate and at times he can't even look me in the eyes, as darker parts of himself emerge. It seems Eli is having difficulty facing this part of himself. I'm having difficulty just facing Eli each morning; I don't know who I will find. I am reminded of the symbology of the owl's magical visit. Reminding me to look behind people's masks. Was this referring to Eli's masks? And to enhance this situation, Eli began calling several woman, one of them being beautiful turquoise eyed Logan, and would spend hours on the phone chatting with her.

Clearly we had been experiencing growing pains together in Seattle, but this dynamic, which progressively brings out his "unsettled side," prompts me to think maybe it's time to make some changes. Do I go my own way? Do I stay and hope he finds his happy self again? As if being kicked 'out' by Sedona herself, even his dream world began telling Eli.....your body doesn't resonate with Sedona's energy.

One evening, while out with friends at the Leaping Lizard evening club, Eli was tired and left early. I stayed with Mara, who

I met through the art classes and her French male friend. We're drinking a bit and the passion began to flow as easily as the wine. She's digging on me and I'm digging on the French dude's appeal and accent. In a moment of passion, all three of us began kissing. I kiss him and she kisses me. Right in the middle of the dance floor.

Since Eli had left early, Mara and her friend had agreed to take me home. On the journey, they eluded to wanting to have a three-some. Although tempting in my wine-filled euphoria, I decline. I am still married after all, even though the winds of change were growing steadily like a storm. However, this dynamic did open my eyes to the truth of our connection...or lack thereof.

The next morning, I tell Eli all about my passionate evening in which I had kissed and enjoyed kissing this 'other' man. A part of me knows what the consequences of this truth will do to him but I can't help myself. This seems to give us a solid reason to separate. I can't hide from the truth of his darkness, as all my color pictures of us are seeming to fade to black and white.

As sure as the Sedona sunrise, Eli leaves; he really leaves and even though I know it is for the best, it rocks my emotional world. We close the door on our relationship and our possibility of becoming a family.

Mara came over to console me as I cried for hours. I felt the loss of my relationship, my possibility of being a mom and the idea of being in a love relationship. It seems to bring up a lot of my unhealed pain from my childhood: abandonment, questioning my worthiness yet again, and feeling very alone. She holds me affec-tionately, which I adore, but it also brought up unhealed feelings of when I was eighteen years old.

As a young woman, my life was a whirlwind of turbulence and bliss. At the innocent age of 18, I was the proud assistant manager at a health food store and restaurant. I became friends with the manager, Jasmine. I invited her to a going away party for one of my dear friends who was moving to Hawaii. Her parents were having the party, complete with lots of Hawaiian drinks, yummy food and fun dancing.

I've always been a bit of a light weight drinking alcohol, as I can feel loopy with one glass of wine. So the flowing of drinks certainly had their effect on me. Feeling exhausted and a bit drunk, I asked Jasmine if she would drive my Saab home? She agreed. We hopped into my car, she behind the wheel and that's the last thing I remember.

I woke up in the middle of the night to find myself lying naked on someone's bed. I cried out, trying to get a sense of where I was, when I looked down at my bare body and saw red marks all over my breasts and abdomen. What the fuck? What are these throbbing red marks on my torso?

"What? Where?" I try to say with a dry throat.

Finding more of my senses, I begin to remember driving my car to the party. Yes, I remember getting into the car with Jasmine driving. Are we at her house? My car must be here. I'm a little relieved, as I cry out to her,

"Jasmine?" I say lightly.

No reply.

"I need to leave, where are you?"

No reply.

I knew I needed to get out of this place. The darkness outside enhanced the rising judgment I felt within me. I didn't care it was the middle of the night. I wanted Out...of...Here. I needed to get to the safety of my own home. I detect a glimmer of light on the dresser, yes, my car keys. Quickly, I grabbed my keys, threw on my clothes, and let myself out the front door, while my throbbing head made itself known. I arrived home safely.

The following Monday, Jasmine and I spoke at work and she told me this situation made her turn to God. As I'm sensing the familiar flow of my invisibility cloak's comfort, I think to myself, really, that's all you have to say? Again I am reminded this is a subject people do not want to talk about.

This event also supports my lack of trust in the world. This scenario reinforces my fear...... I can't trust anyone. And now a co-worker, a woman who I thought of as a friend. Who could I trust?

I come back to Sedona and myself on the couch with Mara. I begin to see a pattern in my life; a pattern of sexuality which seems to permeate my heart, my soul and my Life. What to do with this information?

I shared my Saab ride to Crazytown with Mara, igniting my aching heart and body.

She listened attentively and thought for a long time before speaking gently, "Dear Rhea, imagine all the compassion you are learning from these situations? As I see it, this is partially what allows you to be so vulnerable and available for people, paired with your intuition is a wonderful combo.

And true trust is within You. Learn to trust yourself and that's really all you need. Ignite your power within while realizing you can trust yourself is any situation is the real juice. When you, as Rhea, trust you can handle anything, it makes life so much easier."

"Thanks from my heart, Mara. This will take some time to sink in and I know it to be the truth and I need to trust my intuition also," I say with a shimmer of hope shining through my emotional exhaustion.

Speaking of intuition, a few months later, I hear of Eli and Logan's marriage plans. Yes, Logan with the piercing turquoise eyes and the star of my 'hot tub' dream, which seems to still be embedded in my brain.

Kudos to the wisdom and ignition of my dream world. This I can trust!

— *Flying Abstract*

My ideas about life can be bizarre at times, however, my first Sedona party is beyond any expectations I've ever entertained. What a glorious gathering, ripe with diversity, sharing and love. Salmon sizzling on the grill and a buffet meant for a queen tempts my taste buds. Interestingly, I can only admire with my eyes because I have started a cleanse this week. I have to admit, I'm questioning this decision as every part of me is wanting to taste the grilled salmon. Oh well, I'm proud of myself for cleansing my body, it's part of letting Eli go. Even still, my heart hurts for him, or is it only longing for a companion? I remember what Kellye, the psychic, told me, "Rhea you won't meet your soul mate until later in life." OK, I get it but it still can be lonely living by myself.

I'm proud of myself for even finding the energy to come to this party as I was feeling tired from a busy day of doing my life. Plus, being on the third day of my cleanse has amplified my lack of energy. I felt my Guides urging me to attend this gathering.

This party place is perfectly located by a flowing creek with beautiful open ground dotted with lush green grass and tall pine trees. This is the desert where grass is a rare commodity, so I take off my stylish yet funky leather sandals so I can touch the softness of the green earth between my toes. I stand there in bliss while making small talk with several new faces.

I hear Mara, my lovely, German friend speaking her native language to a young man. His German is quite a match for her German heritage and they seem to have made a connection. I'm also watching vicariously as three men are creating a fire in the distance. The dancing bonfire is casting its blazing embers all around the yard, beckoning us to join its warm and glowing energy. This increasing blaze seems to balance the multitude of stars, which is one of the many wonderful attributes of living under Sedona's skies.

Meeting the woman who is celebrating her birthday is a pleasure. She is a petite, lively woman wearing a tight fitting sarong that enhances her small frame. Unbound hair is flying behind her like an unruly earthy-blonde curtain.

She plants her body and smiles to the group,

"Thank you for coming tonight. Rather than the traditional birthday idea of you giving gifts to me," she says, "I want to gift all of you!"

A wave of anticipation swirls around the spacious yard of intrigued guests.

"Please follow me over to the fire pit and lie on the ground alternating male and female with your feet facing toward the center of the fire."

Being a lovely warm night with a gentle breeze, this is enticing to all. I look around at the many faces and see the playful, curious child within each of us start to emerge. I grab Mara's hand, as we skip over to the fire together, giggling with anticipation.

"I think I've met someone very special."

"Already?" I ask.

"Yes and he speaks fluent German. I'm so excited. Yeah!"

"Well you go, girl!" I laugh, feeling better about my decision to pass on the eating. Perhaps this next phase of the party can make up for my committed perseverance.

We move toward the bonfire and somehow we magically form a perfect circle, easily and effortlessly, as if we had rehearsed this scene many times before. Obeying the suggestion to lay on the ground alternating man/woman, my friend and I separate.

"Thanks for inviting me to this party, but we must separate temporarily," I say very dramatically.

"See the new You soon!" she laughs, as some unknown man lies down between us.

Lying on the soft ground, I begin to look at the array of stars. I am overcome with such appreciation for following my heart to Sedona. Closing my eyes, I'm drifting into my familiar inner world with the comfort of the fire warming the bottom of my naked feet when, suddenly, I also feel hands on my feet. Then my head and neck are being massaged. I look down to my feet and see people moving around the inner circle touching all the willing bodies at the gathering. As I gently close my eyes again, I begin to relax to take in the full effects of this lovely, group massage, energy. "This is fantastic," I think, as I sink deeper within myself.

Beautiful singing ensues by one of the women. As I come out of my world of fantasy, I realize this woman's lovely voice is the same one celebrating her birthday. What a lovely voice; she is truly gifting us. She is singing the Gayatri Mantra:

"Aum bhuh bhuvah svah

tat savitur varenyam

bhargo devasya dheemahi

dhivo yo nah prachodayat"

I have absolutely no idea what these words mean, however, they are so beautiful and full of feeling, they make me move even deeper into my melting pot.

Then a deep bass sound of a didgeridoo suddenly blows across my body. This deep vibrating tone comes from a wind instrument in the form of a long wooden tube that the Australian Aborigines blow into, producing deep and resonant tones.

This highly invigorating combination of music, massage and singing continues for several hours. I feel entirely lost yet more present than ever. It is mesmerizing, magical and highly sensual.

Next, I am being fed raspberries, blueberries and my favorite, the mango, followed by a birthday cake also hand-fed into my mouth. OK, so my fasting ends here but nothing could stop me from receiving this love, in the form of food, at this juncture. Talk about total bliss in every way. Kissing has evolved with the food intake as some are now sharing the cake with their mouths, rather than their hands. Ooh la la!

Feeling the relaxing benefits of the massage and the magical feelings flowing throughout my body, I notice the music has come to a halt. Slowly, I sit up while opening my delirious eyes and look into the burning fire, not finding words to match my multitude of feelings.

I am being helped up. In complete exhilaration, I now stand and stare directly into a man's warm brown eyes. His shoulder length hair shines in the moonlight.

"You're cute," seems to fall out of my mouth. Apparently, these three words work quite well.

"You are too," he smiles, "my name is Harrison."

Easily, as if still having been rehearsed, we grab each other's hands while maintaining eye contact and smile gleefully at each other. We move in the direction of the hot tub where several people are basking with big smiles planted on their faces. We follow their lead and take off our clothes and let the blessings continue as we sink into the heated waters. My German friend follows us into the hot tub as well but she has a funny look on her face. Then it dawns on me that the "cute" man I have connected with, is the same man she was so thrilled about earlier who spoke German with her. Darn, that was entirely innocent on my part, sorry friend. However, now I can understand why my guidance nudged me to go to this party.

The following morning, I'm still spinning from the night's events. I Google "Gayatri Mantra," the lovely song being sung around the fire pit.

I read, "This 5000 year old Hindu mantra is one of the most ancient, sacred and powerful mantras to meditate upon in this world! It is believed that by chanting the mantra and firmly establishing it in the mind, if you carry on your life and do the work that is ordained for you, your life will be full of happiness."

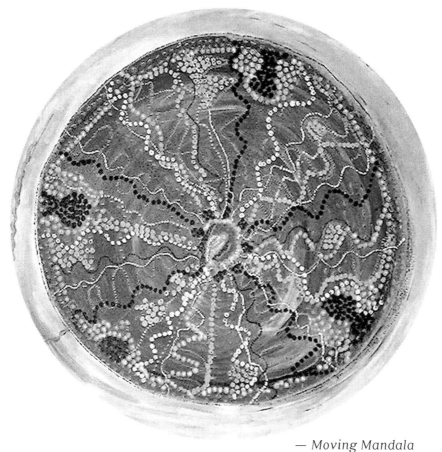

— *Moving Mandala*

When I created this mandala, the painted lines were actually moving. It was very much alive. I had no conscious understanding of what a mandala was or even that they existed. I just paint. It's as if I was re-creating our powerful circle around the bonfire.

— *King, Indian and Child*

This painting was a dream I had shortly after I met Harrison. I believe it is of us in a past life together. Despite our differences, I adore his heart and wisdom. Notice the webbing between the King and Indian, I believe this represents our child.

No one has ever guessed my true age. The person guessing seems to think I am much younger than I am. Probably because I feel young at heart and I know how to have fun! This is another of those situations, as Harrison is seven years younger than me. Despite our age difference, Harrison and I became friends quite naturally and easily. We drank beer and talked for hours the following weekend. When I look deeply into his eyes, I see a child in his eyes. Is this the child of my dreams? Well actually, there is very little invested in the process of getting to know Harrison, as it seems we went from meeting, to being curious about each other, having fun and then to me getting pregnant. Our child was conceived while I was painting my Mandala painting. Harrison was painting as well and the creative energy seemed to enhance the perfect environment to create our child.

The typical time, generally allotted for dating, instead turned me into having a big, huge pregnant belly. Of course, this curtailed the 'fun' part as I was determined to have a healthy child. I changed my diet to cutting out all alcohol, caffeine and potato chips, all which I adore. This withdrawal of some of my favorite food and drinks, brought out parts of my personality I didn't wish to share with anyone, much less the father of my child. This personality shift of mine also seemed to bring out Harrison's worst as well.

Harrison and I couldn't be more different. He's a night person, I'm a morning person. In fact, he could get angry if I spoke to him before 10:00 in the morning. He's the last to leave a party while I could be one of the first to want to leave. The way I see it, I like to leave a great party while I'm still carrying the "high" of so many interactions whereas he wants to stay until it's light outside.

He thinks he knows everything. What? I would literally scratch my head over the reality of this connection. And we're pregnant! What a whirlwind of emotions. How can this be? I had not used birth control with Eli for over two years, thinking I was having a child with him. And I was even starting to wonder if I could get pregnant? Isn't it amazing how some things are truly preordained!

Despite our many differences, I am committed to making this connection harmonious with Harrison, given we have a child on the way. The child I have felt around me since I was in my twenties, is finally making their grand appearance.

Harrison and I do agree to choose godparents for our child. We decide on our neighbors, Michael and Emily, who are an older couple with lots of love to share. They own resorts in Sedona, Hawaii and California called Sunshine Babes. Michael is in his late 60's with balding blondish-gray hair and a short body accentuating his belly. It's clear he was a handsome chap in his younger years. His bold voice and laughter can be heard from their house across the street, despite his short stance. His love of beer and steaks on the grill is accentuated by his cascading Hawaiian shirts.

Emily, follows Michael around, shadowing him, as if wanting more attention than he is able to give her. She is a sweet, shy woman, who when she does speak, has a liberal point of view, which I can relate to.

The four of us have had many meal shares and talks of philosophy, spirituality and politics. The more intense, the more animated we become. We are thrilled to have them be a part of our spiritual family.

Being pregnant is unlike anything I've ever experienced! I've traveled to many new and foreign places, I've tasted new and exciting flavors, I've run the depths of emotions and felt physical challenges of climbing to the tops of mountains, white water rafting, strenuous sports activities and indulged in many relationships. However, nothing in my life prepared me for the perseverance, focus and energy it took to birth a child.

Around my sixth month of pregnancy, I'm playing this pushing game with my child. I would poke my belly gently with my finger, and I would get a poke right back. It's very special to feel this deep connection with my baby each time we engage this way. On this particular day, I poke my left side to begin our game and my baby pokes back rather vigorously, as if to say, "Hey, this is my space now!" I promise to honor this although I'm looking at the humor of it! This is my belly, my body! How can we comfortably share this space?

Soon I realize my child is given this space by my willingness to surrender. Therefore, it is technically his to accommodate his many needs for survival. I'm fully feeling this child's power! We end our game of tugging back-and-forth, and I soon find we can share this space together with love and respect. We find a mutual honoring of each other from this point forward. Is this real love? I feel I already love this little being, I already honor this little Being. I'm so very excited to meet him or her.

My friend, her husband and their three children came to visit while I am eight months pregnant.

"How were your three deliveries?" I ask. "I'm a bit nervous since this is my first child."

"Oh Rhea, all three of my births were so easy."

"Really? How so?" This surprises me after seeing and reading the many possible challenges of childbirth.

"All three were easy and quick, even my husband would kid me that our children just fell out of me."

"Really? I am so intrigued to hear this? I thought..."

"You're going to be quite surprised how natural it will be. Plus you're very physical with your hiking, yoga and bike riding. I imagine your delivery will be similar to mine."

I really want to believe her. Actually, I become a bit "cocky" about the situation, incorporating yoga, belly dancing and my daily kagels. I'm not too concerned about my delivery at all. Little do I know, I'm in for a big humbling!

I understand why so many woman have just one child. Four days before the due date, on a full moon Saturday morning, my water breaks and we're off to Flagstaff Hospital. I've wanted to go more natural and have a home birth but I am "over the hill" according to society and the midwives we spoke with indicated they would not—could not touch me or our baby. I find it so sad how much of our society has negative blinders on around aging. At a certain age, so many constrictions are put onto me. People's interpretations can be so judgmental and fear based! Perhaps that's a topic for yet another book, as I feel emotionally and physically, better than ever.

As we are driving up the beautiful canyon to Flagstaff, which is about 40 minutes away, Harrison insists we stop for dried buffalo jerky, which is being sold on the side of the road by a local Native-American vendor.

You want to stop now?! This being my first child, I am thinking I can deliver any moment. But Harrison seems all too comfortable and insists I need some protein for the birth. "Fine, then make it quick!" I blurt out. Buying the jerky, I gobble the chewy meat but only to appease dear Dad.

As we walk into the hospital and look around the lobby, every chair is occupied by a lovely round woman with varying degrees of emotions. I've wondered if it were true most deliveries are affected by the full moon. If you think about it, the tides are affected by the moon, therefore, since we are about 60% water, certainly we are affected by the moon's placement. Looking at this room full of pregnant woman is compelling evidence.

The hospital staff is clearly struggling to keep up with the many needs of the soon-to-be mothers. Apparently, my doctor is on vacation and they are understaffed. Not the words I wish to hear right now. Did this add to my anxiety? Hell yes! Finally, after about a two hour wait, which translated into walking the hallways and processing my abundance of energy like I'm preparing for a marathon, they call my name.

We are guided into the birthing room. I'm determined to have a natural delivery beyond their persistent attempts to give me all of their wonder drugs. I'm also wanting to be naked, which the nurses did not like. I persevered, as any bit of clothing feels inhibiting to me as I push, scream and surrender. Some fourteen hours later, after maneuvering the waves of emotions and the waves of childbirth, I'm crying and ready to give up. I realize I have learned remaining in control is essential to my safety and being out of control is threatening. This birthing, when I need to trust my body and let go, has become a major issue for me. The entire process is agonizing and exhilarating all at once.

"I don't know if I can do this," I finally reveal to Harrison.

"Sure you can," he encourages, while his eyes say something entirely different.

The baby's head would crown, show itself and bounce back in. This went on for hours. I have to go through the entire process over and over again. It was the marathon of marathons. Having been a runner, I had run a thirteen mile half marathon, which was nothing compared to this energy drainer.

Then this little baby boy pops out, complete with blood and mucous and gooey slime all over his precious little body. It didn't even matter. They hand me my child, our baby boy and all I can do is stare between tears of joy. He is so darn cute, I mean, off the charts cute. I feel love for him immediately. Yes, this is Tatum! The name we considered fits him perfectly. He is perfect! I now understand why I was dreaming about having a boy one night and a girl, the next. He is the perfect combination of sweetness and strength.

I think one of the most surprising parts of this birthing experience was how my body naturally responded with the timing to push this child out of me, after I learned to trust and let go. The natural rhythms of my body's momentum that were created to birth this child, this precious Being, is a total miracle. I realize childbirth is often referred to as a miracle; it is the most profoundly incredible experience ever! And then learning about breast feeding, wow.

Obviously I haven't done enough research around breastfeeding, for when I'm told Tatum will need to eat at least twelve times a day, there goes my entire life as I know it. I am in fear wondering how I'm going to run my art business while nursing. If I could have taken the time off, I would have, like our neighbors, the fortunate Canadians who get almost a full year of paid maternity leave. How smart!

Tatum needs to be breast fed for two and a half years. I develop sore sensitive bleeding breasts only to have him put his sucking mouth on them to reopen the sores. I almost gave up breast feeding entirely. Motherhood is one of the most courageous and loving gestures of the human experience but why doesn't anyone talk more about the real challenges? It is quite a commitment I've made. His little sucking mouth, even though painful, is my favorite entertainment of the moment for he has the cutest little lips.

When I was about six months pregnant, I was given two copies of the same book. Books seem to find their way to me at the opportune moment, so the fact I have been given two of them has certainly peaked my curiosity. While nursing, I finally have the time to read it and I can't put it down.

Essentially, this book is about a woman's quest to understand why Americans are in so much fear? Good Question. Wanting to get more clarity on this idea, she travels to remote villages where they live simply off the land. The author begins to witness a certain type of strength she sees in the children, which is different from her American nieces and nephews. She is intrigued as she documents their ways of raising their children. She notices the young children are allowed to walk on the edge of cliffs and to hold sharp knives. Their belief is we are all born with an innate inner trust and they honor, support and trust it in their children. Also, most importantly, the babies are always physically near their mom or dad or someone's heart at all times. With this idea, the parents sleep with their children.

How these wise indigenous people live is through honoring the child's innate knowledge and trust in themselves. She witnessed most American parents jump in to protect their children far too quickly, thereby denying this natural wisdom to be developed and used as a resource in life. This makes so much sense, particularly with our government, medical establishment, news, internet and TV instilling loads of fear-based information 24 hours a day.

I share this concept with Harrison and we are in agreement that this is how we will raise dear sweet Tatum. And we do, he is so loved. Imagine if each of our children were raised in this trusting fashion, always near someone's heart.

Sadly, yet intuitively realizing the inevitable, Harrison and I do not do well with the 'human' part of our relationship. We are spiritually connected but I need to be heard, coming from my family dynamic of being invisible, whereas Harrison is a talker which served my needs initially. However, he can't hear me, much less really listen to me. This leads to lots of fights and disagreements as we both have our control issues running. I had seen glimpses of a separation coming, but it is still difficult to believe it.

Over time, as I watch Harrison and his diverse ways of living, I become aware of the sad truth. He has challenges with his career of being an architect. Right after we got pregnant, he lost his job and was slow finding another one. And ironically, I found a pile of unpaid bills. When I approach him about these, he becomes defensive and blames it on me, "I told you I would never be a rich man, Rhea!" I am blown away. What bothers me is not so much of his admission of not being rich, but that he isn't even open to it possibly happening. My heart sinks and I must face the truth.

Must I go through this breaking up scenario yet again? I really am questioning myself and my reality. Another breakup, more heart ache; I am on the edge. Something's gotta give. Harrison said he knew we were going to separate eventually, but thought it would be when Tatum was around five years old. Tatum isn't even two yet.

Finally we agree it is best to separate.

So here's nursing Mama, caring for my almost two year old, with house payments reaching $2000/month and I'm hardly working! Am I crazy? Am I making everything worse by asking Tatum's dad to leave? I'm totally confused and uncertain what to do with this situation. How could I run my business with a nursing child? I was down on my knees in desperation, begging, crying, asking my Guides for a solution.

Michael became my knight in shining armor offering me a loan. His stipulation in paying the money back is that I share a fun story about Tatum with each payment. I'm going to be able to take care of this beautiful child with more monetary assurance and sense of security. I found other gifts of opportunities present themselves to assist in my single motherhood. While, I never-ever thought I would consider suicide out of helplessness; I had moments of determining the best way, with the least amount of pain, to leave this planet. Pairing Tatum's innocence and Michael's generosity, I was brought back to my senses. Godfather, you saved my life. And the miracles kept happening, a female acquaintance was looking for a place to live, so she moved into a spare bedroom. And I was able to rent out another bedroom to Yoga Retreat Clients. So I see how I opened to receive help and it came in, in threes. Gratitude. There's always Gratitude.

— *Dream: Trees are Alive*

Continually learning new ways of finagling my single mom groove, I've joined a Mommy and Me class. While our children play together, we Moms do yoga, belly dance, interact and discuss the realities of being a Mom. And I am enjoying the freedom to explore Sedona's many hiking trails and magical spots, with Tatum riding on my back. Harrison and I are committed to keep our differences from Tatum, as we continue to love our child. Tatum seems to get our best in this arrangement. Perhaps, calling it a broken home, isn't the truth.

Harrison and I have established a co-parenting routine for Tatum. He spends two weeks at my house, then two weeks at Harrison's house. After many months of fine-tuning our new parenting roles, it seems to be working quite well.

I've been invited to a friend of a friend's art show or as she calls it, an art unveiling. Apparently, Brie, the artist is a master at creating life size plaster masks which look realistic. She will be showing her latest art piece.

Such a Sedona thing. This town is full of inspiring artists, internationally known musicians and dedicated Healers. It's ironic, anywhere I've lived, I've always felt a bit odd being an Artist and a Hypnotherapist. Now, I actually feel...can I really say it?... I feel "normal" for the first time in my life.

I didn't realize how being unique had become part of my reper-toire, so to speak. It's easy for me to meet people here; we share our stories about art and spirituality quite comfortably and easily. Talking about your astrological sign at the market is comparable to talking about the weather elsewhere. It's so refreshing to be understood for the parts of myself which are very special and dear to me but have been locked away and guarded from people. Also, I notice many of the people who are drawn to Sedona are also considered the "Black Sheep" or the "Rebels" of their families. One of my friends corrected me by saying, "We are the white rebel spirits."

Being a rather cloudy Saturday, I'm questioning even going to this art event. As the evening rolls around, I am showering and dressing, when I realize I don't have directions to her house. I think to myself, I will call Brie and if she answers her phone, I will go but if not I will stay home and enjoy a quiet evening. I had a babysitter for Tatum so the idea of a night alone sounds lovely.

Brie answers her phone.

OK, I have my answer. I suppose my Guides are at it again, nudging me in a certain direction. A few hours later, I found myself traveling to Sedona's Village of Oak Creek and asking myself what is this "pull" all about? Why do I need to be at this party? Interest-ingly, I don't even know the host, as my friend, Tracy invited me. All these questions couldn't change the "feeling" within telling me, "Hey, you need to be there or be square." OK, I am here. I'll go inside, however I am a little apprehensive about going to a party alone.

Lovely Brie greets me at the door with her charming smile pairing well with her beautiful long thick blonde hair accentuating her features. Her creativity seems to reach to all corners of her home. As I look up, I see eyes peeking at me from several of her decorative masks in each corner of the room. Brie is dressed in her Sedona flare of blue and purple flowing material with matching jewelry. We introduce each other as she graciously leads me to her new body sculpture she has created.

It is a 3-D actual size model of a woman made out of plaster and exquisitely painted with hints of metallic gold accenting her ample body. I find it to be stunningly beautiful revealing the woman's left breast. It is done seductively with good taste. Brie is truly an amazing artist. Immediately, I feel at ease with her and her artsy home and I am glad I put in the effort to come this evening. She hands me a glass of vino. This will help me relax, I remind myself so I drink it delightfully while enjoying her home and the lively guests in the other room.

Moving into the kitchen area, I notice an array of lovely dishes. Is this why all parties seem to end up in the kitchen? Because of the colorful appetizing food which acts like engaging magnets? As I move to the large seductive table, I notice the colorful array of spinach artichoke dip, stuffed mushrooms, shrimp enchiladas, curry coconut tempeh and grilled salmon. Reaching for a mushroom, I notice another woman also feasting her eyes on the adornment of food. Feeling more at ease, I strike up a conversation,

"These sculptures are amazing, aren't they?"

I point my mushroom hors d'oeuvre to a winged cherub flying above our heads. She looks up from the spread of food-goodliness and follows my mushroom,

"Ooh, I didn't see that one. It must be the guardian angel of culinary delights," she laughs.

I crackup in mid-bite and wipe stuffing off my chin.

"Well, don't we all dream of some guardian angel flying over our lives?"

"So true," she says, "Do you ever fly in your dreams?"

"I haven't been able to fly in my dreams, but I so want to!" I say.

"I do, quite often, I love that feeling," she says excitedly.

"Hi, my name is Rhea,"

"My name is Chloe."

"What's your favorite flying dream?" I ask.

I feel a presence looking at us. I glance over and this very tall man with twinkling eyes seems to be gliding toward us.

"I overheard the mention of flying in your dreams. Hi, my name is Merrick."

"Merrick, that's an interesting name. I'm Rhea and this is Chloe."

I find a place to set down my wine glass and put out my hand to shake his. Gently, he pulls me in for a Sedona hug. Then he hugs Chloe as well. Everyone hugs in this town.

"Merrick seems to be the name that feels more connected to who I am."

"Well, I'll excuse myself, nice meeting you both," Chloe says smiling, "I have some mingling to do."

"And who are you, Mr. Merrick?" I giggle. I am surprised how natural and comfortable it is talking to him. He simply raises his eyebrows and gives me a quick nod. I think that's his answer.

"OK. So, do you fly in your dreams?" I ask him.

"Well, yes I do. I find it very intriguing but I am also intrigued by you at the moment. My friends encouraged me to come over here and talk to you. To be honest, I've seen you before. It was at another gathering months ago but you were with a man, so I was a bit shy about meeting you."

I like his honesty and his willingness to admit his challenges, as my past experiences with egotistic men has taken a toll on me.

"Realllllly? So now your courage has come into fruition. Is this why they are all watching us right now?" I look in their direction and all three of his buddies look away as if they are busted.

"Yep, that would be them. I'm fairly new in Sedona and they are looking out for me, I guess you could say."

"Looking out for you?" I repeat, "And what are your intentions that they need to be looking out for you?"

"Hmm, my intentions? Well to begin with, I'd like to at least get your phone number before I leave tonight?"

"And what else?" I bravely ask.

"That's a nice beginning," he smiles.

"I think I can handle that however, I'm going to be very busy for the next few weeks, as I am getting ready for my first art show in Sedona," I say proudly.

"Aha! Yes, I'm intrigued again. What kind of art do you do?"

"Hmm, how can I describe it? I guess you could say I paint from within. I'm not sure what will appear on the canvas, however, what I do know is that it will provide some kind of insight for me. I also enjoy painting my dream world."

"Ah, a woman after my heart! I love that you paint your dream-world, as I so enjoy my flying dreams which happen more often when my life is flowing nicely. I suppose I'll fly to great heights tonight," he winks.

It's as if little lovebirds are flying back and forth between us enjoying our undivided attention.

"Am I blushing?" I ask innocently.

Why is this so easy, I seem to keep asking myself. It's so easy to kid around with this tall cutie who seems to be quite the charmer.

To change the subject and take the energy off of me, I say,

"So I notice your interesting eyes, they seem to be very piercing yet different," as I look deeply into them, "What is it? Ah, yes, I see your left eye's pupil is much larger than your right one?"

"Wow, you noticed," Merrick says clearly surprised with my observation.

"You know the eyes are the pathway to the soul. You must be a deep person, yeah?"

"Well I guess you'll have to find out for yourself, hint, hint, nudge, nudge," he pokes my arm gently with his elbow. Just the perfect kind of touch, gentle but with confidence.

Consciously, I pull my energy back to myself. Our energies seem to want to coagulate right between us, as if wanting to stay there and create a third entity. I'd never felt this before.

"Aren't we supposed to be talking about our careers or something like that?" I lighten the mood a bit.

"OK, let's act like we just met? What do you do for a living?" Merrick gets the drift. I like his ability to understand and go with the natural flow. Not that I'm keeping score or anything. Or am I?

"Primarily, I teach art to children and I am a hypnotherapist but here comes the big one, I am the proud mom of an almost two year old boy. So, you can turn around anytime you wish and return back to your friends, who, by the way, are still watching us."

He looks deeply into my eyes, "Why would I want to walk away?" My entire body is flooded with goosebumps.

"I can't just walk away."

"Why not?" I am truly curious now.

"Honestly?" he takes a deep breath. "OK, here it is: It's because I dreamt of you about ten years ago. That's right, and in my dream it was revealed my soul mate would notice my unique eyes. That, dear Rhea, is why I am very curious to see where this goes."

"This? We already have a "this"? I laugh nervously.

"Well, do you want to have a "this" with me?" he adds.

I take a big, long drink of my wine. I'm not sure if it's to give me more time to digest or to help calm my adrenaline rush, which has made its presence known quite well.

As if sensing my need for regrouping, Merrick continues,

"Anyway, I'm traveling to France tomorrow for two weeks, so you will have plenty of time to prepare for your art show and get ready for our 'this."

He smiles a big one, as the candlelight shimmers off the top of his brownish hair. I so enjoy the style of his cut, casual yet flattering and fun.

There's a pause. Taking the lead, I swallow and change directions.

"OK, so what are you doing in France? Business or pleasure?"

"Pleasure, I suppose, it's a retreat in southern France for Trance Dancing"

"A what?" I ask. This man gets more mysterious every minute.

Merrick laughs out loud, "Trance Dance. It's a shamanic practice."

"OK, so what do you do besides trance dance?"

"I've been doing art my entire life, and this has moved me into doing graphic design work and book work."

"Oh, BookMerrick," I say laughing.

Our eyes meet again in our giggle mode and seem to want to linger there.

"And about this Trance Dance? It sounds so intriguing and in France, I've always wanted to go there."

"Well, since you mentioned hypnosis, you are already aware of the power of trance, so imagine dancing to rhythmic African drumming music with blindfolds over your eyes. You feel alone and this can be incredibly insightful to release old patterns and heal your inner self. Plus it's fun!"

I listen with keen interest, "I am enjoying the visual of you moving your body around. Is it safe? I mean, all these free spirits flailing their whatevers around?"

"Funny image, for sure, but seriously it's safe. They have what are called "spotters" watching and they're not wearing blindfolds, by the way. They are well trained and it is professionally run. Besides, I am good friends with the facilitator. He travels all around the world sharing this ecstatic healing practice with people from all walks of life."

He pauses as if awaiting for my response.

"Are you interested?"

"Are you inviting me?" I giggle.

"Can you fit in my luggage?"

"Tatum, my son? Is he invited as well? No time for finding a babysitter."

"Sure, why not? Although he may be run over by a passionate parisian dancer," Merrick laughs.

"Perhaps another time. Whoa, speaking of time..."

I look around at the other people at the party who had temporarily disappeared as I was in the Merrick tunnel. It's as though a blanket of magical super glue is being created between us allowing us to fit together perfectly.

"Yeah, I've probably taken up enough of your time for now, let's mingle a bit and I'll speak with you before I leave. Wonderful meeting you," his eyes seem to twinkle as he holds my hand with both of his. I like the feel of his hands. Clearly, he hasn't used these soft hands for any type of physical work.

"Sounds perfect," I smile genuinely at him, wondering if he notices the slight moisture on my hand. I watch him as he kisses my hand and then spirals around to venture outside, ever so gracefully.

I'm delightfully spiraling inside as well. I feel so comfortable with him! I marvel at this idea. I'm enjoying thinking of how he was so endearing and open and what a great listener. He really seems to know how to engage both my spiritual and my personal needs. Who am I with this man? I recall a part of myself comfortably being presented that would not, could not come out with other people, particularly with other men. This was so unusually easy, yes that's the best word I can find to explain our exchange, so naturally *easy*!

Through my mesmerized eyes, I look for my lovely friend, Tracy. She is a stunning beauty, who can reveal her cleavage in a classy way, enhancing her attractiveness. I want to thank her for inviting me to this party.

"Rhea, how are you?" giving me the Sedona hug and a kiss on my lips.

"I'm spinning at the moment," I appreciate my honesty, even though it can get me into trouble at times. People think they want honesty until it is staring them in the face.

"Earth to Rhea," Tracy laughs, "I saw you with Merrick. What WERE you talking about?"

"Oh just stuff, you know" looking for words is a bit more complicated at the moment, "We spoke of art, trance, France, and dance. Hey, that rhymes."

I laugh easily as if releasing some of my adrenaline still lingering from my conversation with Mr. blue eyes.

"I was watching you."

"What? Why? What did you notice?" I ask.

I am reminded of Tracy's ability to see beyond this dimension and her intuitive abilities. However, still I wasn't quite so prepared for her next words,

"As you were talking, there was quite a light show happening. I saw your auras full of vibrant colors aligning with each other. It was incredible to witness and stunning to watch!"

"What does that even mean?" I want to know.

I look around the party room to find my eyes on Merrick and Brie, the Artist Extraordinaire, talking by the hallway. She is swaying her glass of wine as if it's a microphone, while laughing at his every word. She moves in for the infamous Sedona hug and then kisses Merrick right on the lips. It seems a bit longer than my kiss from Tracy? Or is it my imagination? Yuck, my body is reacting to this scene. Is this jealousy I'm feeling? Really? I don't like this part of myself.

I take my attention back to Tracy, "Simply put, your auras connecting means you two seem to have quite a connection, quite a journey together of learning and growing. You realize he is my boyfriend's brother?" she continues, "I understand Merrick is very picky. He's never been married. Several of my friends have attempted to go out with him and he has no interest," she continues, "So him spending that much time with you says a lot, Rhea."

"Is he gay?" My heart is beating a bit faster.

"I really don't think so. According to his brother, he's just picky."

"Hmm, interesting. Tracy, he says he dreamt about me ten years ago."

"Yeah, not too surprising, I understand he is very intuitive as well," she adds.

"Fortunately, I have two weeks to consider this, since Merrick is leaving for a trip to France tomorrow morning."

Tracy nudges me, "Speaking of..."

"I am back," I hear as I turn around to blue eyes, "Did you really think I would leave without getting your phone number? My flight is early in the morning and I haven't packed yet...hey, are you OK?"

He notices my face has changed a bit from our previous conversation.

"Yeah, sure. I have a business card in my car."

"I'll walk out with you."

Somehow I'm able to move my attention from Merrick, "I'll talk to you later, Tracy and thanks."

As we turn toward the door, we are met by Brie's piercing eyes, as she notices Merrick touching my arm ever so lightly. Moving in the direction of the front door, I pass Brie and thank her for a lovely party.

After giving Merrick my business card and a sweet hug, I follow his maroon SUV all the way down I-79, as I realize I want to be in his energy the whole way home. Later Merrick would tell me he watched me in his rear view mirror and he could tell I was interested in him because I stayed within car range. Boy, was he correct, I was interested.

Later that night, safely in my world, I'm curious about Trance Dance and I Google it:

'TranceDance is a unique blend of body movement, healing sounds,

dynamic percussive rhythms, transformational breathing techniques and the use of a blindfold - together stimulating a 'trance'
state that promotes spiritual awakenings, mental clarity, physical
stamina and emotional well-being. TranceDance takes participants on an 'inner journey.' Ritual trance journeys have been a
vital part of shamanic and eastern dance cultures for thousands
of years. Trance Dance's primary focus is on healing and spiritual
evolution.'

Preparing for my art show requires all of my undivided attention. I am making little touches to each of my paintings, my babies, while adding wire to each of them to hang. It's fascinating how my vulnerability has been peaking out of the closet, pairing with the idea of showing them to the public. It is much more than sharing my artwork, it is revealing a part of my soul!

Two weeks later, I get a call. Having returned from his trip to France, it's Merrick,

"Hi Rhea. How are you?"

"Bonjour, Traveler. How was the Trance Dance?' '

"It was a Tour de Force," he laughs.

"Really? In what way?"

"There's so much to it, let's see...well, southern France is beautiful and," he pauses, "I'll tell you about my favorite part and then I'll share more when we meet in person, I mean if you still want to meet."

"Sure."

"I suppose my favorite part was a bit frightening at the time, yet very empowering."

"Go on," I prod.

"Well, I became aware of unhealed emotions of my childhood and found a boogie."

"A what?"

"A boogie, you know, that stuff that keeps holding us back from our full potential. The challenging subconscious beliefs we carry; I like to call them my boogies."

"You're talking my language now. That's a big part of my evolving and my own personal beliefs, too."

"I know."

"What do you mean, a bit egotistical dear One?" I laugh. Did I just call him dear One? Did I also call him egotistical?

"Really, seriously," he continues as if thinking about it first, "I hosted seminars and had a private hypnotherapy practice years ago."

I think my neighbors, Emily and Michael could hear my jaw drop.

"Time out. You're an Artist and a Hypnotherapist? And you're open to change? Three of my favorite topics of conversation."

"Yes indeed," he replies rather proudly.

"OK, I surrender. You have my full attention at the moment."

"Well before we discuss details....how are you, Rhea?"

"I am great. Remember my Art Show I was telling you about? Well, it's approaching quickly, in fact it's in three days and I'm frantically framing, retouching and getting all my paintings ready for the show. So as to how I am doing? I am nervous and excited equally."

"That's cool. I'd really like to see your paintings; talk about a perfect opportunity to learn more about you!"

There's my warm fuzzy feeling again. It wasn't my imagination after all. I relax a bit more on the phone.

"Would you like to meet for coffee?

"Sure, how about Thursday. Do you know where Ravenheart is?"

"It's a date," he says, "I'll meet you there, how about 10:00ish?"

"Perfect. I'll be wearing my smile just for you."

"As they say in France, Au revoir Mademoiselle."

"Arov-a-rear," I attempt to say as I hang up the phone, laughing and thrilled to be alive. This is an ear-to-ear smile kinda day.

Ravenheart, Sedona's quaint caffeine and go-to community spot, finds us on Thursday at 10:00, sipping our drinks on the lovely patio overlooking the fountain and exploring our "this."

"Rhea, I have a confession. I saw you months ago at a gathering. I was stunned how familiar you looked and shy about approaching you. You left and I promised God that if I ever saw you again, I wouldn't be so uptight. I know, it sounds crazy."

I listened in awe. What could I say to this heartfelt honesty?

"Somehow I knew of our reunion," Merrick admits easily, "I do have woman friends in town but I haven't been romantic with anyone in years."

"That's so sweet of you to wait for me," I say, "Although I'm a bit shocked at your honesty. Most men wouldn't admit this about themselves."

Merrick looks embarrassed and I change subjects quickly,

"So, you were going to tell me more about Trance Dance."

"Oh...yeah. Well, we did have an agenda. I'm starting to feel it really doesn't matter what we chat about. Have you noticed how easy it is for us to talk?"

"That is so true, does it surprise you?"

"As I said back at the party, I dreamt of you about ten years ago! You were wearing green shorts and a cute tee shirt, you know, hiking clothes."

We talk and talk or shall I say he talks and talks. Humorously, I listen as I try to make sense of all the emotions I'm feeling while looking at his cute young face. For even though he is a bit older than I, he has a baby face with round cheeks. I want to squeeze them as he shares his version of life.

"This Trance Dance event was so empowering even though this is my third one. Each time, as I let myself become the dance, rather than doing my usual moves, I find some insight from within me. It allows me to see more of the false ideas I am carrying from my childhood."

"Aren't we all?" I say seriously, "I mean, I am still moving beyond all the unworthiness I've carried from my childhood. Sometimes it feels never ending and then the sun pops out once again."

"And so hearing your understanding of all the wisdom within us," he glances up toward his left side and continues, "I'd like to share a very special experience I had," he looks at me for the green light.

"Of course, please continue."

"Well, you'll need to open more of your already open mind!"

Now I am curious.

"I was having a conversation with one of my friends and we were discussing some of the basic human questions like, Who am I? Where are we from? Where do we go after death? What is death? You know the basic little questions about life."

I giggle out of delight, as I notice his excitement of the subject. I so appreciate passionate people, as I am discovering more of this part of myself through my painting.

"So, our conversation eventually lead to Terrence McKenna and his research with psilocybin mushrooms."

Merrick looks at me for a reaction, as if noting my interest level, he continues,

"After some research, I decided I wanted to try these magical mushrooms for the spiritual benefit. I wanted to open my heart and mind and see what I could learn about myself and my life."

"Intriguing."

"Before I go into the whole experience, I need to visit the little boy's room. Be right back."

As I watch Merrick go inside, I spot a friend of mine across the courtyard. He waves and comes to our table.

"How are you Rhea?" Sedona hug, no kiss.

"I'm great, I am in an interesting conversation with my new friend, Merrick."

"Really, speaking of interesting, can I share something with you? I have a few minutes before I have to run."

"Sure," as I say this he finds Merrick's seat across from me.

"I had the most amazing spiritual experience this past week-end, I tried magic mushrooms for the first time, it was so enlightening!"

"No way," I sputter.

"Yes, way, and I am still high from the entire experience. It has changed my life and has allowed me to relax into myself more. It's as if I can accept myself and my life. Truly the best gift I've ever given myself!"

"Interesting! I was just talking about..."

"Sorry to interrupt, Rhea. Here comes your "friend" which I can imagine will not be a friend for long, if you know what I mean," he winks at me, "Let's catch up another time, I need to run to work right now."

"Ciao," I say.

"Ciao," he echoes.

As Merrick returns to the table, my face must have told a story.

"What is it, Rhea? Is this topic too much for a first date?" he asks.

"No, please continue. I am so interested, it's just that my friend came over and shared a little of his experience with mushrooms. Coincidence? I think not, just the Universe doing its weaving dance," I continue, "You truly have my full attention NOW!"

Merrick begins as I sip my chai tea,

"When I was living in Colorado, I felt the desire to do a mushroom journey. I set up my spare bedroom with a futon and some pillows. After taking them, I laid down and felt myself being overwhelmed by swirling patterns of color and sensations. This was a very uncomfortable place but it eventually gave way to a feeling of floating in a vast ocean."

"A familiar voice came in to speak. It was my higher guidance but more present and distinct. I began asking what they wanted me to do. They said simply. "Give up your body." That was easy since it seemed I was drifting deeper anyway.

Then they said, "Give up your life, family and friends. Let them all go...give up your identity as Merrick...give up your beliefs and everything you feel is the truth."

This went on for a long time; with each "giving up" I released another part of myself until I felt I was floating in a black void.

"Now you must give up LOVE."

"What? How could I give up Love. It's all there is!" I cried.

They said, "This is as far as you can go if you can't let go of love. You can have back everything you just let go of." Hearing those words, I felt deep despair for what seemed a long time. Finally I gave up; I let go of Love and breathed it away... gone."

"At that moment of release, I am slingshot into the void of space at frightening speed. Rhea, it was like a roller coaster with rocket engines! And as fast as it started, it ended full stop. I was floating in blackness but I felt the voice except much closer as a presence."

Listening intently to Merrick, I must move my legs and arms to feel some circulation. Who is this man, I ask myself?

"So the voice says, "turn around."

Before me was an overwhelming sight! A vast field of lights was spread out to the edge of my vision and made up of sparks of iridescent colors. They moved in unison toward the center where a huge fountain of light pushed them upwards. It became brighter the higher it went. Upon reaching the top, the lights exploded outward in all directions to the farthest ends of this immense field where they each started their journey again, only from a different position."

"What was this?" I ask after a needed sip of my tea.

"Creation. Each individual light was a spirit moving through their own life." Merrick explains, "You see, I realized life experiences are infinite. One life may be "Mother Theresa" and another "Hitler," but there's no judgement of one's experience for there is no death.

I had to give up love—to see this—but it wasn't Love I gave up, only my conception of love."

"WOW, I'm speechless," I say slowly.

"I am surprised I told you this entire story, Rhea. I haven't shared this with many people. This really says something about our connection."

Merrick pauses and looks at me, "Have I found love again?"

This warms my heart as our eyes hold our connection.

"I am so amazed and thankful you shared this. What an experience! I feel so satisfied about my life after hearing this, even worrying about things like money seems insignificant."

"Was this experience the last time you did mushrooms?" I ask.

"Yes, and what a grand finale!"

"Most definitely, I'm shaking inside imagining meeting the Creator, meeting Creation. How long did this experience last?"

"Many hours as you can imagine."

"Wow and I've spent so much of my life judging others and myself. I feel your story is a game changer. You are a game changer," I smile a big one and look into his unique eyes.

We hold this moment and begin to really grasp what our connection can be together.

I break the intensity, "I want to go to there," I laugh, "Really, I'd like to try mushrooms some time. I think I'd like to try many things with you!"

"Now I think you have answered my question," he smiles in return.

24

I've often been told, "I am too much." I guess it's because I enjoy talking and sharing from an honest place, with heartfelt emotion. My many ideas about life are endless. I like discovering new places, eating at new restaurants, enjoying coffee, wine and having a good time. So with Merrick, could I have possibly met someone who could keep up with me?

I planned a picnic in the lovely red rocks with Merrick. I knew of an ideal place with a wooden picnic table and a spectacular view for our dinner escapade. This chosen spot provided a peaceful ambiance facing the setting sun, surrounded by red rock encampments. The subtle lighting is perfect for a romantic night of wining and dining with my new intriguing friend. I made a lovely pot roast paired with mashed potatoes, gravy, caesar salad and red wine.

As we sit under the fading sunset, I notice Merrick isn't eating much and is a bit more quiet.

"Are you OK?"

"I don't know. I had dinner with some friends last night and they were warning me of dating you. Not you personally, but dating a Mom with a child."

"Were these your male friends from Brie's party?" I am curious.

"No, these are some female friends of mine."

"Yeah, what else did they say?" My radar is listening.

"They said Moms with children do not date, they are only looking for a Dad."

"Beyond what your friends think, what do you think?"

"It did make me look at our situation from a different angle."

"And what angle would this be?"

"It made me think about the responsibility of dating a mother, if you want to call it that. It made me think more seriously about what dating you involves since it is a package deal with Tatum. I've never thought of myself as a Dad type, is all."

"I'm sure your friends are only looking out for you."

I'm remembering his friends watching us at Brie's home.

"And I'm curious, are they wanting other things from you?" I need to go there.

"What do you mean, other things?"

"Perhaps they are interested in you romantically? Tracy was telling me some of her friends had wanted to date you."

"I consider them only friends, but one particular friend did act strange, now that I think about it."

"Merrick, you're so open and sweet, perhaps women find you appealing; I certainly do!" I notice the sunset has left and the crescent moon has replaced it perfectly.

"Perhaps?" he chimes in.

"Hmm, think of it this way; I believe everyone is searching for some form of love. Am I looking for a Dad? Not necessarily a Dad per say. What I am looking for is someone to share my heart and soul with. If that's the case, I suppose I'm guilty as charged."

He laughs, somehow breaking some of the tension in his taut body.

"I suppose I'm thinking way too much about this entire situation," he continues, "Let's dive into this beautiful roast." He adjusts his butt cheeks on the hard bench and I take this as the perfect time to unpack my favorite blanket.

"That's a bit forward, a blanket?" he says.

"It's for my sore bum, would you like to share it with me?"

"Sure thing, my blanket buddy," he smiles.

"Now that's nice to see you smile again; you were getting a little uptight."

"I'm back."

After eating a bit, I pick up our conversation, "I suppose I do understand their concerns for you. It tells me how much they care about you." Pausing for more time to think, I continue, "Please know that, Yes, I'm searching for love just like most people I know. And I have learned the real love I am searching for is to love myself more and more each day. This is my first priority, then my spirituality, then my son. If you happen to feel compelled to jump in with us, it will be because of our natural connection which we both have already felt. This is your choice and I honor your decision either way. Tatum and I will be fine with or without you. If the energy goes in favor of our being together then, yay. I am wondering when two souls have found each other, if they can really separate. Love seems to have a magical way of tapping into the core of each one of us and birthing that place deep within us that has longed for expression."

I ended my little sermon with a question, "Wouldn't you wonder what you may miss if you don't at least give us a try?"

Merrick ponders my words then says, "I admit the conversation last night scared me a bit and I let my doubt override my heart. Yes, you're right, I wish to see where this takes me and of course, I wish to see where this takes us."

"You help me to see with my heart, as I don't feel judged by you," I am pleased to reveal.

"Are you strong enough to handle my female friendships?" Merrick asks.

"Sure," I say with confidence. Not realizing what I have coming.

When Merrick meets Tatum, which happens almost immediately, it is adorably humorous. They are complete opposites. Six feet four Merrick and little two year old Tatum; what a sweet combo! They connect easily and this creates a warm feeling in my heart. I can feel their instant comfort with each other. We go on a hike around a large pond and they play and splash and became kids gleefully together, marking the beginning of a special connection.

Merrick says, "Uh Rhea, by the way, the shorts, t-shirt and converse you are wearing, are exactly like the clothes you were wearing in my dream of you ten years ago!"

25

My little trick to staying physically fit, is to not make my body 'a thing' to worry about. I simply enjoy my body and appreciate the magic of it. Often times, women ask me how I stay so healthy and thin. It's easy for me. Simply put, I don't make the idea of my body into an idea to stress about. I find this type of thinking makes it metaphorically become heavy, like concrete. Generally, I love my body because I know it will be fine. I don't dwell on it and I definitely do not believe in dieting.

Allowing my body full expression, Merrick and I are going trance dancing! Our ten day retreat is on the big island of Hawaii. After Merrick's powerful experiences while dancing, I am thrilled to be flying across the Pacific to learn more about this moving process! Ideally uncovering more of my jewels from within.

Everything for our physical needs is within walking distance. We are comfortably situated on many acres of green paradise with banana, coconut and guava trees galore. Our little wooden cabin has two separated living quarters and is sweet and easy to call home. I look forward to meeting the other trance dancers, Alex our guide and our neighbors next door.

The main room has a couch, a few chairs and connects with our little kitchen, which I doubt we will be using. Not because of a lack of love for cooking or eating, but because our outdoor dining area provides a gourmet spread of organic food and drinks for every meal. With so much physical movement, appeasing our appetite is necessary. The bathroom is intriguing with an open shower; there is only a full length screen between my naked body and the trees outside. This entire environment speaks of transparency and openness.

Our first day in Hawaiian bliss, Merrick and I walk to the beach, which is basically across the street from our resort. Shiny black sand awaits our adoring eyes, as the sound of huge waves make their presence known. It is dotted with many suntan bodies, some of them in their birthday suits. A double rainbow spreads its beauty across the horizon, as African drumming ensues and joints are being passed around like Halloween candy. I think we have arrived in heaven!

A legend is told to us by one of the locals. It is revealed there are black male and female rocks scattered on the beach. If you take a rock, another rock will not be able to make babies and the beach will eventually disappear. It opens my mind to consider the rocks as living beings.

Gloriously, we spend the day sunbathing, swimming and enjoying our Hawaiian welcome. As the sun sets, we glide back to our cabin to get some needed sleep before the dancing event begins the following day. We honored the legend and left all the lovely mating rocks to continue basking in the moonlight.

That night, being so enthralled by wondering what is to come, I found myself struggling to find sleep. I hear some commotion next door. Apparently, the walls are very thin between us, as our new neighbors have arrived. Their screams and banging on the walls becomes louder and I think, wow, this couple is a having one big fight. Even Merrick is stirring from his sleep. As the shouts get louder it dawns on me; Oh my, these are sexual noises, as their wild cries and moans pierce the night air. This dance, of sorts, seems to go on for hours, as I turn and try to enter my dreamworld. I wonder if they are with our group. Oh yeah, this coming week is going to be fascinating. This has the power to unleash my wounded ego that tries to snatch me into thinking I am entering into dangerous sexual waters. I do my best to come back to my original intention of being in my curiosity, rather than my fear.

The meeting space is a huge open area with a white canvas roof and no walls. This allows the ocean breezes to be a part of our shaking and sharing. The weather is perfect every day, with droplets of water falling perfectly when it seems to be getting a bit too warm.

We dance every day. Imagine darkness so intense and so complete it makes me see with my heart instead of my head. Beyond doing my default style of dance, my dance of comfort, I open to become the music. This is liberating and for the first time in my life, I enjoy dancing without having the need for alcohol to take away my self-consciousness. I love every step as I am moving around the large open space. The more confidence I find, the larger I become.

A different chakra of the body is discussed and emphasized each day as well. Eastern nations, as well as aboriginal people all around the world are aware of the seven chakras, the centers of spiritual power in our body. The chakras are vital to our health, as negative feelings can hamper the spinning of these chakras, resulting in sickness and dis-ease.

Each particular chakra movement brings up more insights about my life. Our group talks openly about our experiences and their ramifications. We dance like wild animals and claim our animal totems. My personal totem is a tiger, which I've always appreciated all creatures of the cat family. While dancing the second chakra, the sexual chakra, I'm feeling primal. I throw off my shirt while dancing wildly. It feels so natural and liberating.

On the seventh day, we are meeting at night for a full moon

ceremony only we haven't been told where we are going. Our group meets late in the night and we all drive through dark, bumpy dirt roads to get to our mysterious destination. Finally there, we are guided to walk across sharp lava mounds that shine like black glass under the bright moonlight. Each step requires my full concentration. The lava is the newest earth of the island and requires as much attention and respect as a new born baby.

Where are we going? My curiosity is highly present as Alex stops and points to a mountain off in the distance. I turn my gaze and see fire coming out of the mountain! It is Pele, the Fire Goddess. Pele is also known for her power, passion, jealousy, and capriciousness. Alex explains the significance of this full moon and why he wanted to bring us here on this auspicious night. Pele is erupting for the first time in three years! What magical timing.

There is a modern legend invented by a park ranger which says Pele will curse people with bad luck if they take rocks from this spot. It is against Federal law to take anything from our parks, so the ranger gave it an emotional twist. Apparently, it works quite well.

As soon as we lay our blankets on the ground and turn to face Pele to give our respects, the moon shines overhead and spreads multiple colors across the black sky. It's as though it has been drawn perfectly for us. This auspicious sight is the first and only time I've ever seen a "moonbow." We lie on our blankets and drumming commences, taking us each into our own world of insights and opportunities. With many of us becoming emotional, our tears find a place within needing some healing. I am proud to say I find my magical place, realizing my optimism of life and feeling free. Could I really be healing? I ask myself.

Spending our time dancing, swimming in private spots and enjoying Hawaii's many jungle treasures is easy and pleasurable. On day nine, it is time for the rebirthing part of the retreat. At midnight, we are guided to a nearby lagoon. Each person is immersed into the water, for a period of time and then brought back up. It appears to be harmless and relaxing.

It is my turn. I am held under the water's depths by Alex. This is so pleasing, with the warm water and its gentle movement around me. I'm nudged by an idea that I'm not in control of how long I stay here. With that simple thought, I am paralyzed with fear. I feel myself being buried alive. I feel like I have been under water much too long and I am really going to die, right here on this grand island. After panicking, I let myself experience this dying process, pondering the idea of coming back a lot more evolved next time. This is so freeing as I surrender completely. I am brought up to the surface, coughing and perplexed at the power of this dynamic.

The next day in circle, I share my rebirthing experience and ask if I was held under the water longer than the others. Clearly the facilitator is moved by this and says, "less than a minute." He shares with us that the Native Americans perform this type of ceremony in varying ways, to face their fear of dying. The idea is when letting go of our natural fear of the unknown, of death, this allows a new level of liberation and freedom to enter. To live life to the fullest.

It was only a few moments in time, but this rebirthing has the power to awaken me a bit more and reminds me to not take life so seriously. I am ready to dive in fully, a bit more aware. This amazing trip solidifies my connection not only with myself, but also with Merrick.

Merrick and I are spending almost all of our time together, since returning from Hawaii. Realizing our ease and comfort while traveling, we decide Tatum and I will move in with him. It seems the perfect setup for everyone involved. Within a week, I have moved out of my house and into this beautiful space atop a hill of gorgeous red rock views.

Challenges emerge with Merrick's little group of woman friends. For several years, they have had weekly gatherings in Flagstaff to paint, sculpt and be creative together. Merrick insists they are all just friends and I truly want to believe him, however my deep inner feelings tell me differently.

"You don't know these woman," he says.

"Precisely. Perhaps it's time for me to meet them?"

Pause. The silence is palpable.

"You're reluctance for me to meet them is curious to me, it makes me wonder even more what their intentions are, I mean two years is a long time to have been meeting with these women," I conclude.

"OK, I'll ask Ellen about us visiting her in Flagstaff," he says.

This ought to be interesting.

"If you are creating together that's fine and Sweetie, you did mention there was a blowup when we started dating."

"Rhea, I feel we have talked about this dynamic enough, we all are just friends."

Déjà vu takes me to these exact words spoken by Eli. Then I find out Eli married the woman he was just friends with. Why is this happening yet again?

"Then why was there a big debate when you told them about us? Was it all the women or just certain ones?"

"I hadn't said anything to anyone about us dating until I was sure of us. It came as a big surprise to, well, a few."

"Are you obligated to tell them everything about your life?"

"Rhea, come on."

"I understand this is how you view your connection with women, however, I'm not so convinced. What about Ellen; does she feel this way since it's her house you meet at? Just the other day, your brother's girlfriend told me Ellen considers her time with you as sacred and will not make any other plans with anyone else. Even Tracy thought it was peculiar and also wondered about Ellen's feelings for you. Just saying."

Merrick stares at me, "Let's say she does have more feelings for me, I need for you to realize I'm not interested in her. So just trust me."

"Why would you want to play in those dangerous waters?"

"They aren't dangerous to me," Merrick comments.

"I see how open you are with women and you've told me so many stories about how women have misinterpreted you. Plus you're easy to talk to, women love that; I love this about you. It's interesting how the thing I fell in love with in you is becoming our biggest challenge. Psychology 101!" I comment.

"I am with you, honey that's all you need to remember," Merrick says. "I'm off to Flagstaff to play with clay."

The deep feeling within me seems to crush my heart. Even after hearing his commitment to me and our relationship, I'm still apprehensive. What is underneath this I wonder? I want to say have a great time and really mean it, but the words are stuck to my heart with some sort of weird glue.

"Bye," comes reluctantly through my lips.

Merrick comes over to kiss me and says, "Rhea Sweetie, I'm with you. See you soon."

The next several hours move slowly. Usually Merrick's back by now. Tick. Tick. Tick. I'm remembering what he had told me about Ellen and her upset over us dating. Of course, I can't think of anything else. My ego mind won't let me out of this painful loop, my little pity party. With this bit of information, he still insists they are "just" friends? I'm confused. I'm totally baffled by this situation.

As I watch the clock, Merrick is late. One hour goes by, painfully goes by, then he's two hours late. How long does it take to drive back from Flagstaff? Holy crap, now I'm imagining he and Ellen are in bed. I can't get the image of him caressing some other woman out of my mind. He could have at least called. I'm freaking out, I can't do this! The pain is too much like my childhood. I couldn't trust anyone. I want to trust him, but there's too much subtle evidence!

I decide I need to get out of here, the waiting is driving me crazy. I pack a few things, put Tatum in his car seat and leave. I drive and drive and cry and cry. Why would he do this after our talk? Why would he be so late? I'm even questioning my judgments and most importantly, the real pain is that I'm questioning myself.

Miles later, as I witness darkness envelop the sky, I surrender it's time to return home. I'm pretty sure he'll be home by now; if not I'll try to handle what's next. I'm coming back to my senses, as I drive through the beautiful red rocks. Why don't they look so pretty right now? The rocks seem to be reflecting the intensity of my cloudy feelings, rather than shining their usual beauty.

I pull into the driveway and Merrick comes out to the car to meet us. Seeing him has brought out my wounded little girl again. Even if he slept with what's-her-name, at least he didn't stay for the cuddling, I remind myself. I am so in IT.

"Where did you go?" Merrick says as he meets me at the car door. He is way too smiley.

"I went for a ride," is all I can find to say.

"What is it, Rhea?" He stops and looks at me.

"Did you have a good time with her?" I say sarcastically.

"Yeah it was our usual sculpting, painting, and creating. Then we all had a glass of wine; it's how we end our time. Is this why you left?" He's catching onto my mood.

"You sure were gone a long time?" I probe.

"We got caught in a conversation."

"About what?" I ask.

"Spiritual relationships," he says.

"Fill me in, kind sir, are you having one with her? The one who shall remain nameless!" I ask with my less than nice voice.

"Oh, here we go, down the rabbit hole again?"

"Are you? Just be honest with me, Merrick?"

"Rhea, I'm here with you. What does that tell you? If I wanted to be with her I would be with her."

"Why were you so late again?"

"We were talking about spiritual relationships which don't require having sex to feel complete."

"Oh God, sounds so perfect."

"People can have relationships without sex," he adds.

"Is this what you have with her? I mean do you consider your connection with her a relationship?" My voice is quivering.

"Our friendship, sorry," he adds.

"Freudian slip if I've ever heard one."

"OK, you need to meet her."

"I trust you, I just do not trust her."

"Rhea, once you meet Ellen, you'll see she's not even my type. I like you. I love you. I'm with You," he smiles and pulls me in for a hug.

"And I want you to remember I grew up mainly around my sister and mom. I am very comfortable with women and they seem to feel this and they open up to me. Often times, I find women are more interesting then men for they speak openly and honestly. I know you like this about me as well."

I'm shaking inside, this overwhelming feeling is so scary and seems to gnaw away at my senses. Any logical thought goes out the window and in rushes this craziness and I feel out of control. It's so scary and makes we wonder about having a relationship with this man. Wow, relationships have the power to bring up everything that is unhealed.

What I did not see coming was the power of the law of attraction. When I met Merrick, I believed I had discovered something I had searched for yet despaired of ever finding: a man who is my equal. Merrick is my soul mate, the partner who can share in my visions of a better world. He has the passion and courage to make these changes with me. Like me, he carries a rebel spirit, a discernible force of nature. Because we are so alike in our spiritual quest, it is a double-edged sword, as we try to forge a relationship. If we can learn to work together in harmony and harness our shared desires for truth and for each other, we can create an unstoppable energy toward positive change in ourselves and in our world. But these same passions have the power to be singularly destructive.

26

I really do want to overcome my envious feelings about Ellen. I am hopeful a visit can bring some harmony into this female friend debacle. The plan is we'll drive together to Flagstaff and I'll go visit my favorite art teacher, while Merrick and Ellen have their creating time. Afterwards, we'll meet for a light dinner.

At the last minute, my art teacher isn't available due to a personal situation, and so now I'll be spending the entire evening with Merrick and Ellen.

Her home lies within a perfect view of the San Francisco Peaks. Ellen's house is immaculate and everything is perfectly in its place. During our introductions, Merrick maneuvers his 6'4 body over to her and they greet with a hug and a kiss...on the lips! It seems to me their hug, with her on her tip toes, is a bit longer than the designated hug time. Feeling right at home, Merrick excuses himself to get something from the art room.

As she is leading me into her eclectic living room, she looks into my eyes and says,

"You realize, Merrick and I would be together if I were taller."

"Really?" I say as I shake her hand.

She is an impeccable older woman, about five feet two inches tall. Merrick was right about one thing, she does have the 'I need to look perfect' look, as every hair is exactly in place, everything is tucked in and her home also reflects this innate perfection.

The only thing she hasn't perfected is her ability to hide obvious feelings for Merrick. As he joins us in the living room, his presence brings out her charming smile. All I received from her was a tight grin of sorts.

After this bizarre welcome, I couldn't find comfort with her, or even like her as I had hoped to. I'm thinking to myself, I've gone this far in my crazy life, looking for my soul mate and this woman is basically threatening me because I'm taller? I wish I could say I handled it with a bit more grace, however, this meeting was awkward.

"Rhea, did you go to college?" Ellen asks as she hands me a glass of wine. I look over at Merrick and notice even he is surprised by this mundane line of questioning. I surrender to play the game.

"Yes I have a degree in Education."

"Oh," is all she can say.

"And I am a certified Hypnotherapist."

"Oh," once again.

"What are you doing now, as I hear Sedona can be challenging to make a living?"

"I'm currently teaching art classes and doing some hypnosis sessions as well. I have come to see creativity as a force of enchantment!"

"Oh."

"I hear you have a son, how old is he?"

"He just turned two."

"Oh."

Pause. Uncomfortableness abounds.

"You know, Merrick's never thought of himself as a Dad type."

There's an awkward silence.

It. was. so. Unbearably weird.

"Ellen, come on!" Merrick finally says something. I look at him and he is clearly irritated as well. Why was she asking me these questions? Clearly she could care less about me or my answers.

Is this really the same woman Merrick has told me about? He has talked about her with glowing reviews. How can she be one of his good friends?

Pause. I take a big gulp of my wine.

"What are you currently sculpting?" I believe this is a safe question.

"Nothing really," Ellen responds.

This is going to be a long evening.

"Oh come on Ellen, you're sculpting this amazing piece right now," Merrick grabs the object he brought from the art room and shows it to me. As I take the sculpture, I notice he has taken a fairly large gulp of wine as well.

The statue is abstract with many colors demonstrating a flow of sorts, inviting my eyes to follow the pattern. I really like her style of creativity.

Again trying to make some connection, I comment, "I really like this Ellen, it seems you have created this from that mysterious place within yourself. Can you tell me what it means to you?"

"Well, my statue is OK," she smiles sweetly at Merrick. Has she forgotten I'm sitting right here?

Pause, new attempt.

"I notice your many intriguing masks hanging in each room, what do they mean to you?"

"Oh, I really don't like masks. I feel they represent you're hiding something."

"But...I..." I look at Merrick's face and I stop. There is no need to try and communicate with this woman, as she is clearly not interested in me. I want out of here and now. I look at Merrick and he is twirling his fingers together, a sign of his anxiety and feeling of malaise.

So here's the irony of this situation, I was wishing I was wrong in my accusations about her feelings for Merrick. Quite the contrary, as she clearly is in some form of love with him. Her pupils look dilated whenever she looks at him. When he speaks, all of her focus goes to him as well. I wasn't even in the same room with them, or so it felt. Before I materialize into invisibility again, I choose to remain present and aware, even though my little girl is begging me to hide.

I tolerate the rest of our visit in her perfectly orchestrated home, while trying to push away my gnawing feelings of insecurity emerging within me like a tornado. Where's my fantasy reality that states, once I find my soul mate, I get to feel automatically happy and joyful? Ha Ha. Sure, I have my wonderful moments, but this is like beauty and the beast. I have found him and how could I be feeling so miserable at the same time?

Two hours later, I'm really not sure how I've made it through this completely bizarre dining escapade. We walk to her front door to leave and she stands on her tippy toes and kisses Merrick on his lips again and completes her good-bye with a hug. It looks so natural between them, I want to puke.

"Nice to meet you, Rhea," she says as she shakes my hand.

Where's my kiss on the lips I'm thinking to myself? At least I still have my sense of humor. I've been told by many friends what they like about me is that I can laugh at myself.

Nice to meet me? I really don't believe you, Ellen.

"Good night," I say.

On the drive back through the canyon, I ask Merrick about this kissing on the lips dynamic and he says, "Oh everyone in the group does this. In fact I thought everyone in Sedona did this."

"Well do you like it?"

"Not necessarily, but everyone does it,"

"I'm sorry Merrick, that is a lame excuse, that's what a six year old might say."

Where's the man? I wonder.

"I'm wondering if you would be willing to change this with your woman friends. I feel it gives the wrong impression."

"I agree, I've been wanting to, but having just moved here, I wanted to fit in as well. Thanks for helping me to see a healthier reality. This feels better to me already."

"No more kisses 'on the lips' for You!" I laugh, "except from me. And I'm realizing that jealousy is simply an indicator of what I want. I want to be abundant financially like her. It's a green light reminding me to go for it. Knowing what I wish for exactly... is important for me to open to receive abundance."

"Bravo," Merrick says with a huge smile making its way across his entire face.

27

"You what? I'm not sure I heard you correctly?" I say.

"I connect with my Higher Guidance, you know, my Higher Self." Merrick repeats, "Remember the mushroom story, when I mentioned my Higher Guidance? That's also called my Higher Self in metaphysical studies. It is like an oversoul to all the lives and experiences you have had since becoming a spark in God's creation."

"Oh yeah, like Kellye connects with her Higher Self. I am so intrigued with her, not realizing you would be able to do this as well!"

"So can you, Ms. Rhea!"

"Can you show me?"

"Of course, but let's chat a bit more."

"First I need to find that special place within me that feels peaceful, my truth. This is where the practice comes in, because our Ego wants to start telling me all the things that it knows can get me unraveled."

"Yes, the good ole Ego....I've been training mine and it has less and less power over me. I've taken the shouts and made them into whispers."

"Great Rhea, this is what I mean. For me, I had to lessen the pull of my Ego in order to be able to connect more effectively. It's as though the two work against each other, so to speak. The Ego can mimic our higher guidance if we're not careful and all kinds of misinformation spews out. So basically, the less the Ego's words are taken as the truth, the more authentic our higher guidance's information can be. Actually, the process of channeling is as old as human history and is based on timeless spiritual law. People channel not only their higher guidance but spirit guides, angels, and the departed."

"Interesting, I'm starting to get it. The best way for me to attempt this is by trying it, as I am a hands-on learner."

"My degree of awareness affects what comes through, for example if I am tired, or hungry or feeling distracted, these aren't the best times to obtain information. But whether the signal is weak or strong, my wise spirit beings never attempt to control me. They warn, protect, encourage, and inspire, but the rest is up to me."

"Do you really think I can do this?"

"Sure you can, you already speak from this place at times."

"I'm starting to understand why we couldn't have come together any sooner?" I reflect, "Because I wouldn't have been ready for this part of my spiritual path until now."

"Aw, that's so sweet and so true," Merrick says and continues,

"Plus I don't think I would have been emotionally ready for you any earlier."

We hug as I realize the home I have been looking for since age seven is in Merrick's arms!

I am in awe and perplexed watching Merrick speak from this place within. He closes his eyes and seems to move into another dimension. I remember the first time Tatum was sitting with us for a "check-in", as these meditations have come to be called. As

Merrick closed his eyes and connected inward, Tatum looked at me and said,

"Where did Merrick go?"

This reveals how much his bodily energy shifts. Not only is he an amazing artist, a graphic designer with a successful business, he is a kind and loving soul! He began to mirror all this for me, not to mention the spiritual part as well. We really are destined to be together.

However, what is needing attention is this uncomfortable feeling with Ellen. I am wise enough to realize it has nothing to do with her, as these are my feelings and my feelings alone. I've asked another practioner in town by the name of Josef to do a session with me. We meet and talk for his understanding of my challenge. He is kind and a great listener.

I am determined to find out how to deal with not trusting people, both men and women. It's especially painful seeing Merrick's demeanor when I reveal this truth to him, of not trusting him.

Josef guides me within.

"Josef," I say trying to find the correct words, "You are not going to believe who is here in my inner world with me?" I exclaim.

"Who?" Josef asks.

"Well it's one of my Spirit Guides. My female Guide from my childhood visits," I say as tears touch my eyes.

"She's so beautiful and she's wearing her little hat, just like when we met so many years ago."

I see her aura of blue and purple vibrating around her as if this is a natural part of her presence. She walks slowly to me and hugs me. I feel her warmth and love go deep within me. I feel a familiar bond and am brought to tears yet again. As she pulls away from me, she looks deeply into my eyes and says, "Rhea Dear One, we've been together before in other lifetimes. We've been friends.

We are friends."

"Thank you for coming in today!" I keep my focus on her. I feel the tears flow, as I communicate without words as well.

"Rhea, I want you to realize how special you are. You have chosen a very challenging life and it has taken away any sense of who you truly are. I am pleased to see you finding more of your beauty, more of your truth."

I am balancing my curious nature as a Hypnotherapist and my wonderment of standing here with this lovely female presence. I find this situation a bit humorous and yet juicy with possibilities. By now I am aware anyone and anything can happen in this magical world within!

"Wonderful," Josef sighs, "welcome and thank you for coming in for Rhea today. What else would you like to share with her?"

"I am here for her. She has helped me many times," she says out loud in her sweet voice.

I'm taking in the depth of feeling this woman's presence so close to me. She's breathtaking, not in a beautiful way, but in a radiant way of being. I so enjoy her and want to be with her without talking.

I find it difficult to speak from this place.

"What else would you like to share with her?" Josef asks.

"Rhea's greatest challenge coming from a wounded child is removing her Ego. She no longer needs it."

"How can she do this?" Josef asks.

"She needs to be aware that her Ego is well trained and is on guard 24/7, even at nighttime. This requires vigilance to see how it has taken over her life."

"OK, thank you. How can she deal better with people she doesn't trust?"

My Guide says to me and I repeat to Josef, "Tell her to treat people like she treats her plants. Nurture and love them, sing to them and give them what they need in the moment and then let them go."

"That really makes sense. Thanks. Anything else you would like to share with Rhea?" Josef asks.

"She will continue to meet other people that I am connected with. Tell her that I am willing to come to anyone who is open to me and I'm always around her for support and guidance. And one more important reminder...she must write her book, this is her legacy!"

"Thank you so much," Josef says.

Slowly, I come back to this reality wondering what the heck just happened. Josef is smiling and is pleased with my inner journey. I am thrilled beyond words to have her support and love.

Over the next few years, we continue to meet on a white leather couch. My Guide is available for any of my questions, as she sheds light in many areas of my life. I feel such a connection with her. After many visits, she began showing up wearing jeans and a red t-shirt and no hat.

I ask, "Where's your little hat?"

"Oh I wore it so you would recognize me. And it worked, yes?"

After one of my Guide's visits, I tell Merrick what she revealed to me, "I have to figure out how to value my own vision, sort of like donning that cape again. I need to find comfort with myself and embrace who I am, even if it seems the rest of the world can't see it? Of course, I am referring to my family. I have to realize they will never be able to see the real me, especially my Mom who still treats me like a child. I have to realize it's OK and accept this about her. I realize I don't want them to judge me so I need to stop judging them."

"You got it, Rhea!"

"This is a game changer!"

"Congratulations Padawan!"

"What's a Padawan?"

"You know...from Star Wars."

"Aw, I take that as a compliment," I say as I hug my home buddy.

— *Soul Portrait*

*When I am balanced, connected to my Higher Guidance and in my true Light,
I can manifest Magic.*

Surprise, surprise! Lightheartedly, Merrick hands me a card for my birthday. I'm thinking a card, this is intriguing, I'm getting a card from my Beloved. As I begin to open it, I notice this isn't a typical birthday card as it is written in French. I look at him with curiosity and mystery all over my face. I'm not familiar with the French language beyond Bonjour; I wish I were. Therefore, I can't interpret its contents but it's beautifully written in teal ink, whatever it says. He is wearing his playful look and says with an outstretched hand,

"Do you want me to read it to you, Mademoiselle?"

"Yes, of course."

Taking the card, he begins reading it to me slowly with a lovely French accent.

'Bonjour, Je suis voyage avec vous au Paris
pour votre anniversaire.
Je t'aime, Merrick'

"Wow, what about Paris?" I ask curiously.

"Would you like to visit Paris this March with me?" He smiles.

"Are you serious?" I say wanting to fully capture the immensity of the words written on my card.

"Yes, Sweetie," he replies calmly. I run into his arms and kiss his lovely neck about seventeen times.

"I'm going to Paris, we're going to Paris, we're going to Paris! Happy Birthday to Me," I chant while skipping around the kitchen.

Merrick watches me and his smile broadens. I like how he appreciates my enthusiasm!

I'm thrilled as I've always felt some form of connection with Europe, especially France. Given my French ancestral line, I'm truly ready to meet this part of my heritage.

Whether we're strolling along the Seine or soaking up the city life from a sidewalk café, Paris is synonymous with the word: style. Paris is a city of villages, the place of dreams, the one that calls to us from afar and encourages someone to buy the plane ticket in the first place. This is what I'm about to witness and much more!

Our first evening, feeling jubilant and hungry, the combination has us on a mission to find our first dining experience in Mouffetarde. The cafe is called Maison de Viande and Merrick chose this cafe because it is one of his favorites. It requires a bit of a walk to reach, however, walking is part of the experience, even a prerequisite in Paris, which I thoroughly enjoy. We're heading to our dining spot, when we pass this beautiful old marble statuesque fountain in the middle of a circular roadway. Beyond it is one of the many glorious old churches prevalent in Paris. I am moved to a halt as I breathe in the beauty of this Church. As I approach this cathedral, Merrick is following close behind as I look reverently at the looming exterior, with its mixture of saints and gargoyles.

"Something special happened here. I want to go inside," I reply to Merrick. He gives me a look.

"I'd rather stay outside with the gargoyles, where I belong," Merrick adds.

I need to go into this Church, as if it is calling me to do so. There's something about this particular building that is pulling me into it.

"But Rhea, usually nothing gets in the way of eating."

"You're right, that's exactly why I must go in there."

Merrick hesitates, but I grab his arm and pull him alongside me.

"Come on. I promise to be quick and I'm sure the walls won't tumble down as you enter."

We reach the entrance and the Church is called Saint Medard a Paris. We enter as the setting sun streams through the huge stained glass window, illuminating Merrick and myself in brilliant light streaked with crimson. Merrick ˙wanders, face elevated to the windows. I walk slowly beside him, trying my best to remind myself that this is a building of enormous historic and architectural significance, and not just another church.

A French Priest walks past us, nodding a solemn greeting. I stumble slightly as he passes. The priest stops and holds out a hand to steady me, addressing me with mild concern in French. I smile and put my hand up, indicating that I am fine. Merrick returns to my side as the French priest goes on his way.

"You okay?"

"Yeah, just a little dizzy all of a sudden. Jet lag, perhaps. Hunger possibly?"

"It's true, we haven't eaten much all day," Merrick reiterates.

I point to one of the side pews that is in line with the lovely altar.

"I'm just going to sit down here for a minute and enjoy the stained glass. You go look around."

Merrick looks concerned, but I wave him away.

"I'm fine. Go. I'll be right here."

Merrick nods and goes off to explore the cathedral. I sit in the pew, steadying myself. I don't want to admit to Merrick just how unstable I'm feeling. It had come on so fast, and I knew that if I didn't sit down I would have fallen. I didn't want to tell Merrick since we had been anticipating this trip for so long, I didn't want to spoil it for anything in the world. I am sure I'm fine.

I wipe my hands over my face, trying to shake off the dizziness.

Kaleidoscopic beams of colored light from the stained glass window shine on the altar, illuminating a large crucifix. I blink. The crucifix appears to be growing, looming larger and larger in my sight. I say Hello to my friend Easa, Jesus, giggling to myself. And I thank Jesus again for guiding me to move out west.

I grab my head as dizziness envelops me and this vision takes over:

"I'm in a nun's body wearing a black habit and veil adorned with only a rosary around my neck. I'm in the exact same church, where I feel right at home as I'm praying. A sharp noise echoes throughout the cathedral bringing me out of my reverie. Determined to see what the noise is, I scramble to the large wooden door. Alarmed by the smell of smoke, I open the door. A man is lying on the concrete bench by the fountain. He has been shot in the chest. Feeling concerned, I slowly approach the man, calling out to him.

"Cher homme?"

No response.

I repeat, "Cher homme, êtes-vous bien?"

Still no response, no movement from the man.

Step by step, I walk toward him. Keeping my eyes solely on his body at all times, yearning for any type of movement. Suddenly I know the truth. The man is dead. I could sense his soul was no longer in his body. Frightened, I attempt to run in my long habit looking for someone to tell of my revelation.

Entering into the cathedral, I find the Monsignor in his office.

"Monsignor?" I catch my breath from running, "there's a man lying next to the fountain outside. I think he's dead."

Appearing alarmed, the Monsignor responds, "Oh my goodness," then calms himself, "we will not tell anyone. We can not get involved or people will stop coming to our church and we will lose their money."

I am thinking to myself—the Monsigner's words are the words of God! I can't even question him."

I feel a gentle tug on my arm, as Merrick is looking at me with his concerned look, "Rhea, Rhea are you OK?"

"What? Where am I?" I say slowly, as I find my present vision coming back to me.

"You're in a Church in Paris, remember?"

"Yes."

"What happened? You look so far away?"

"I need to leave here," I say without hesitancy.

"Come on, let's walk, I know a breath thing," Merrick says providing comfort.

As we are leaving the Church, I look at the marble fountain again fully expecting to see the dead man's body. The body is gone but the memory will be with me forever.

Merrick listens intently as I share the vision with him, while walking to dinner. After some introspection, he suggests we return there again to speak with someone at the Church to obtain more information. I like this idea. Finally reaching our destination, we enjoy a lovely dinner of grilled salmon, rice pilaf complete with wine and dessert. Returning to our quaint hotel, I feel sleep knocking even before hitting the French pillow.

"Bonjour," our hotel manager greets us the following morning.

"Bonjour," I say happily. I love the feel of this word in my mouth.

"What do you think about your experience at the Church?" Merrick asks over fresh coffee and pâtisserie. "Do you still want to return there and speak with someone who works there? It could be interesting."

"Yes, absolutely. I do want to return and as far as the experience, it felt so real, so absolutely real. Since I awoke, I've been going over the details in my mind and I have no doubt this was me as a nun in a past life. I could feel her; I knew her. Actually, there are parts of me that are her in this life time. She felt a bit rebellious of the traditional ways but she couldn't do a thing. I'm guessing she "me" became very suspicious of the Catholic Church after this realization about putting money before faith. I sense she went through a form of depression after this situation and made an agreement she would find her own religion, despite the fact that she was a nun. This helps me to understand how I came to want to find my own religion this life time. It is the "Rhea Religion" and I get to choose bits and pieces and create my own religion."

I continue, as we find our way to the door, "Sounds a bit humorous, however, I truly believe this is where I am this life. Would you like to join my religion?" I say lightening the mood a bit.

"Sure thing," Merrick says while grabbing my arm to skip off to the Museum with me. "As long as part of your religion requires having fun with you."

"Yes indeed," I giggle.

We find it easy to play and have fun together.

We visit the Musée d'Orsay for a whole afternoon but it is the smaller Musée Marmottan Monet that captures my passion. It features a collection of over three hundred Impressionist and Post-Impressionist works by Monet, Berthe Morisot, Degas, Manet, Alfred Sisley, Camille Pisarro, Gauguin, Paul Signac and Renoir. In addition it houses the Wildenstein Collection of illuminated manuscripts and the Jules and Paul Marmottan collection of NapoCameronnic era art and furniture as well as Italian and Flemish primitive paintings. We are in creative heaven.

"Merrick, come and look at this painting with me," I say looking at Monet's 'Water Lily Pond.' As we are standing directly in front of his painting, it literally looks like a bunch of paint thrown onto the canvas.

"Now walk backward with me," I suggest as I grab his hand.

"Keep walking...back...more...more. There's nobody behind us."

Suddenly the image of water lilies appears clear as can be, as if we had adjusted an old TV antennae. We are now about 20 feet from this magical Monet painting. How does someone paint a painting like that unless they are connecting with their inner wisdom?

"I truly believe he was channeling his paintings," I smile at Merrick, "like I do. Not that I'm comparing myself to this artist extraordinaire; it seems we use a similar process. I did read that Monet paints energy."

"I so agree with you. And I'm pleased you have taught me how to let go and just paint. Being a learned artist, I have let my thinking mind get in the way too much. So watching you paint so loosely, truly inspires me!"

I so love this man at this moment. If I could stop time it would be in Paris with Merrick, my sweetheart.

"As Monet inspires us, I so adore you right now," I say.

"Aw, sweet!" he responds.

"The painting or me?" I laugh.

"To be safe, I'll say both," as he hugs me while admiring the genius nature of Monet!

It's time to return to the infamous cathedral again. I think I'm ready yet a part of me is concerned about a re-occurrence of the last visit. And I'd really like to talk with someone about the Church's history. We walk into the vestibule and right there are brochures about the area, its culture, amenities, services, and most important to us, the history of the area. We grab a brochure feeling this will be ample information to appease our curiosity.

Returning to the fountain, we sit while listening to the flow of water behind us and begin to read. Basically, it says,

'This area in the late 1800's and early 1900's had a rather dark history. The area was known for Paris' lower class where crime and prostitution occurred. This resulted in violence and murders."

Well that's confirmation, indeed! Confirmation of my resistance to a religion, of my discomforts with money, of past lives in general. I love you Paris for much more than your art, food and culture.

— Mother & Child

My life seems to have found a flowing groove. I can comfortably sit back, eat a little popcorn and watch through my wise observer eyes. I am running my Creationship Art program in thirteen grade schools in Flagstaff, three elementary schools in Sedona, one school in Cottonwood and three schools in Phoenix, Arizona. I've trained the art teachers and the children love the classes. The little artists have learned there is no right or wrong with creating. They can copy from each other and they enjoy this freedom.

This exquisite program provides a need for so many little artists to open up to their creativity as well as their spirituality. Some of my students have begun to ask for quiet time, as they are getting in touch with their creative magic from within! Plus Creationship is providing many jobs for teachers and wannabe artists. I am thrilled.

I am flying high; my vivacious dreams are coming true when suddenly, literally everything collapses. A lawsuit within the Phoenix School District prevents me from sending my flyers home to the children. The Flagstaff Director apologetically reveals to me they no longer have the funds for the program and the Principal who hired me in Sedona has moved to another town. The new Principal has no interest in supporting the arts. All of these changes happened within days of each other!

Watching my entire world seemingly crash and burn, I am truly devastated. There is still a part of me that refuses to allow the luxury of sustained success in my world. Why, oh why, can't I become fully successful? This question haunts my entire being. I want to scream, I want to cry, literally I feel so confused.

I have to look at my life realistically, I'm starting to see yet another pattern, when I get close to full on success, I sabotage it some how, some way. I'm smart enough to see this happening and this realization adds to the complexity of the situation. I know I am creating this, however, here is the big rub; it's on an unconscious level. Do I still believe I am unworthy or is it something else? I can see how I had to become invisible to protect myself as a child. My invisibility cloak is dripping with no sense of worth and I know this; I see it and still this makes me feel out of control inside and out. I have to change this about myself. How can I be a parent if I can't even feed myself? CRAZINESS runs through my veins and I have to find a way to vent all this energy. I am on my knees praying for guidance and support once again.

Finally, Merrick and I do a "check-in" and all our guidance would say is, "Go within."

"What?" I'm hysterical by now. My entire business world has disintegrated right before my eyes, thus threatening my survival and this is all my higher guidance could say,

"Rhea, go within."

"Really?" I am furious. Why don't they just give me a practical solution or a business plan or the name of someone who wants my program.

"Dear One, Just...Go...Within," they repeat.

After much heartache, multiple discussions with Merrick and rampant tears of frustration, I'm actually entertaining the idea of these two simple words, "Go Within." And what will I find there? It seems the more I look, the more scary it can be. I have no other choice but to go within. I have tried everything else.

I surrender to my inner world, having no other alternative. I commit to myself to meditate each morning, rather begrudgingly. Coming from my "do-do-do" family, I find this very challenging to stop my well learned "busyness' and to explore my inner world on a deeper level. I know in my heart and soul, this is the best gift for myself, however, the reality of it is that it's challenging to spend that much time alone. This idea of time alone is difficult initially and I can see it will take some practice indeed.

It takes many months for me to begin to really find a comfortable place within myself. Still, there are days when it's uncomfortable; it's a process. As I attempt to meditate, I still struggle with the idea that "I should" be actively doing something. I should be making money, I should be cleaning the house, I should be creating, I should be doing yoga, I should be exercising, on and on. It's endless.

Months later, given this solitary dynamic I've committed to, I'm meditating in Tatum's room when in comes a romping horse with a man's head and torso! I'm completely surprised. Here is this Centaur galloping up to me and it says to me quite naturally, "Tatum is carrying Jesus' energy."

"Whaaaaat?" I find it difficult to even form words from this inner place.

"Tatum is carrying Jesus' energy."

"What does it mean?" I ask again while not missing the irony I'm trying to communicate with an hallucination of a Centaur.

"Watch Tatum as he is your teacher!" as he gallops out of the door.

I'm in a whirlwind of wonderment. Did I really just see this figure? Where did he come from? Wow, this is a lot to digest. I close my eyes again, as I am learning to appreciate this peaceful feeling that I can find inside, if only occasionally. When I open my eyes, Tatum's room is the same as usual, with all his sweet ideas of life.

Later, I share my deeply moving experience with Merrick and after much contemplation he says, "Wow, how cool, I think I get it. Tatum has always carried a specialness about him, this really makes sense. I mean everywhere we go, people come up to Tatum and want to interact with him and his dazzling personae. Children come running across at the park, at the grocery store, to wherever we are in excitement to see Tatum. I am beginning to expect this dynamic when I enter a store with him, I expect to hear "Tatum, it's Tatum!" I feel as if I am with a celebrity."

"You're so right. And even as I think about it, I felt his sweet presence even when I was pregnant. I didn't have anything to compare it to, being my first and only child, however he's always felt so special. And so many intuitive people told me they wanted to touch my pregnant belly and told me of his eminent power."

"And remember the garage sale story?" I say excitedly.

"Remind me?" Merrick asks.

"Tatum and I were at a garage sale when he was around four years old. The man who was having the sale was enthralled by Tatum. He kept watching him intently and then asked,

"How old is your son?"

"He's four years old."

"When was he born?

"He was born August 20th of 2000," I say.

His excitement is palpable as he says, "I knew it, I just knew it."

"Knew what?" I ask.

"Would you like to hear a story?"

"Well after your noticeable excitement, yes, of course."

He begins, "My son was also born in the summer of 2000, in the month of July," he said as if he could still feel the pride of this moment in time. "My wife and I were traveling in China when he decided to come a bit earlier than planned. After his early birth, many Chinese people were lining up outside our hospital room.

I asked the person in front of the line why they were so interested in meeting our American son."

The Chinese people in line responded, "Because according to Chinese folklore, during the summer months of June, July and August of 2000, any child born during this time is considered to be the Kings of the future, the Golden Ones." He continued, "Golden Ones mean the best of the best. The year of the Dragon."

"Remember Sweetie? Then the man gave Tatum a Chinese kite as a gift."

Only in Sedona! Even my friend, while on a trip, asked me referring to Tatum, "Why did you get the good one?"

And of course, we did a check-in for further understanding and confirmation:

> *"In this year 2000 when Tatum was born, there were 256 souls born around the world carrying Jesus' energy to assist in the needed transition and rebirthing of this planet. You may meet another female soul in Sedona that also carries this Jesus energy."*

— Full Moon Magic

I have never looked in the mirror and said, "I'm a jealous person," because it implies other people are better than me or that I am weak somehow, and I am always trying to protect my ego. Because it's so hidden, jealousy is one of the most destructive problems of all.

At a lovely Sedona gathering, I am in the bathroom washing my hands, when I overhear voices through the closed door,

"So Merrick, what do you do?" inquires a woman's lovely voice.

"I'm a graphics and book designer but I also like to paint. I wanted to move here many years ago but couldn't find a way to maneuver my business as I needed to meet my clients in person. Now it's so wonderful to be able to use the internet and email."

"Interesting, so you are an artist and a graphic designer. I'm impressed."

I'm imagining her lovely lips as she says, "So when is a good time for us to get together?"

"How about next week for lunch?" Merrick says.

Oh no, freak out.

Here I go again, that feeling I so despise seems to have grown a body and legs and has found me again. It is moving all throughout my being in rapid progression. It feels like terror and enough energy running through me to hurt someone. Pretty scary and there is no escape.

I look around and there is no window in this bathroom. The only way out is through the door that leads right into their private conversation. I must open the door and face Merrick and his new woman "friend." I take a deep breathe, find what composure I can and remind myself, 'I can do this; I have to do this.' People's bladders are on the line.

Having only two bathrooms in this house of fifty plus people, I have enough sense to realize I can't hide in here forever, even though I desperately want to crawl into the bathtub, turn on the water and slide down the drain, with hopes I will simply disappear.

Gathering my nerve, I open the door slowly. I can't even look at either of them in the eyes. I feel so wounded and invisible. Making eye contact would only show the harrowing state. I proceed to the living room and start gathering my things to leave. I find Merrick and still can not look him in the eyes, as we walk out to say our Good-byes and head to the car. As soon as we are out of listening range, I ask him the question my pounding heart wants to know. Or does it? For it could mean the end of the life I had been experiencing and enjoying with this man.

"Why the sudden need to leave?" he asks.

"Who was your lady friend?" my voice quivers as I say friend.

"Who? Which one, Rhea? Are you OK?" Merrick asks.

"The woman you were talking to when I came out of the bathroom."

"Oh her, I just met her. Uh, let me think of her name?"

"Funny, you can't even think of her name yet I overheard you both, Merrick. She was asking you when you were going to get together? I find your behavior baffling."

"Oh! Wow, Rhea. Is this why you are so upset and your sudden need to leave? You're shaking."

He reaches to take my hand and I pull back my hand to my heart for comfort. I'm remembering a photo of me when I was about three years old, with one hand covering my heart and the other hand was over my yoni. Protection?

"Well, duh!" My wounded little girl has stepped in right on cue.

"Wait a minute, Rhea. I think I know what's happening here. Listen..."

"No you listen, I heard what I heard, and she sure has a lovely voice. Is she pretty also?" I say sarcastically.

I am officially in "it."

It's as though a button has been pushed and there is no turning back. I'm hurt and confused.

"Rhea. Please. Listen. We were talking about her and her husband and you and me getting together! We had been talking with the three of us for quite awhile before she and I walked through the hallway outside the bathroom. That's when you heard us."

"Well I heard you talking all about yourself, no mention of a woman in your life or a child, nothing? That's also what punctured my heart," I add.

Merrick reaches for my hand and I allow him to hold it this time, "Rhea, you only heard the end of our conversation. I told them all about you and Tatum and our lovely life together."

"Oh, well, I only heard..." I begin to cry as the release button has popped open. I can't hold back the flow of tears any longer. I can only hope this is the deep pain I have been running from my entire life. Perhaps I won't need to run any longer?

Finally, I decide I need some intervention for this situation keeps popping up in my life. I have met many wonderful Practioners in Sedona. I call a friend and reveal I need a past life regression around my feelings of betrayal with Merrick. It's starting to effect both of us and our relationship so deeply that I don't trust him. I want to trust him, but it is as though something keeps getting in the way.

I am reminded of my past life training and the belief is that if you feel sad, sick or anxious or you're frustrated by chronic pain over and over again, it's because you are reincarnated with these unresolved emotions and symptoms. They were the last feelings that you experienced during a traumatic, past-life death. As a result, confusing survival patterns were unconsciously instilled in our past lives and reinforced at conception through birth, childhood or adolescence. If you're exhausted by relationships or work, it's because you died tired and confused by someone or something that drained you. You died stuck, trapped or emotionally blocked while feeling miserable. By resolving past lives, you will end the unnecessary struggle and misery. If not resolved, you will carry it into your next life.

When confusion in your unconscious mind is resolved, your mind/life will become aligned with the clarity. You don't have to continually suffer as a victim or as a victimizer, hurting others with misdirected anger. Past life regression is most effective because it lets the human mind lift its boundaries to look wherever it needs to look to find remedies.

I set up an appointment and find myself at a friend's house for my Past Life Regression session. As she gently takes me into that comforting place within myself, I feel very relaxed and at peace. I'm asking myself if anything is going to happen, when suddenly I see myself and Merrick somewhere in Europe long ago:

'We're on an island and we are wearing clothes of the late 1800's. My large bonnet, protecting my delicate facial skin from the sun rays bouncing off the water, matches my light blue gauzy outer garment. I am deeply in love with this man, who I can sense is Merrick, as I look deeply into his unique eyes. As I breathe in the aroma of the salty air, I notice the twinkle of the water reflecting the movement of the ocean. I remove my white cotton gloves to hold his hands and look lovingly into his eyes, thinking this is the

moment when he will ask me to marry him. It's the perfect setting, romance seems to be blowing in the wind, on this perfect day.

I look over to another smaller island and see a woman. She is waving at me, at us? I try to imagine who she is and why Merrick's attention has gone to her instead of me. "Come back," my eyes are wanting to say to him. Bring yourself back to our connection. The comfortable time to gaze at another woman has come and gone. His energy seems to be glued to her, as he turns to me and says,

"I must go with her. My heart is with her."

"Why?" I cry out.

"I must go with her."

In my inner world, I am devastated and begin crying. This scene within has become so real and the feelings I have within my body match the scene. I am balling now and must let go of his hands and his attention. Perplexed, I watch him get into a boat and row over to her. I tell myself to look away, I do not want to watch their coming together, however I cannot move my gaze anywhere else. I watch him go to this mysterious woman in the long flowing dress and little umbrella.

I am sobbing by now and my entire body is pulsating with the seeming power of some kind of machine. I am distraught and devastated. I will never trust him. I tell myself, I will never trust opening my heart to love again. This disheartening situation has me questioning my entire existence. The pain is so excruciating and deep. It bespeaks a misery beyond words.

As I collapse onto the ground, I am wondering why this man would leave me? Did I do something wrong? Who can I trust? Who am I without him? All these questions have me actually considering killing myself. I can't face my life without him. Am I enough? Can I continue onward? Every part of myself says no, life isn't worth living without him, without his love. I must seek a way out of an extraordinary amount of pain. Yes, I will do it, but how? Through the miasma of anger, guilt and despair, I recall someone telling me about a deadly plant known as belladonna.

Next scene:

And so I do it.

And so I kill myself.

I airbrush myself from that life.'

My observer is taking all this in, as I feel great sadness in my heart, resting right next to a pile of understanding for myself. I can begin to have some empathy and forgiveness for myself. Aho! The beauty of the inner world. I am guided back into the room in Sedona. At least I know why I have been affected by the feelings of envy, jealousy, betrayal, abandonment, etc. It has many faces and many weapons. Now I can open to yet another layer of healing.

Transformation arrives in my dreams! It seems I am owning my feelings of empowerment as I dreamt I was in this office building with several other people. A tall assertive woman walks up to me and says, "Rhea, it is time to fire your Attorney and get a new one. This one no longer serves you and your needs."

I look at this striking woman with wonderment in my eyes and despite my confused look, she continues, "And you need to fire your cleaning lady as well. Quite frankly, she's exhausted."

I awoke from this dream to the early morning sounds of a variety of birds in our yard welcoming me to the new day. For some time, I reflect on this dream. Yes, I'm aware of this part of me, the Attorney, that judges, critiques and makes a case out of situations in my life. Well, mainly those situations which involve people who can hurt me. Which is just about everybody!

Judgment has been my learned and needed protection. I see I have to find something wrong with everyone, in case they reject me. Then I can make it all about them instead of feeling the pain of the unworthiness or admitting to myself that maybe something is wrong with me? I know at a deep level I am protecting myself to make sure I am safe, to pursue every possibility of being hurt, before it can get me. But what a huge dose of energy it takes to keep this dynamic running all my waking hours. OK, I surrender! I will fire the Attorney and the Cleaning lady. I feel more freedom seeping in as I make yet another commitment to myself to let go of those parts of myself which no longer serve me.

31

I am inviting a ray of hope into my life. While meditating, I make an intention to see my life through healthier eyes. It seems when I make a declaration of this type at the front door, a new challenge follows and greets me at the back door, also known metaphorically as "the peeling of the onion." But I still didn't see this dynamic swooping into my world. Merrick tells me he is going to visit another longtime female friend who lives in Phoenix, which is about a two hour drive from Sedona. Prior to our coming together, Merrick would meet her and then spend the night. He insists they are only friends and he sleeps in her guest bedroom. They have also taken many trips to seminars and workshops together with their other friends.

Using my healthy eyes, I choose to believe Merrick and this other woman are truly friends and support his independence. I believe him and yet I have been so conditioned to see a man/women connection through sexual eyes causing me to slip at times. Clearly this is a spinoff of having been introduced to the idea of sexual play at such an early age. Therefore, I still find it difficult to imagine, as I've had the complete opposite experience; usually one of us wants more than a friendship. I do want to broaden my narrow point of view. So with a fresh attitude, I support Merrick's Phoenix trip and move through my day with an open mind and an open heart.

However, as I enter into Merrick's home office, I glance at his computer and there is an open email from his Phoenix friend.

She writes, "I am NEEDING some Merrick time..."

As I'm reading this one little sentence, my hands start to sweat and my heart has made its presence known, as Merrick walks in through the door.

My face must be revealing my confusion, as I wonder if serendipity is at play?

"What is it Sweetie?" he asks.

"I was coming in to talk to you and I found this?"

I point to the letter with the new evidence, hanging Merrick as far as I'm concerned. Fear has a way of seeping in through the windows, especially when it is a core issue for me. My optimism from earlier has darkened and in its place is a booming cloud that has covered my ray of sunshine.

After Merrick glances at his computer, he turns to me and says, "Oh, she's referring to talking with me. She doesn't have anyone she can talk to about certain things, you know, spirituality and current events."

"So she really does need you, that's lovely. Do you need her as well?"

"Come on Rhea, you're being silly."

"Am I? Why do you have to spend the night with her?"

"I'm not spending the night with her, I'm sleeping, emphasis on sleeping. You know it's a long drive down and back, it's just easier to stay at her house."

"Where do you sleep?"

"I've told you before, in the spare bedroom."

"I think you're being so naive, yet again."

We are reaching the scary part of our journey when our egos are vying for air time and there's no going back. Our voices have gone up a notch.

"Rhea, be nice. Good lord, I've known her for 15 years."

"This is me being nice. Can't you see it's obvious she's SO into you."

My body feels sick as I realize I have said these exact words to Eli, ugh?

"She has said we're just friends."

Deja vu.

"Remember your history of thinking women are friends and then you find out differently. What about Brenda? During your visit, she said "Let's go upstairs," and that woman jumping onto you on the boat trip, and last Christmas when one of your drunk friends jumped across the couch and kissed you on the lips right in front of me. I'm so sick of this."

"I'm sick of it too."

"Well, what do we do?"

"Wait a minute, don't you even try to give me an ultimatum!" Merrick warns me loudly.

In my mind, I do want to say, "It's her or me," but I know I would not be OK with someone saying that to me, so I resist this idea, even though my ego wants to go there. Instead I say,

"Don't you see this is a pattern, one woman after another misinterpreting you. What is your part in all this?"

"I see people as people, not male or female," he says very loudly.

"Oh God, is that supposed to be comforting? Why do you want to play in those dangerous waters?"

"They aren't dangerous for me. I know how I feel about them."

"But what about them? How can you be so sure?" I plead.

"I need you to just trust me. I'm hurt that you don't trust me."

"I trust you, just not the other women. I see how open you are and they love that, they feel safe with you and want more time with you but guess what? The bedroom awaits you both."

"Oh God, that's your version, not mine," Merrick says sarcastically.

"Well, what about Ellen, she's still into you!!" I scream at him, letting my emotions come into full throttle.

"Oh God, we're on her again."

"You're asking too much of me, damn you Merrick," I'm screaming with hurt.

"I asked you in the beginning if you could handle my female friends," he screams back.

"Well, I had no idea there were so many of them. I foolishly thought I was enough and you would change your ways."

Fight fight fight! As our egos are brought into full attention in this very vulnerable area. Merrick is afraid of losing his life as he knows it and I'm in fear of losing my life with him as I know it.

Finally, I come to some form of common sense and see we are in the hole, in this painful cycle where we are both hurting inside so unconsciously, we want to hurt each other.

"Let's continue this conversation later at dinner," I say sadly.

I look out the window and see the familiar Sedona rock formation of Mother Mary holding baby Jesus. This fuels me somehow, bringing me back to myself as I leave Merrick's office taking my humbled pain with me, "What else we can say? I'm not sure we can come to a comfortable place with this."

Dinner is at one of our favorite outdoor restaurants. It is called the Hideaway and quite an apropos name for what we are really needing on this auspicious night, to hide away our egos!

From our table on the long wooden deck, we are eye level with the tops of the sycamore trees and a stunning view of the setting sun's reflection on the red rocks in the distance making this a perfect weather evening. Our large pizza matches the quality theme, however our conversation finds its way back to the reality of our emotional stalemate, Merrick's woman/friend situation.

Anger slowly builds as our voices go from whispers to louder and louder arguing. It doesn't matter too much what words are being spoken at this point. As Tatum says, "You two are fighting about such stupid things!" The other diners are glancing in our direction and then looking away, just as quickly. Their concerned faces seem to be saying, "what the fuck?" Even in our state of flurry, we are aware enough to realize we need to go elsewhere to try to resolve this situation. We are both determined to win as our egos have put on their boxing gloves. We request a carryout box for our mostly uneaten pizza.

The drive home is a whirlwind of repressed energy with no words except for accusing eyes. We seem to have come to a place where all the hurting words have been said and we both need to reflect in our confused little minds. Why must we keep coming to this? Our home brings little comfort, for we have both arrived with our carryout box of pizza dripping with hurt and anger sprinkled all over it.

"She's just a friend!!" Merrick's scream can be heard a mile away. He hops out and slams the door, shaking both my car and myself. He goes directly to his SUV and, as I am watching him climb in, he flips me off.

What! Really? How did we get here? He skids out of the gravel driveway faster than usual and leaves into the night taking my heart and soul with him.

The clock has stopped moving entirely. Or is it my life that has stopped? The hours crawl by, wondering where Merrick is? Is he OK? Is this really the end of our relationship? My entire body hurts just thinking about this possibility. I attempt sleep, but it is very far away as my mind has taken over my body and has taken me to the grand feelings of guilt and shame. I am being harsh on myself, trying to figure out who is right. Does it really matter who is right? My ego seems to insist I am right. Even if I am 'right,' it still doesn't provide any comfort, as I look at the empty side of our bed. I am not able to sleep in the middle of the bed, almost as if this would be an admission of sorts; that our relationship is over. I cry, feeling the pain and sadness and then drop into that still, expansive place within me, allowing me to finally go to sleep.

Around midnight, Merrick returns. We makeup, kind of, which is enough for now.

The next morning, Merrick is silently preparing for his trip to Phoenix and he is gathering a variety of supplies for doing some graphic work for her business. His color printer is sitting in the hallway, two feet from the front door when Tatum runs through the tiled hallway and decides to stand on it, breaking off a piece of the printer. Holy crap! This only embellishes the intensity of the awkward parting moment. I want to say have a wonderful trip and mean it, however, I can't say anything except, see you later with a brief hug.

I move into my familiar working mode, which brings much comfort by taking my mind off of what Merrick and his friend are doing. I have a few of my own hypnotherapy clients arriving throughout the day. Currently, I am working with Gabby, a 69 year old woman, who has the energy of a spry 22 year old. Gabby has quite the story. She has been sentenced to go to prison in three months. After a grueling month long trial, she was found guilty. How can I help this lovely woman who may loose her entire life as she knows it?

Gabby has done two inner journey sessions and has met with her deceased parents and made peace with her brother, while crying buckets of tears forgiving them and then letting them go. She has certainly moved lots of old pent-up feelings, ideally freeing her to create a healthier outlook as she enters a very different reality than she has known.

I ask her if she ever thought of suicide?

"No way, I enjoy life too much!" she replies without hesitation.

I appreciate her response as it inspires me to look at the true meaning of life, rather than being taken down by its challenges. I embrace this idea and it brings a smile to my face. Who is helping whom? I giggle to myself as I entertain the idea of enjoying my life again. I come back to my place of Gratitude! Always Gratitude!

Alleluia, I've found a comfortable place within myself, even knowing Merrick is spending the night with another woman. Perhaps I can handle this situation? Despite my optimistic attitude, I still wonder about future trips to Phoenix? Can I find comfort with these? Am I being fair to myself?

32

I am at one of Sedona's many gatherings—called parties every-where else—where I meet an intriguing woman, Annie. We both value the connection to our intuition and agree to meet to do some channeling for each other. While our Higher Selves are talking with each other, many ideas are exchanged. Besides sharing this process with Merrick, this is a new experience for me. I find it very exciting to be able to communicate with another being from my higher place.

During our conversation, it becomes clear her guidance is suggesting it could be beneficial for me to work at the spiritual retreat company where she works with her brother and his wife. She spoke of a position referred to as a Retreat Guide, which means I would be designing spiritual retreats for people. Also, I could offer my hypnotherapy sessions again. This sounds so perfect as I'd been looking for an avenue to express my organizational and hypnosis skills simultaneously.

I got the job; I'm feeling hope again. My responsibilities include meeting people from all around the world and talking about what changes they wish to make. I design a personalized retreat for them, implementing growth and change in their lives. Also, I would be offering my own Hypnotherapy Sessions. I'm going to be paid to do what I love and there's no better gig on earth than that.

It is a colossal relief for our little family! How beautifully perfect, yes indeed. I'm manifesting a spiritual opportunity to create financial security and I love my new job. I'm feeling more powerful in my new found financial basis while being able to express my spiritual side.

A few weeks into my career, a personalized retreat has been designed for me. Part of my training is to experience the different Practioner's modalities that they offer to the Clients. It consists of three sessions a day over four days.

My Opening Session is done on the beautiful red rocks inviting me to create my intentions. An Emotional Clearing session brings me to tears forgiving both of my parents, while realizing they did their best. A Human Design Session reveals I am a Generator in life with the Practioner reminding me to appreciate my inner power and intuitive abilities. The Family Constellation session reveals family dynamics. In this session, I've placed a pillow representing my dad all the way across the room from me, reminding me of the distance I felt with him while growing up, again inviting more forgiveness.

The best Cranial Sacral massage I ever had allowed me to completely relax into myself and release on a physical level. It was followed by a Breathwork session, which brought up lots of images of my childhood with my siblings, allowing a letting go of the pain and abandonment I had felt. I'm diving into old childhood stuff yet again as I obtain new insights about myself as well.

For example, I'm seeing how my pain and suffering has created an angry delivery of my words. When I feel hurt, unconsciously, I want to hurt others with my pain. My communication needs some polishing, as my protective Ego mode no longer serves me. I'm feeling a bit more confused one minute, as I am sensing the depths of my challenges and parachuting into the next moment of feeling empowered. What a roller coaster ride of a retreat! I'm enjoying every minute of this glorious unveiling of myself.

While learning the Practioner's offerings, I'm buzzing along looking at my "stuff." Then I meet an Astrology/Psychic who is highly recommended for her work. Kayla is a lovely, dark haired woman who I find to be pleasant and wise. Her trustworthy demeanor allows me to feel safe and her contagious laugh opens me up even further to my joy.

She had created my Astrological chart before I arrive and it is confirming the apparent emotional and physical drifting between Merrick and myself. Kayla is right on although her reading is a bit scary and a little too real. Because we connect so deeply and quickly, she describes my relationship with Merrick like she is reading our personal diaries. It's unnervingly precise. What is revealed astrologically is a need for separation from Merrick. Frightening to hear yet this is a relief at the same time. Can I give up on love again? And what about Tatum?

The rest of the day, I am spinning with both freedom and fear trying to dance together. Despite this feeling, I am moved to share these predictions with Merrick later in the evening.

Sitting on our large king bed together, I'm setting up my iPhone to play back Kayla's session. I say, "Kayla, the Astrologer/Psychic referred to our relationship as the "perfect storm.""

"The perfect storm?" He ponders it for a minute, "That seems accurate, yet kinda creepy."

"I know, I haven't been able to think about anything else all day," I add.

"You...really...want...to...separate?" he says in slow motion as if he is trying to digest the meaning.

"I'm not sure about anything, I do know the way we are doing our life is so dysfunctional. I'm not blaming you or me, it seems the third person we create together needs to grow up." My attempt at humor falls dead, given the seriousness of the conversation.

"Is there any other way?" he continues. "It seems we have tried and tried and we keep coming back to our wounded core issues. And all we are doing is continuing to hurt each other."

"Well, I do agree with you. We seem to be caught in a spiraling that takes us back to a fight again and again. Your desire to connect with your female friends triggers my own core issues and insecurities. I really don't want to stop you from living your life fully and I am so wounded from my childhood of being sexually, emotionally and physically abused. What to do? It hurts me at such a deep level. I want to trust you. I really do. Actually, I feel I do trust you, it's the other woman I can't seem to trust." I pause to clear my throat.

"It's probably from the time I came home and found my friend rolling around on the ground with my first husband, laughing and enjoying each other. If I hadn't come home, who knows what would have happened? And, you know this same friend had an affair with her best friend's husband. So I know I have issues with trusting. I'm doing my best, that's all I can offer you and it hurts me emotionally when I realize I am "not enough" or my little girl tells me so. I know it's not the truth yet it still hurts."

I begin to cry as my shoulders are shaking with the oncoming pain again.

"I don't want to hurt you, Rhea, but I don't want to hurt me either. And you can't control me, I know you learned this so well, however, it doesn't work with me," he says calmly.

"Could you stop being so stark raging calm?" I ask him. "This is our relationship we are talking about."

"Rhea, let's be honest with ourselves, we've known this stalemate was coming. I suggest we consider separating for a period of time and come back together when we're in a healthier place."

We both sit there in a momentary silence, contemplating what has just been said out loud. Merrick suddenly looks lost.

"Wow, so we are really going to do this? Are we really separating?" he says stiffly. "We have to do something but I'm really feeling sad."

"Let me play the recording and then we can talk more after," I reply.

We listen, as our minds try to wrap around the idea of separating. Afterwards, we look deep into each other's eyes.

"Let's sleep on it and do a check-in tomorrow? Does that sound good?" he says as he takes my hand.

"Well it's terrifying and yet we seem to be so stuck in our dysfunctional ways together. It really is the perfect storm. I feel being understood is over-rated, what I need is to feel safe with you. And the love isn't missing, we just need to do some healing, perhaps it would be best to do it apart from each other."

"It is but I still wonder if this is REALLY the best way?" he questions again.

"I don't know, all I know is that the reading with Kayla felt so accurate, even though a part of me doesn't want to admit what it all means." I sit back and brush hair off my forehead, I am exhausted trying to imagine my life without Merrick.

"I agree her interpretation felt so amazingly accurate, it's difficult to deny its authenticity."

"Wow, you're really going to just accept all of this without a fight?" I'm growing angry in my pain.

"Rhea, I'm doing my best to come to terms with ALL of this?" he adds.

While thinking to myself, where's the man in this scenario? Where is he? Merrick's way of so easily accepting things without a fight can be a mixed bag for me. Of course, it is wonderful when things are flowing, however, I crave to see the part of him that really stands up for himself and his beliefs. This is one of those times, I wish to see his passion for me, feel his desire for us to be together. Where is the man? I repeat to myself.

When Merrick was a young child, his mom would continually tell him, "Don't grow up to be a man like your father." This seems to have contributed to many nights of Merrick rejecting me sexually. It enhances my wondering if he is desiring other woman sexually. This idea was clearly embedded within him, yet it still hurts seeing him resign to our next move. I still have hope he may want to fight for us tomorrow after a night of sleep and reflection.

I will only be disappointed. Not really wanting to break our connection, but feeling at a loss for words, we attempt to sleep. Sleep is not coming my way any time soon. Merrick didn't even reject the idea of separation, which is additional pain to my opened wound. This scares me even further for I thought, or better, I hoped he would resist such a breakup transition. Yet I see how fed up he is with handling most of the money situation, our arguing, and especialy with my own insecurities around his female friendships. Could this be his challenge in withholding 'sex'? I desire honesty. My fear is clinging to me like slime, as I attempt to find sleep. I'm terrified of what tomorrow will bring.

The next morning, we agree to do a check-in, feeling mainly exhaustion trying to examine this next move with our thinking minds only. The check-in was rather blunt and to-the-point:

'This separation is needed for both of your evolutions. You are both caught in your childhood dysfunctions and you need to separate. You will come back together. However, we suggest for Rhea that you date other men and Merrick you need to do some soul searching...alone.'

Both of our Higher Selves reveal it is for our best interest to separate for awhile, allowing us to move beyond the dependencies we have created and our dysfunctional ways. OK, we will officially separate, we decide. Did I hear this correctly, that Merrick needs to spend time alone and I need to explore the world of dating again? What? Could this be possible? Is this fair? This conjures many spiraling conversations between us.

Our many questions, hypothetical or not, along with our raging fears and concerns are all discussed. Even in the midst of such turmoil, we are still able to communicate openly and as honestly as our hearts will let us. This ability to converse so beautifully is appreciated.

So with the suggestion for me to date and for Merrick to spend time alone, I found myself asking the obvious question,"What am I to gain from dating?"

I've never really enjoyed dating to begin with, but I'm being asked to dive into this world again. What will I find from others that I can't find within? It is confusing and yet I am learning to trust this guidance. Believe me, I need confirmation before I risk losing Merrick for good; Tatum's soul daddy.

"What if you meet another woman?" my shaking voice wants to know.

"What if you fall in love with this man you are supposed to date?" Merrick asks.

— *Four Directions*

I am crying soft tears, as I pack my pots and pans. I'm scared, even though I am finally making a steady income. My wings are growing and spreading, enabling me to fly alone, hopefully, allowing me to find more of my truth.

We agree to separate harmoniously despite the mystery of the unknown. Imagine, I'm leaving the man I love, my soul mate to do some soul-searching, to be open to create a healthier more connected, less dependent relationship. Merrick and I continue to support, love and learn from each other, even while separated. Tatum continues to spend one week-end night with him, to maintain their sweet connection. Even this loving action reveals what a special man Merrick is and compounds our peculiar commitment to each other.

With a newfound trust and our few belongings, Tatum and I move with Merrick's assistance. A friend helps as well and he keeps repeating, "you two are meant for each other," particularly after he looks at two paintings we had each created separately.

The paintings are sitting together on my new kitchen floor and they compliment each other. It seems they are meant to be together as well. Despite my art training in Seattle, I still prefer to paint from my place within, the unknowing place. So to bring our unique paintings together that resonate and are compatible, color-wise and energetically is a bittersweet send off for our souls.

I'm digging our new house. It is cute and small; perfect for my new life. It is the complete opposite of our old home, where all the rooms are divided by many walls, connected by long hallways. Tatum and I each have our own bedroom and bathroom and to complete the picture, there is a charming little back yard. One day we find at least 50 sea shells in our backyard, given the fact that this area was once an ancient ocean floor.

Tatum's little room, that we decorated together, is perfect for him and he loves it. He enjoys giving input on where he feels his things need to be placed. He's a bit confused by life without his buddy Merrick and yet he's always been very adaptable.

Over time, I learn to make the best of my new situation, living without Merrick, but I find it is difficult to truly call this house a home. This seems only temporary, or is it? I want to believe it is and yet my life has taught me anything can happen and everything changes. Even though we are apart, I'm still seeing Merrick for casual dates and sharing Tatum. In fact, it seems our relationship is bringing in a new form of appreciation. Our higher guidance seems to be neglectful in telling us the whys, for there seem to be many. OK, we'll trust, we'll go with this, for we can only follow our guidance. If not for that, then what else is there to rely upon? By this time, our guidance is about 95% accurate.

As a Retreat Guide, I spend my days designing spiritual retreats for all types and ages of people. Most are in the middle of a personal crisis such as a divorce, the death of a spouse or loved one, health issues, or simply feeling disconnected from themselves. Being a hypnotherapist, I can offer my understanding of the importance of looking within for healing. Too many traditional therapies focus on the outer circumstances as the source of pain which is why a spiritual retreat is so effective in looking at the whole picture; inner and outer. Being a retreat practioner, I am able to use my hypnotherapy with the retreat client; to go directly to their life's crisis or pain and release them from these unconscious chains.

One morning, I answer the phone at the office and it is a man from Canada who is coming for a Spiritual Retreat for his birthday. He reveals he is bi-polar and therefore, I need to talk to his Therapist first. Talking at length with the Therapist, he believes his client, Grey, would benefit by coming to Sedona and doing a retreat. In fact, his Therapist minimizes his bi-polar condition reiterating that he has learned how to handle it quite well and is a very successful man.

Grey is recently divorced and is arriving in Sedona in one week. We chat easily and I promise to create his personalized retreat for him. Through email, Grey sends me a photo of him looking quite conservative while standing on a golf course.

A week later, I drive to the Hyatt to pick him up and he is standing out front with a lovely smile; he is cute.

"Hello, I'm Grey, you must be Rhea," he says jumping into the front seat next to me. Ironically, one of my favorite colors is gray. I notice the synchronicity. I shake his hand and look into his eyes; dark soulful eyes seeming to sparkle in the Arizona sunshine. He is clearly excited about his upcoming retreat as he is playfully wiggling in his seat, which suddenly feels too close to me.

Thank Goodness I'm wearing sunglasses in the Arizona brightness or my eyes may be giving away too much. We continue to the spot I have chosen on the land to do our Opening Ceremony. A special area is chosen overlooking the lovely red rock valley below, complete with the flowing creek and many Juniper and Pine trees aligning its pristine banks. I lay the Indian blanket on the ground and set up the Four Directions Ceremony. I ask Grey to choose a spot to sit outside of the Circle. He chooses the West, which is where the sun sets, symbolically representing where the old beliefs and patterns can be released.

I choose the opposite side of the Circle, in the East, which is where the sun rises, representing what's coming. Crisis or opportunity? Even the Chinese have one symbol which means both Crisis and Opportunity reminding me that in every crisis there is also an opportunity.

I explain the concept of the Medicine Wheel; it is a life process that we move through many times in our life, depending on how open we are to change. Our soul comes to Earth in the South, which is our Authentic Self, our innocence and purity. We move counter clockwise into the East taking on beliefs and ideas from our childhood. As we experience crisis we need to move into the North, where our Inner Wisdom resides, providing insight. Moving into the West, we let go of the old ways of being, the untruths we have come to believe about ourself. This allows a natural movement back into the South to become more of our truth, more of our Authentic Self. The more challenges, we have in the form of crisis, allows an opening to our truth.

After honoring all of the four directions, I ask Grey to write anything he wishes to let go of on a piece of paper. He then burns it in the ashtray in front of him, releasing that which no longer serves his life.

I am in a whirlwind of emotions after I drop him off at his hotel; is this the man I am supposed to date? As much as I am questioning this, I know in my authentic self, the answer. But why him, of all men? He's certainly a handsome chap, part African American, part Caucasian which equals a lovely color of skin with dark hair and eyes. He's tall and slim, like I like. It's clear he is personable and charming, as we connect easily. I remind myself I'll see him again for two other sessions.

We have our second appointment together which is to be an Inner Journey hypnotherapy session. As we are talking, he tells me he is feeling very upset; his ex-wife has just taken one million dollars out of their joint account without asking him. I am thinking, wow, that's a lot of money. Bringing my focus back to the session, I guide him within asking for some insights around this anger that has presented itself. I have learned when anger is present, it's rarely related to what we think it is, it's usually something much deeper. As he sinks deeper into his past, he touches some long-forgotten childhood trauma and I encourage him to feel the pain. As it comes up to the surface to be embraced, he cries many needed tears from these old memories. Once he has moved through these old feelings, I explain to him how powerful this is to have released this old baggage. He even seems lighter, as he attempts a smile.

During our Closing session together, he reiterates he is going through a divorce and he continues to tell me of his story. He is a CEO managing hundreds of people; he also reveals he has fifty-four million dollars in the bank. His broad smile with perfect white teeth has suddenly become sweeter. Really? Fifty-four million dollars! I honestly have no concept of what having this type of money would be like. How can someone who has access to this amount of abundance be unhappy? My intrigue level with this man has been amped up to 10!

I encourage Grey to talk about each session and we create a personalized plan for him to take home. We have a little time left, so I share some of my paintings with him, which I have never done with a Client before this moment. He's clearly moved by my creativity. Am I trying to impress him?

As he is leaving, he asks me if he can see me again.

"OK," I say slowly, realizing the ramifications of these two little letters.

A few days later, I receive a surprising email from Grey. He asks if I would like to meet him in Phoenix for the week-end? I agree. I set up arrangements for Tatum to stay with his Dad.

Friday afternoon arrives and I drive to Phoenix in a whirlwind of anticipation. Will I like him? What will this be like?

As I'm arriving, I can't seem to find the casita so I phone Grey.

"Where are you?" he asks, "I'm so excited to see you again."

"I'm here in the complex, where is your casita?" I ask.

"'Our' casita!" he emphasizes. I like the sound of this. I giggle as Grey gives me directions and I realize I'm eager to see him as well. He is standing in the driveway with his charming smile.

"Hello You. Did you know I wanted to kiss you at my Closing Session? Finally I can." he gives me a sweet kiss on the lips. "Would you have let me kiss you then?"

"No, I don't think so; I was working," I answer easily.

"I appreciate your honesty," he adds.

I look at him through my observer eyes and he is wearing olive green cut-off shorts and a black t-shirt, with a sterling silver necklace; casual yet classy. It is as if he dressed perfectly for my artsy eyes. I am so glad I came to see him.

"Please show me around our casita for the week-end," I smile as I take his hand. He gives me the grand tour. Our casita, for the next few days, is a gorgeous display of Mexican flair. It has five bedrooms and three bathrooms, complete with an upstairs deck overlooking the beautiful Arizona skyline.

He then guides me to the patio and offers me a glass of wine as we get to know each other away from the client-therapist relationship of the previous week. This is incredibly freeing as we talk, laugh and enjoy what's left of the setting sun. By the time it's dark, we can't seem to get close enough on the patio bench.

Later, we dress up and walk to the Resort's restaurant, where he orders a $2000 bottle of wine to compliment our lovely meal. Apparently, this bottle of wine is the same year he graduated from Harvard and it holds great significance for him. I have to admit, I was thinking of all the things I could spend that money on that's much more practical. Nonetheless, I certainly enjoy every sip of my lovely red wine.

I'm also noticing the attention he commands from the waiters. Trust me, when someone orders a $2000 bottle of wine, all the restaurant help is available to kiss our toes, so to speak. The meal is phenomenal! I am mesmerized; I feel like a queen being waited upon by the entire restaurant. After our meal, we stroll around the beautiful courtyard, holding hands like we've known each other forever.

The following day, the swimming pool seems to be calling us with its pleasant thought of fresh clear water and sunshine. As we stroll to it, holding hands, Grey asks me, "So how does it feel to date someone who has access to millions of dollars?"

Still digesting this fairytale reality I'd stumbled into, I look at him, "Well, I really do like you for you, and the money is certainly a perk!"

He presents his charming smile, "It seems women are always available to me because of my money, so thanks for your honesty. I like you also." We find time to connect more on our lounge chairs and equally take time to enter our own little worlds of bliss.

Later that afternoon, we drive to my favorite outdoor artsy mall in Phoenix. All the central area is outdoors, and the wet misters are spraying randomly to cool the desert air. After strolling around in a kind of euphoria, we find an air conditioned movie to get out of the constant sun and heat. Ironically, we have now become shade hunters.

The movie is about a man and a woman who meet after having broken up with their partners. They decide to be together. Synchronicity? It is enjoyable and light, yet has hints of depth just when you think there won't be any real meaning. As we walk out of the movie theatre, Grey grabs me and pulls me in real close to give me a kiss and a tight hug. It appears the movie stirred some deep feelings of our coming together.

Dinner is a bit of a blur as we find words to match our new feelings toward each other. In the back of my mind, I am still wondering how I'm going to tell this to Merrick. He knows I am seeing someone and it is a bit emotional for me to imagine if the situation had been turned in the opposite direction.

"Earth to Rhea, where did you go?"

"Well, I was thinking of Merrick and how I am going to tell him about this week-end. I'm feeling way too comfortable with you."

"And this is a problem for you?" he laughs. "Nice problem to have."

"Well, I've been honest with you about my situation with Merrick. Even though we're separated, we're still seeing each other and he has Tatum over every weekend for a sleep-over."

"Yeah, well we may need to talk about this a bit more."

"Sure, what are you thinking?"

"Well, I'm wondering if he's doing this to have a reason to see you?" he says.

"Possibly and I want to honor their sweet connection as well."

"Let's save this topic for later, let's enjoy our precious time together," he says as he takes my hand into his for a little squeeze.

When back in Sedona, our next phone conversation reveals Grey has decided he wants us to be exclusive. He will break off all ties he has with women he is dating and wants me to end my connection with Merrick. Enthralled by the newness of an entirely different type of life, with the freedom of travel, shopping and moving beyond the stress of everyday expenses, I agree with us becoming an item. We agree to date exclusively and I agree to talk to Merrick.

On my list of things to do, I write:

√*Meet with Merrick and update him on the latest with Grey.*

I have to laugh, "Right. As if I would really forget this one!"

However, I am shaking as I realize the ramifications. This means he can date as well. Can I handle this? And what does it mean to our relationship? It feels as if I have one foot in one reality and the other foot in another reality. Which reality will capture my heart and soul?

Merrick and I arrange to meet at Sedona's local Thai Restaurant to talk about the latest details of our unusual journey apart. I'm wondering if he has any idea of what's coming? He phones me to tell me he's running late as he is coming from his new apartment in the Village of Oak Creek. Actually, this isn't unusual for Merrick to be late, however since our separation, he has been ready and willing every time we've made plans to meet. Isn't it interesting if a situation becomes a bit precarious, people seem to step up with their best? What would our world be like if everyone stepped up with their best all of the time?

"Hi Merrick," I say as he sits right next to me at our table.

He leans in for a kiss and I decline. Well here we go, I say to myself. This agreement I've made with Grey will be apparent pretty quickly I realize.

"Rhea, are you OK?" he asks.

"Yes, I'm good however let's order and then chat."

There's an awkward silence as we peruse the menu.

"I'm ordering the curry and coconut milk with chicken and veggies." I say, to break the silence. "Do you want to share like we usually do?"

"Something tells me we've stepped out of our usual place," he says looking at me inquisitively.

Saved by our waiter's need to take our orders, he arrives as if on cue. We order Thai iced teas and our meals; there will be no sharing of food today. Our meals arrive quickly and I notice Merrick isn't the least bit interested in his food. This is highly unusual for him. I'm ravenous and begin eating.

"So, go ahead and tell me about your week-end with what's his name?" he says sarcastically.

"Well, I do like him. I enjoyed myself," I begin.

"Go on," Merrick urges me.

"I tasted wine that costs $2000 a bottle." As soon as I said this I'm reminded of needing to be more aware of the delivery of my words. It's as if I picked up the salt shaker off the table and poured it right into his open wounds. Immediately, I regret this.

"Oooh, so he really is wineing and dining you!"

"Well, as I mentioned to you he does have a lot of money," I justify my words.

"What else? No...wait...I really don't want to hear any more about your time with him. What I would like to know is where does this leave us?"

That's it, the real question. I take a deep breath,

"We are going to continue seeing each other," I reveal.

"OK," Merrick whispers. Are those tears I see forming in his eyes?

"He wants to meet Tatum," I say.

"Go on..." Yes, those are tears and his fork has found its place back on the table.

"We have decided to date exclusively."

There it is, I said it. I'm not sure if I feel relieved or sad, as so many emotions are moving through me.

"Really?" he murmurs, "I knew this could happen but I didn't know it would happen so quickly." The enthusiasm is long gone from his tone. I notice Merrick has become solemn. His voice feeble.

"I know. It's so confusing to me, Sweetie, and we have to keep trusting what our higher guidance has told us, that there's something for me to learn through this dynamic?" My voice squeaks on the last few syllables.

"We have to keep trusting," I remind his wounded eyes.

"Easy for you to say, and I think we are beyond you calling me "Sweetie." You're the one out having the fun part of this experience. I've done my best to honor this and it just isn't easy for me to watch you, knowing you're with another man," he says.

"I understand and if it were switched around, I don't know if I could handle it either," I remind him.

The waitress arrives at our table to see how our meals are, she notices Merrick hasn't touched his food.

"I'd like a box to take this meal home with me," is all he can say.

"Let's go somewhere more private, Rhea." he says, "I need to get out of here."

"OK, where would you like to go?"

"Anywhere without people. Let's go sit on the deck at the Sedona Grille. We can be outside and have some privacy."

It's sunset as we drive separately to another restaurant with an outdoor deck atop the building. From this high deck, we watch the top of Brins Mesa and Wilson mountain burn from a wildfire that engulfs the National Forest. An army of helicopters fly over head, dropping repellent on the flames shooting high into the air. It is both mesmerizing and scary, as if we are watching our own relationship symbolically burning away.

After talking a bit more, it's clear we are getting nowhere. What's to talk about when I'm revealing to Merrick that I am interested in dating someone else. It's very fragile ground as he stares at the mountain in flames.

The inevitable occurs and we decide to go back to our separate cars. Going our own way is painful.

"I adore You," I begin to say.

"No Rhea, you don't get to say that right now. I don't know what to do with it."

"You don't need to do anything with it, except keep it in your heart. Nobody knows what's going to happen. However, I promise to tell you the truth throughout this situation. That, I can promise you."

I drive away with a colossal pain in my heart, resting right next to my adoration of Merrick for supporting and listening to me. My heart is still warm from his presence.

Because of a curious delight, I continue to engage with Grey. His soul calls to my world, perhaps offering something richer, more textured, more varied. Is this enough to lure my heart and soul from Merrick's presence?

Grey returns to Sedona. I have invited him to revisit my world and meet Tatum for the first time. A fun activity that all of us can share is to go bowling in nearby Cottonwood, which is about a 20 minute drive. I mention to Grey that I'd like for Tatum to get a nap on the way, so he'll be rested for bowling.

As we are driving the long stretch of road to Cottonwood, Grey looks back at Tatum; "I bet you're a great bowler, yes?"

"I dunno," Tatum replies.

"I bet you can't go to sleep right now?" he continues.

Four year old Tatum looks at me and then back to Grey, "You're trying to double-talk me."

Grey stops talking and I notice his demeanor has changed. I felt so proud of Tatum in that moment; he caught Grey's attempt at reverse psychology. However, Tatum did surrender by taking a much needed nap. While Tatum sleeps we can speak more candidly.

"How do you feel about Tatum? I mean your children are all grown," I inquire.

"I'm not worried about Tatum liking me, that's the easy part. I'm more concerned about hurting him as he's already lost his real dad part time and now Merrick."

I admire him in that moment, as his concern for Tatum is real. Grey and I agree we will act as friends 'only' in front of Tatum.

Bowling is enjoyable as is swimming the next day, followed by a lovely dinner at Cucina Rustica, one of my favorite restaurants in Sedona. It has a European flair and feels as if we have arrived in Italy. What a freedom to order whatever I want without having to add up the total to see if I can afford it. It's an absolute delight for us to sip on wine and enjoy each other's company.

Our next trip is an annual event Grey makes with his friends to Las Vegas. Ironically my friend, Kayla, the Astrologer, is also in Las Vegas. She and I have become good friends since she predicted Merrick's and my separation. That she will be in the land of gambling with her boyfriend, Anthony, is more than I could hope for; what fun!

Once again Grey makes all the arrangements. I love the idea of someone taking care of me so I can flow into my feminine side naturally. Grey has booked a suite at the Bellagio overlooking the fountains that spray every hour.

We meet at the Phoenix airport so we can fly together. I am continually shaking myself to make sure this is my reality. A sweet embrace feels natural and then off we go to our first class seats enjoying champagne and hors d'oeuvres on our flight. We hold hands while chatting about life's many mysteries.

Our suite has three bedrooms and three bathrooms. It's essentially a house, complete with a huge living room and dining room. I'm mesmerized as I feel so alive with all this exquisite beauty surrounding me.

The six of us, including Kayla and Anthony, meet for dinner at a Japanese Restaurant, where the cook sautes the steaks, shrimp and vegetables right in front of us. The champagne flows and we are all enjoying the light conversation and fun. Afterwards, we go to back to our lovely Suite and partake of some pot his friends brought along. This opens my playful side. Grey and I begin chasing each other around our large Suite while laughing and capturing each other in our arms. The reward is a full body embrace with passionate kisses.

Floating into sleep world in the fine Egyptian cotton sheets is heavenly. That night I dreamt my childhood nightmare again. Walking around the darkly night, I meet the tall, shadowy man with no apparent face. He will kill me if I am still in the dream when we return to the corner. Each time I have this dream, I wake up just before we arrive back at our corner. Terrifying! I awoke this time wondering why now? Why am I having this dream right now! This creates a feeling of fear within me that I have a difficult time shaking. I haven't had this frightening dream in many years, so why now? I let it go as I peer around the room and look at the man next to me in bed. Is this a prophetic dream? I feel a moment of dread wanting to climb my spine and hang out there for awhile. I dismiss it as I hear Grey's gentle voice,

"Would you like to go out for breakfast or have it delivered to our room?" his smiling face asks.

"Oh, that's easy, let's have it brought to us and we can dine in those lovely cotton bathrobes I've been admiring in our bathroom. They look so dreamy and comfortable. Like You!"

"Aw shucks," he says shyly.

And so it is, room service brings us fresh brewed coffee, fresh squeezed orange juice, perfectly cooked omelets, home fries with onions and peppers and warm croissants with real jam. This all appears in our reality.

I think I could get used to this kind of a life! It helps to remove this feeling of fear and dread that seems to come with me to breakfast. Darn this dream! I'm trying to be in the moment and continue the feelings from last night's fun. I so want to enter this world of blissful living but it is a bit challenging to shake my dream's remnants.

Of course, being in Las Vegas, we had to try our hands at some gambling and some drinking. Having had little sleep, the alcohol has a stronger effect on me than normal. The cards are dealt for a game of 21 and we make a natural team with Grey's friends joining our table. It seems our intuition is guiding our choices nicely. We are up $2800 when I take a bathroom break. I return to the table and that is when all hell breaks loose.

Grey's mood has changed and he snaps at me,"Why did you leave when we are in a winning streak?" he demands.

"I had to use the restroom," I answer truthfully.

"Well it's not a good time to leave the table, we need to make up for the lost time." It's amazing how tones can carry so much leverage.

"OK, Dude," I snicker, as I salute him. My lack of sleep is clearly getting the best of me.

As the cards are dealt, Grey is changing our way of playing. Suddenly, he is wanting to make all the decisions, even about my own cards.

"Hey Grey, I appreciate your advice, however, I would like to make my own choices, since these are my cards."

"Rhea, I insist you listen to me if we want to win," he orders.

Whoa, where did Grey go? I want to ask. It seems a new shade of grey has taken over while I was gone. Fifty shades of grey is cruising through my mind.

"Excuse me but I would like to have the freedom to make my OWN decisions."

I'm realizing this is about much more than playing cards. Where is that free flowing feeling from last night, I wonder?

"Fine! Let's take a walk," he insists.

As we are leaving the table, we let Grey's friends know we'll be right back. This lively couple who leaves the building as a couple never returns. Who returns is a controlling millionaire and his independent girlfriend who is standing up to him; something he is clearly not used to.

In all fairness, it is his money we're playing with. However, I'd played many variations of card games my entire life with my family and my grandparents so I feel confident about my skills. Add drinking alcohol. OK, lots of alcohol, and having had very little sleep has created Emotionally Sensitive Rhea. It seems "she" swept in from the Bellagio water fountain when I wasn't looking and took over. Simply put, I would not allow him to control me. So, this is what it feels like to be controlled in a relationship. This is also what feels like the beginning of the end.

That afternoon, I return to our room after a lovely massage and "Controlling Grey" would not even talk to me. He is angry and apparently his way of coping is through passive aggressive behavior. This is exactly how my Dad would treat me when he was upset with me. Oh, the pain runs deep.

Somehow I make it through the evening, wearing my beautiful flowing black and brown dress with my metallic shoes. Honestly, I would rather be wearing my sweats to match my mood, as Grey continues to ignore me. We have dinner with his friends but I feel sick inside. He will not talk to me, just like my dad. Ouch, the pain of my little girl is erupting within me again.

We have front row seats to Cirque du Soleil and watch the most amazing water show but I can't really see it for my childhood blinders are protecting me from seeing this excruciatingly painful world being created around me. We walk back to the Bellagio and I end up with blisters all over both feet from my new silver heels. Ouch, this is turning into one heck of a painful week-end in every way.

I call my friend Kayla from the hotel hallway. I cry as I say to her, "Grey won't even talk to me about anything, just like my dad. His silence has become noisy!"

"Rhea...honey, you have to talk to him," she says. "This isn't fair for either of you to not have some kind of discussion. You may not like what he says but you're a big girl and, let's admit it, you shared in this problem. Plus dear, you have the tools from your years of looking within and healing to rely on. He doesn't."

I hung up the phone not sure of anything anymore.

"Grey, at least tell me what you are thinking? What you're feeling? Something?" I say as I reach to touch his head. He pushes my hand away,

"I can't Rhea. I don't know."

"Well, tell me anything, this silence is ridiculous," I plead.

"If I have to make a decision about our relationship right now, in this moment, I'd say we're over. I need some time to think and we'll talk later this week."

"That's really all you're going to say after all we've shared?" I'm distraught at this point.

"Yes," with a stern stare I hadn't seen on him before. I knew in my heart this was the end of any possibility of a glamorous lifestyle for me, with him anyway.

We flew home the following day in first class, yet it felt like the lowest class ever as his silence seemed to envelop me and my apparent insecurities. We parted at the airport without even saying good-bye.

I was totally devastated. It was no surprise when I took a wrong turn out of the airport and headed south toward Tuscon instead of north to Sedona. I didn't arrive home until after 2:00 am feeling depleted emotionally and physically.

I remember one of the symptoms of being sexually abused is

that the "victim" will not let anyone control them ever again. I feel tears of understanding and empathy for myself.

Merrick is away visiting friends in Colorado when I return from my Las Vegas "enlightened" nightmare. I think I got the beauty of dating this millionaire; I make an agreement with myself that I would not attempt to control anyone ever again. Especially Merrick, IF we get back together.

I need windshield wipers for my eyes. This unraveling of my controlling nature will take some practice, however I will make an honest attempt.

I'm watering Merrick's plants, per our agreement, with my many tears. As our unique connection continues, I leave him this note:

"Dear Merrick,

Welcome home, your plants are watered and happy, they just miss you like I do.

Guess what? My rendezvous with Grey is over, call me and I'll tell you all the details. And I think I found out why I was supposed to date him, wow did I ever!

Big Hugs,

Rhea"

"We did it, we survived the ordeal of separating!" I say gleefully to him upon our next meeting. At first, he looks at me like a blind man seeing light for the first time, then his pain washes away the spark, "Rhea, I need to be honest with you, hearing about you dating another man, um, that was more difficult then I would have ever imagined. Knowing you were with another man, wow!"

Tears are forming and running down his cheeks as he continues, "I need to take this slowly so I can move through all the emotions that are coming up for me. I accepted this was going to be a long haul, probably years, so this is a shock to hear it is over so soon."

"Of course honey, I'm just so happy we can be so open and honest with each other. Do you realize we have climbed a huge mountain and perhaps now we can relax at the top?"

"Are you really over him?" Grey doesn't get a name I notice.

"Well that's a worthy question and of course, I have feelings for him and the idea of living the "good" life had me hooked for a bit. However, I know in every part of who I am, that I can not live with someone who needs to control me and can't even communicate his feelings with me. And I realize having money doesn't make anyone happy. As it turns out, the more I got to know him, I saw he could be pretty miserable at times. And when I saw his way of coping with a challenging situation, well, that was so revealing to me. I couldn't even imagine doing a relationship with his passive aggressive nature. I've come too far working on myself to be punished for being me. I have a new appreciation of our relationship that we can talk about anything and everything and we do!"

"Yes, that's true," he adds.

"The way I look at it, if we can survive this emotional roller coaster, I feel we can survive anything!"

"Well, that's a good point. Just be patient with me, OK?"

"Absolutely, you got it! And I must say again that if we had been in the opposite situation of you dating, it would have been very difficult for me as well. I get it, Sweetie."

Merrick looks at me with relief in his eyes.

I attempt to sing, "Yeah for us, yeah for us, yeah for us!"

Our reuniting sparks a new flavor, a new tone to our commitment with each other. This creates new avenues to explore, new parts of ourselves to emerge. We held each other in a new way, we open up to each other in a new way. We both want the same thing from our relationship, therefore, this makes our journey easier, clear and clean finally. I am home!

One day a few weeks later, I was watching Tatum at the skate park when I look down at my left ring finger and I visualize a ring. I even felt its metallic energy. I share this with Merrick and he has been thinking about the idea of marriage as well. This leads to a realization, if we're going to be together, we really need to commit, to fully commit to each other. We decide to get married.

We find a beautiful home on Sunshine Lane and move back in together. It's a large home with a back deck the full length of the house, overlooking green fields and beyond that looms Sedona's towering red rocks. It's gorgeous and the perfect place to begin playing house together in uninterrupted marvel!

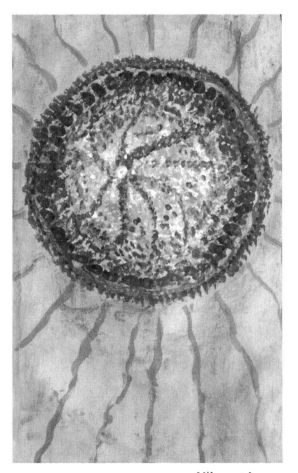

— *Vibrant Love*

Beginning our new journey includes an intimate outdoor ceremony in our spacious backyard. I found a 'lovely' dress off the rack and it cost a grand total of $25. It is beautiful with shiny clear sequins decorating each form fitting curve. We wish for the purity of white, as Merrick chose to wear all white as well.

On a perfect weather day, all our guests have been guided to form a Circle of Love with Tatum and five of his little buddies sitting on oriental rugs in the middle, each wearing white Indian style shirts. It is uniquely real and inspiring as Merrick and I walk into the already formed circle of friends and family to read our personalized vows to each other.

Rhea: "This gathering is so special for me because, although I've been married before, this union with you Merrick is very different from anything I've experienced. It is clear we create together very naturally. I look forward to much more of this magic as our connection is ripe with personal growth, love, beauty and realness. I feel our separation last sumer was the best thing for both of us. Although I left, my heart never left you. We have something so deep, so ancient, what I yearn for in my life. My commitment to you, to "Us" is to continue to do my best to love myself more and more each day, so I can share the gift of that love fully with you!"

Merrick: "Today is a celebration of Rhea and me in marriage. I cherish this day to love her with all my devotion toward our overflowing future together. As many of you know, this is my first marriage. It took a personal journey of self discovery to find my own commitment to someone very special. But along the way, I've received some memorable advice from friends. I want to acknowledge my friend Evan. Years ago he challenged me to look at my solitary pursuit of personal growth. He said, "Merrick if you are really committed to your growth, be in a relationship." I've learned way more about myself by being with Rhea. Thank you Evan. Last year, Rhea and I had difficulty resolving issues together. Another friend here had some profound advice to bring the love that Rhea and I had for each other through those delicate times. Alex, who I've known for 25 years, reminded us of having the courage and trust to separate and heal so we could be together again. That leap of faith allowed us to find ourselves and led to this marriage today. Thank you Alex for the depth you've brought to my life and for the movement that shakes us up.

I can't fully express all the memorable talks with my friend Will. For over 20 years there is always magic that emerges. Will told me how he knew when to marry his wife Carmen. "When I already felt married to her in my heart." I thought about that over the years. I realize I feel this with Rhea which is why this day is natural. I take to heart another message: "Be totally willing to feel everything without resistance." This was important for last year. Thank you Will and especially thanks for our friendship. Finally, I want to acknowledge someone who has had significant impact during our relationship. Harrison is Tatum's Dad. I thank Harrison for his "open-hearted allowing" of my presence in Tatum's life. It says a lot to me about a Father who can so fully share the impact of another man with his son like Harrison has. This marriage would not be the light it is today without Harrison. Thank You.

So now dear Rhea, let's plunge into this beautiful event together!"

Rhea, "I appreciate: Your strong spiritual belief and connection with your Higher Self, your complete acceptance of me "in love and in fear," your constant consistent belief in "Us" and our little family, your strong integrity and openness to grow and change, your endearing embrace where I feel I am home."

Merrick, "I appreciate your genuine joy, your humor and your laughter, your passion and realness in our love and in life, your endless creativity in everything you do, feel and think, your deep spirituality and the desire to continually grow, and your bringing Tatum into my life and the wonderful mother you are with him."

Wine is passed around to all the adults for the final toast to our union. The children in the middle are given grape juice to drink. Amongst the toast and celebration, a child's voice is heard,

"My juice tastes funny."

One of the adults takes the glass from his small hand and sips it. "This is wine!" Everyone bursts into laughter. Apparently, the bearers of the wine had accidentally given it to some of the children. Ironically, it was revealed that two of the guests, whom had been challenged with alcohol and had given up drinking, decided to drink it in honor of our wedding. Both of them had been given the grape juice, creating the perfect culmination of our Circle of Love.

Spending the week-end with all our friends and family, many of them confirm how perfect we are together. Some acknowledging how much we look alike, saying that they had not noticed the similarity until we walked into the circle together. After everyone left, we look at each other and I say, "We really do need to go on a honeymoon, we're so high and happy, personally I don't want these feelings to end."

Our ocean front resort in Puerto Peñasco, Mexico matches my desire for beauty. Our lovely room with a balcony overlooking the beach, is perfect to continue our celebration. The large swimming pool is surrounded by huge beds with canvas roofs and sides for privacy. We make out like teen-agers on a bed facing the Gulf waters. Laughing, we feast upon the warm ocean breezes, the rhythmic sounds of each wave hitting the shore, and the ungainly pelicans diving for their food.

We have come to realize healthy spiritual loving has very little to do with the pose. Sure, changing and trying different angles is enjoyable and provides nice variety, however, when two loving, connected souls engage with each other, it is that which is truly sacred. A real uniting beyond our human words. This is what my husband and I have together as making love is a very sacred place indeed! We fit so perfectly, literally and symbolically, as we share life's simultaneous orgasm time after time. I am truly home!

36

It seems there could have been some warning, but I felt none. Events are already in motion. There is no turning back.

I'm attaching the mini microphone's clip on my cotton shirt, as I squirm in my seat trying to ease the all too familiar pain in my right hamstring. Who wants to feel that constant pain, especially when it is raining. Fortunately, that is rare in Sedona. I come back to the present moment.

The woman interviewing me paces back and forth temporarily blocking my view of the modern metal podium, while her excitement is rapidly pushing the button on her ballpoint pen in and out, in and out. While noticing the click, click, click sound, I am watching the filming in this small chapel, located next to the Creative Life Center. This is where our writing retreat will be held. I can hear the multitude of outdoor fountains with their subtle splashing of water in the background. What a relief, hearing water flowing in the desert.

All eyes in the room are on me in my artsy, black shirt with teal, fluffy sleeves that allows me to feel more of my feminine nature. The photographer wears a "what the bleep?" t-shirt, as he looks at me from his intimidating video camera. His smile seems to calm my inner heartbeats somehow.

"What is your name?" the interviewer asks. Click, click, click.

"Um, my name is Rhea," I answer after clearing my somewhat dry throat. I attempt to appear confident by maintaining eye contact with her.

"What inspired you to come to this day long writing retreat?"

After pausing and gazing a little past her to the window behind, I say, "I feel a book within me."

The large window capturers the spotted green foliage against the red rock beauty of Sedona. I gaze to the left at the bold vibrant abstract paintings on the walls. I appreciate the green and red hues indicating a nice use of complimentary colors.

"Are you attached to the subject matter of your writing?" she continues, "considering you will be pulling this information from deep within you?"

"Well, I sense it will be about my personal journey and I'm open to see where my writing takes me," I respond.

"Thanks and good luck," she concludes the short interview.

I leave the warming chapel, feeling my unstable knees find their strength after sitting so long. What is happening? I ask myself. Why am I having such a reaction to this writing process? What is unfolding?

Thrilled to begin this experience, I make my way up the circular walkway to the main building of the Center. As I enter the spacious "Great Room," I gaze around at the circle of thirty-two wanna-be authors. All of us have made a commitment to write for a full day. While taking in this circular room, I notice its unique beauty. I look up to see a large colorful depiction of abstract blooming flowers. The massive stained glass window illuminates from the ceiling carrying its beauty to every corner. It is about fifteen feet long by ten feet wide. Adrift with a multitude of streaming colors, it seems to be bringing in a constant flow of light. How perfectly symbolic, I think to myself. We will be bringing in our own light from within or will it be our darkness? Either way, it provides more insight and learning.

The large room is comfortably round in shape with a smaller circle of folding chairs, one for each of us. On the stage off to the right sits a baby grand piano, revealing the room's diversity for creativity in all forms. Concerts of every type of music, spiritual speakers, Indian Gurus, Native American Ceremonies and even Trance Dance. I have fond memories of Trance Dance, as Merrick and I had shared many events in this room, watching and honoring people's expressions of their personal interpretation of the dance.

Continuing to move my eyes around the room, I notice, each of the walls surrounding us has large windows, inviting the beauty of the red earth to evenly intersperse with the room. There is a distinct sense of anticipation in the room.

Looking around a room full of strangers, except for Kayla. I want to appear open to the others yet I realize I am wearing my protective armor today, so that nothing is able to pierce through. I realize my slightly offbeat nature and totally individual personality still wants to fit in the group somehow.

I'm finding this process is asking me to reflect upon my life. I am aware of a deep appreciation of my relationship and my current career path. My sessions with Clients from around the world and from every walk of life feeds my soul. These searching souls are willing to look within, to see both their shadow and their brilliance; wishing to become better people as a result of their searching.

Interrupting my thoughts, Taylor, our writing Guide, emerges. As if directing his question to me personally he begins, "Are any of you feeling the least bit nervous?"

A lifting of almost all of the hands in the room reveals I'm not alone.

"Please realize, this is very natural, for you will be divulging a part of your soul over the course of the day," he explains, intending to have empathy for our feelings. His long blondish hair seems to emphasize this point as it moves across his shoulders. He pushes his wire-rimmed glasses up on his face, as he continues, "I can attest to this. From years of writing myself."

He is a best-selling author, I remind myself, as I notice his attempt to appear preppy with his plaid shorts and matching collared shirt. Somehow, his appearance doesn't quite fit with my previous conversation with him. We had spoke on the phone for about forty-five minutes earlier that week, for both of us to get a sense if this was what I was looking for. Clearly, the answer was a resounding Yes!

"Consider your intentions for your writing."

There's a lengthy pause so we can answer internally. I'm considering my intentions when, I am brought back to the room by Taylor's deep voice.

"You will be guided into your creative space within and write from this place. I suggest there be as little talking as necessary while you're writing."

Taylor gently guides us within. Lost in my images and senses, I can only half listen to Taylor, as my attention is on the sounds of flowing water and the alluring aromatherapy of the fresh green earth. In my inner world, I am on Vashon Island, feeling safe and nurtured. I notice a big burly man approaching me from the distance. How long has this man lived in my imagination as this massive and powerful presence? As he approaches, I am reminded of Hagrid in the Harry Potter movies. His kindness, combined with this large size, is a rarity. He says as he looks deeply into my eyes, "I come to you with love and joy. I have always been with you on your journey."

I begin to cry as I see this man, as I sense his presence again. "How do I know you? How do I feel such love for you?" I ask through my tears. His presence feels Divine as he says to me, "Remember the many nightly visitors of your childhood?"

I shake my head, words seem unimportant.

"I wanted to connect with you then, to let you know that you are never alone. I am always with you. I'm one of your Guides."

"What can you tell me about my life? What about all of my challenges?"

"Stay with your feelings and trust me when I tell you, you will discover more of your truth through your writing. I chose to meet you by the nurturing waterfall because I knew you would open up to your writing here, as you did in the past with your painting."

"OK, we have a deal," I say inwardly to my new, yet familiar guide. "Let's see what we create together."

"My question pertains to me finding how to forgive myself for being unable to be truly successful and hold onto money?"

Taylor gently guides us within. I begin writing.

'I'm being asked to write right now so I shall...keep writing until it feels like someone else is taking over...let my hands relax and then let the flow begin...why am I challenged with lack of money? Or rather holding onto the money...I make more cash and more bizarre things happen that requires the need for more money.... mo money...I'm letting go to whatever wants to come through me... my first communion, Oh Wow, are we going Catholic now? Am I writing these words correctly? Well, hell yes, we are going to the Catholic world...I mean it was a part of my growing up years... sorry Jesus! nothing personal. I really see you so differently then the Church likes to portray you. I mean, when I met you in California, I saw you as a nonjudgmental, caring cool man, as a man...anyway talk to me about my First Communion....which was when I must have been about 7 years old...what is with me at seven years old? This age keeps coming up?'

I continue writing after shaking my cramped hand.

"All of my large family has come to the party for me, I'm so

thrilled to be saved from Hell. The belief is that when we receive our first Communion we are taking Jesus' body and blood through the host and the wine. So we are yet saved again from that mean God in the sky. Thunder, Kaboom rings in the background. I'm dressed in all white, complete with what looks like a wedding gown for kids from Kids-R-Us, patent leather shoes, turn me over, so the frills hang over socks, and my white veil.

I'm getting so much attention it scares me. Why must I cover myself with my invisibility gown? I want to show my cute white dress, show my cute self, but I'm afraid to, but why? Oh my! It's time to open all my gifts. I bet there are 50 of them from all the relatives, neighbors, friends, boyfriends, and whoever else my mom knew at the time. These parties are big and open to the public, it seems. I'm excited to open my gifts: beautiful charms for my new gold charm bracelet, one is an angel and one is a golden bell. There are a few rings and a few necklaces and lots of money. I'm thrilled to have so much money. What shall I buy with it?

Then the bomb drops, my parents need the money for bills and groceries. Sorry Kiddo, they actually take all my money after the celebration has ended. You really don't deserve it any way is what I tell my lil' self again.

"I don't deserve it" rings in my ears, in my body, everywhere. As I write this I'm beginning to see the depths of this creation in my life. I've been carrying this belief that I don't deserve money. Wow, what a revelation!"

After lunch break, I find my spot and sit down while organizing my large unlined notebook, many pens and my water bottle.

Taylor again guides us within. I begin writing,

'As if physically taken to my childhood, I see myself in my grand-parent's basement. I am sitting in a circle of relatives on my Mom's side of the family. We are in a bigger circle and it's Christmas season with the well-decorated tree shining in the middle. There's a multitude of gifts beneath it. I smell my grandma's anise cookies. I am not sure if I like the licorice flavor or merely the memory of her loving nature. I tap my black, patent leather shoes with my white fluffy socks together while I wiggle in my stiff red lace dress.

I'm having the exact same jittery feelings emerging. My five year old self has to pee and I am so afraid to get up and walk through all of these relatives who feel like strangers to me. Noise, commotion and anticipation pierce the stiff air. The only way to the bathroom is through the middle of the large circle and up the wooden stairs. I am confused as I feel myself becoming invisible. I realize this because my mouth seems to be stuck again. Finally, I muster enough nerve to move and notice my upper legs are stuck to the metal folding chair. I hear a pop as my little legs release from their grip, as if trying to keep me here, keep me safe. I notice myself moving toward the tree with all the eyes on it. Or are they on me?

Both ideas frighten me equally. Perhaps everybody is looking at me or nobody is looking? Perhaps nobody cares? This maneuver takes every bit of my courage to walk into the middle of this circle. I cross to the steps to go upstairs. Many of my cousins are sitting lined on both sides of the stairs, whom I must pass in my haze of urgency. I do it again, I feel myself officially becoming invisible.

Somehow, I make it to the top of the basement stairs without needing to talk directly to anyone. This is made easier as all eyes are anticipating what is in the decorated gifts below. What a relief! I turn to the right to pass through the kitchen, noticing the porcelain *stove with the additional aromas of turkey, gravy and pecan pie, swirling through the stagnant air. I smell my way across the quaint kitchen adorned with my grandma's sweet ideas of life. My eyes comfortably meet a magnet that reads "Love is all you need" which is posted on her olive green refrigerator. As I merge through to the other side of the kitchen, I notice to my immediate right a line of relatives in the narrow hallway to the bathroom. Of course, with forty plus people, there always seems to be a line to the one and only bathroom. I cross my little, sweaty legs, to keep myself from peeing right there. My bladder screams to get me out of all this bizarre energy.*

The line decreases one by one, as I finally reach the bathroom door and find my way inside. After relieving myself, I make my way back to the family circle. As I wiggle on my cold metal folding chair, someone touches my arm. I am brought out of my world, as my protective invisibility cloak falls to the floor. I jump and peer at the man next to me. It's Uncle George. He gazes as if looking through me.

"Little girl, it's been at least twenty minutes and you haven't said a word, are you OK?" he asks.

I am stunned that I'm not only being seen, but I am being spoken to as well. This breaks my protective reality and I can only stare at him. I can't speak, I am so deep into the perceived truth of who I thought I was; taken easily to the place within where my confusion and pain play together.

Why is he talking to me?

I've mastered talking to myself. If anyone heard me talking to myself, and how often, they'd probably lock me up as being declared crazy for hearing voices and talking to the air around me.

Doesn't he realize I am the mistake of our family?

As I am continuing to stare deeply at him, with no foreseeable words finding their way to my lips, I see the look in his eyes change from curiosity to bewilderment. Even if I wanted to speak, I don't feel I could at this point. I'd created an entire world within myself, where I was the only one who knew the password. This man seemed to want to penetrate my illusionary wall of protection.

I am perplexed with his tall eyes overshadowing me. At that point, I am not quite equipped to speak. Isn't this odd? I mean what does it mean I can't speak.

I am jolted back to the Creative Life Center, shaking from head to toe.

I shake my hands as I'm digesting what has been revealed to me. How ironic, given all the inner work I do with Clients and their belief systems. I really hadn't remembered this dynamic at all. Would my parents really take my money away from me? Perhaps they paid it back, but I really can't remember ever having any money when I was a child, not even an allowance. I realize I must begin to forgive myself for thinking I was a failure all these years. My shoulders drop as I say these powerful words to myself.

The rest of the afternoon is spent sharing our powerful revelations from writing from within. I feel the information received is so valuable and I feel satisfied with my day of writing from within. Thanks Taylor!

Later that evening, feeling blissful and content, I hop on the couch across from Merrick. I notice his demeanor is different.

He looks at me with wounded eyes as I sense something is off with him.

He begins rambling about what happened at work that day. He is clearly upset and can't stop talking about it. After I present several possibilities to his situation, suddenly, his dark words have changed and are being directed at me. He is blaming me for his upset while pointing at me. His voice has increased to blaming and shaming.

In the midst of his distraught position, I attempt to explain, "Merrick, this is not about me."

I remain calm as I witness all this taking place. In the past, my skin would have started flinching and my insides would have prepared to protect myself.

"Merrick, this is not about me," I repeat calmly. "Your hurting inside and this isn't about me."

Suddenly he throws a pillow.

I sat and listened until he was done venting. Many tears followed as I hugged him. This is a huge step for our relationship, as I was able to remain in my observer mode and not take this personally.

37

We are moving, yes, we are moving again. We are becoming Master Movers as it is part of our regular world. This day seems to present multiple light possibilities. Merrick and I are excited about our new home and an incredible Art Studio.

I have mixed feelings about Harrison's new home life. About two years ago, he moved in with his girlfriend, Ada and her two daughters, Ava, 14 and Olivia, 9 years old. Tatum has created a special friendship with Olivia, however when he returns to our house, he sleeps for almost an entire day. I've asked Harrison about this dynamic and he reveals that he lets Tatum, a 9 year old stay up as late as he wishes. This disturbs my Mommy part and I've learned that I have to accept this new reality when Tatum is at his Dad's house. I have to let it go and trust, yet something feels off to me and I'm not sure why this feeling continues to haunt me.

Our new home is a beautiful, newly remodeled, green adobe home. Each time we've taken more boxes over to it, it welcomes us with loving arms. After mastering the flight of steps, it opens into a large room including living room, dining room and kitchen. The kitchen is complete with a gas stove on an island with a granite counter top and artsy dimmer lights hung perfectly above. All appliances are stainless steel and are the best-of-the-best. Across from the kitchen is an equally large fireplace. All the walls are lined with windows that stretch from floor to ceiling with incredible Sedona views. It'll easily become home.

We can see Brins Mesa, where the top of the mountain burnt for several days. This was devastating to many of us locals for the authorities had to close the Canyon road to Flagstaff for weeks to follow. When I look at Brins Mesa, I am still brought to that specific memory when Merrick and I witnessed the glowing flames as we spoke of separating.

Our other views are symbolically beautiful representing our new blossoming relationship. We can see Coffeepot Rock which appears like an old fashioned percolating coffee pot. Set below the rock is an entire area of streets with names that relate to coffee. For example, Sanborn, Maxwell House and my personal favorite, Coffee Cup Road. It speaks to me personally because I am a java lover, as I appreciate coffee is good for my awareness and thinking skills.

Towering above Coffeepot Rock is Thunder Mountain in all its glory. I can see the white at the top of the mountain; the limestone which erodes at a slower pace than the red sandstone caressing the bottom half of the mountain.

I remember how our home was manifested. Approximately two months earlier, I'm conducting an Art Training. We are in the Art Studio which sits next to our house. I'm showing my client the many techniques of the different art mediums. In addition to the learning aspect there is deep trust that needs to be found from within that can allow the creativity to flow naturally. I'm introducing different brush strokes using acrylic paints, sharing how to bleed inks, feeling the moisture and pliability of sculpting clay, molding plaster, smudging oil pastels and playing with charcoal.

We are enjoying this process as we are sharing our lives' stories which have brought us to who we are today. I took her on an inner journey to find her Creator within. I hung two pieces of white paper, each about seven feet tall and three feet wide on each wall. One for her and one for me. We traced our real life sized bodies on these papers. As we experienced different feelings in our bodies, we would draw these on the paper. This was insightful as it opened the doors for verbal exploration.

Lunch time came upon us very quickly. We glided into the beautiful home, as if opening to our creativity was assisting our movements. As I was standing in this modern spacious living room, appreciating the zen like quality, I excitedly exclaimed,

"I could see us living here."

She confirmed my sentiment as she replied, "I could see it too."

I let the idea go, as we flutter to lunch and then back to our creationship of flavorful delights.

Let it go and it comes back to You. We are moving into this magical house with a vortex near the art studio. We are aware of this energy because of the large juniper tree standing right next to it. Its trunk is swirling in a counter clockwise position revealing the mass of energy below. Scientists have been able to measure the vortex energy and reveal its power.

The following day, we can officially move into our house. We're unloading boxes as our movers move all the heavy furniture. Needing a break, Merrick and I leave. At a local restaurant called the Coffee Pot, we are ordering breakfast. If you like omelets, they serve 101 different types. As we're sitting in our cozy booth, I look around at all the southwestern tchotchkes as we are waiting for our breakfast. I feel a need to listen to my phone messages, even though I hadn't heard my phone ring. There is a voice message from Ada. I detect she has a different tone in her voice.

"Hi Rhea, it's Ada. It's important you call me back."

Rather vague, but enough information to motivate me to walk into the lobby for some personal space. Tatum is spending three days with them while we move. This is day two. I wonder what could have happened that I need to pick up Tatum from school, was he injured? My mind wanders through the possible injuries, a broken leg, a broken arm, etc. for Tatum is very active and adventurous.

I ring Ada with shaky fingers. What could it be? Surely I'm over-reacting. I remind myself to take a deep breath, it's all fine, everything seems to have a way of working itself out, right?

I find my composure and my voice as Ada answers the phone, "What's happened to Tatum, is he OK?" I hear myself asking quickly. Her voice is calm and methodical as she says, "Well Rhea, you need to pick up Tatum from school today because Harrison has been arrested."

"Arrested? For what?" I'm now officially allowing myself to feel concerned. Harrison has never had any problems with the police or the law, that I am aware of.

"Well, there's no easy way to say this," she continues as if reporting the weather, "I was awakened around 1:30 last night by Olivia and she said Harrison was touching her down there and she didn't like it. He was kissing her and she was not feeling OK with it. Apparently he was very drunk. Rhea, she's only nine years old," Ada began crying.

My mind is swirling as if a ton of bricks have just hit me. Am I going to fall over? Where's the ground when I need it? I never saw this coming.

"What? What do you mean? Where was Tatum?" I say while searching for a counter to lean on.

"I approached Harrison and asked him about this development. Oh Rhea, could this really be happening?"

"Where is Harrison now?" My heart hurt, as I care deeply for him.

"They've arrested him and he's at the police station."

"Is Tatum OK? Did he see anything?"

"No, thank goodness, he slept through it all," she relays. "I took him to school today without saying a word."

"How can I tell Tatum this?" I say to no one in particular, feeling my heart becoming heavy. "What can I tell a nine year old?"

I realize Ada isn't in any position to help me; she has enough of her own situation to deal with.

"Ada, how are you holding up?"

"I'm in shock, not quite sure what to think? It's still so fresh."

"I'm so sorry for you and Olivia. How is she?"

"She's coping, as well as she can. I guess time will tell. Yes?"

"Yes, I suppose...are you comfortable talking about it?" I ask.

"Sure."

"How far had the situation gone?" I found a way to ask this as I remember the first time I met her daughter; a five year old, little giggly girl with a runny nose. My mind also raced back to the last time I saw Harrison, he brought her to our house when he was picking up Tatum. As a 9 year old, Olivia was wearing a fur coat and fur covered boots to match, strutting like a teenager, or even like a young woman. I recall even mentioning it to Merrick after they left, how grown up she appeared and acted.

"Apparently, Harrison confessed everything to the police. I feel so guilty that I didn't even know anything. I'm still in a state of shock, I paced the floors for three hours after Harrison left the house saying he was going to kill himself. I had to find comfort with the decision to put him away for a very long time. I finally called my friend in Indonesia who fortunately was awake because of the time difference. He helped me to put things into perspective, that what Harrison did was seriously inappropriate and he needs help. So finally, I found the courage to call the police and they found Harrison this morning in his office. He admitted everything to the police. I guess I already said that. Rhea, I'm feeling a bit lost. Can you imagine how this can affect my beautiful daughter?"

"I can only imagine," I say grasping for the right words, "I really feel for you and her," I say empathetically.

"Rhea did you ever notice anything unusual about Harrison? Anything at all? You work with people?" she asks on the verge of tears again.

"No, honestly Ada, I haven't noticed anything like this, apart from him talking about his challenging childhood, but he's done that in the past. No nothing." As I search my mind for some clues, some hints of something, anything?

"I need to go, my sister just arrived," she says quickly.

"Just know I'm here if you need me. And I'll definitely pick up Tatum from school today. Thanks Ada and take good care."

I sense an empathetic closeness with her as I press the button on my iphone to end this call.

There really aren't words to explain how I feel right now. So many questions as I'm brought back to the present. My mind is trying to absorb all of this twilight reality that's suddenly our current reality. "Harrison has been arrested!" Some version of this sentence keeps running through my mind on repeat, like a news feed on the bottom of the screen. It never stops and underscores every moment, as if I have to keep saying it or it isn't real. I have to keep reminding myself that this is really happening because it's just too fucking unbelievable.

What about Tatum? What does this all mean I wonder? I am aware Harrison is deeply wounded, isn't everyone in some way, but why this? Why her; why an innocent little girl? I'm so relieved that Tatum didn't have to witness this as I feel a sudden need to hug and protect him from what I have to tell him. And I must entertain the idea of why this sexual dynamic is once again entering my world. Clearly, I still have more healing to do inside.

The delight of our dream house seems unimportant as it has lost some appeal. I try to imagine telling Tatum about this new development with his Dad. So many questions are flying around in my head, what could possibly compel a grown man to find a little girl attractive, much less find her sexually appealing? I realize this is enough for now, I will learn more as it unfolds.

I shake myself back to the restaurant and realize Merrick is probably wondering what is taking so long. Especially, to take me away from one of my favorite hobbies, eating. He knows I passionately enjoy my food and usually won't take calls or allow any interruptions during meal time. I wander back to our booth and sit down, needing the grounding of the seat while eyeing my fluffy omelet.

My face must be revealing something as Merrick's smile changes.

"What is it, Rhea?"

I can't seem to find the words to match my soaring mind.

"Ve haf vays ov makin you tok," he smirks.

I feel out of control as I realize I can't do a thing about any of this. I am still digesting the ramifications of this one phone call as I turn slowly to him.

"I'm not sure where to begin."

How does one prepare someone for the depth of what I am about to share.

"Harrison has been arrested," I spit out these words.

"What?" Merrick exclaims.

" Harrison has been arrested."

"For what?"

I begin to cry, no longer needing to remain strong for Ada.

"What is it, Rhea? It can't be that bad," he inquires with serious eyes.

My storyteller-self takes over quite naturally for me. While feeling a depth of sadness for Tatum, I relay the phone conversation. Despite his best efforts, Merrick could not control his growing agitation. Authentic fear is beginning to swell within him.

"Did Tatum see anything? How are we going to tell Tatum?" he asks, as he has grown to love him as his own son.

"No, thank Goddess. Ada said he slept through it all and she didn't say a thing to him this morning. As far as telling him, I don't know, I really can't even fathom," I say with a dry mouth.

I drink some water and say, "It is indeed a sad time when the persecuted become the persecutor." Recalling Harrison's stories of his childhood and how his mom and dad exploited their sexual behaviors and sounds throughout the house on a daily basis. They had little if any boundaries with their sexuality and their five children, Harrison being the oldest child.

Merrick never misses the opportunity to express the truths he holds close, "We must forgive Harrison for the sake of Tatum."

I love Merrick so dearly in this moment.

"I will need some time for forgiveness, however, I do agree with the idea. My intention is to do my best and practice what I've learned and what I teach. And I do want to make a conscious effort to look at this dynamic from the higher place, for Tatum's sake and it will be great practice for all of us. Spirituality is a practice, right?"

"Yes, let's do this together," he says as he squeezes my hand.

Then more questions emerge, as the total realization of our predicament now becomes a full reality.

"How is her daughter?" Merrick is genuinely concerned.

"It's too early to tell, however, I do admire the courage it took for her to go to her Mom and tell her. Can you imagine how different so many people's lives would be if this were the case? Imagine if I had the courage to tell someone at the time it happened to me?"

We look at each other for a moment of reflection.

"And I am pleased Ada believed her daughter and did something about it, to stop the passing on of the sexual dysfunction," I conclude.

"Damn, what was he thinking?" Merrick's words strike a deep cord within me for he rarely cusses. His words bring me back to the present moment in the restaurant.

"I'm so relieved Tatum didn't witness any of this or had he?" I can't bear to imagine this, as sweat finds my body. This is one of the most precarious moments of my life, for I realize I have a choice how I handle this situation. I can analyze it to death, trying to understand it and make some sense of it, using so much of my energy and time OR I can choose to accept this reality, understand this is what's happening and learn to accept it, forgive and view it from the higher perspective? I choose Door Number Two, I choose to implement all I've learned and look at this from the higher point of view. This allows my entire body to relax.

I attempt to eat my omelet just because it is there and I need some energy for our moving day. Ironically, I feel a strange rather hard sensation in my mouth. I pull out a little foreign object and I look at it closely. It is a piece of plastic wrap from the cheese, I guess. This is the perfect segue I need for my appetite is gone. I show the waitress what I have found and she offers to get me another meal. I decline as I realize my body is already way too full.

That afternoon, I lay down for a quick nap before picking up Tatum from school. Or am I merely trying to escape the next conversation with him? I fall asleep contemplating my choice to look at life from the higher perspective. I begin dreaming almost immediately,

'I am teaching in a large, well lit classroom with windows on both sides of the room. Two rows of six desks are lined next to each other in the middle of the room equaling twelve desks, thus allowing open space all around the rest of the vacant room. My assistant, an older competent lady, is moving the trash can from the end of the desks to the corner of the room. I tell myself, "How brilliant, now the trash isn't near the students or me." I feel surprised I had not thought of moving this can myself.

There is a ringing sound of a phone in the classroom. I hear the Headmaster's voice as he is lying on the floor in the doorway. He answers the phone and says, "Rhea, it's a gentleman for You," in a somewhat disgruntled tone. I could sense he did not like that another man was calling me, as I pick up the phone closest to me. The man on the line says to me, "I am calling from our group and I wish for you to come to the Serreall building at 4:00 pm." I knew

I had to go, even though I had no knowledge of this group, nor had I heard of this building and yet I feel a genuine curiosity to go.

Magically, I arrive on the roof of a large city building with seven other women. Four of the woman are stunningly tall and slim with an air of confidence. I found myself admiring their state of being. The other three women seemed to be in my situation; they had also been asked to meet here.

One of the four woman says, "OK, let's go!"

No explanation, no introductions, nothing. I am quite perplexed.

"But what are we doing here?" I ask.

They look at me and say, "Rhea it's time, it's time to follow us. We know the way."

I am suddenly catapulted into a large white SUV with all the women. It is a state of the art vehicle with leather seats and it seemed to be flying. The main woman is driving, or shall I say flying, this vehicle and I am still questioning this entire experience. Then, I am driving this huge car, to where I am not even sure. At one point, the road becomes very steep, narrow and curvy, so much so that I had to put my foot directly onto the pavement to balance all of us.

We finally make it to the bottom safely and arrive at a large vacant parking lot with a beautiful view of the ocean. However, this is not a typical ocean; it is filled with a variety of types, sizes and unusual dimensions of sailboats. The sailboats are not sailing on top of the water either; they are sailing under the waves, deep *down in the ocean. The sailboats seem to be fine even though they are turned sideways and upside down.*

"What?" I implore, "Why are we here?"

"We are going skydiving," the main woman replied with her steadfast sense of confidence.

"But...but...who are you?" my question lingers in the air, as there is much anticipation amongst the women. The circle space opens to welcome a lovely man. This man, Jesus, walks into the middle of the circle. All eyes are on him, as he is clearly the leader of this group.

"Let's go," he says excitedly as he stretches his lovely hands out in front of him, as the women proceed to take off his rings for him. All this is communicated intuitively. He is a magnetic presence with his tall, proportioned body and brown hair. His whole being is electric.

"Yes, let's go," Jesus says.

Again no explanation as to what is happening.

"Rhea is reluctant and is resisting," one of the women tells him.

Jesus turns to me and takes my arm very gently to move away from the circle so we can chat privately.

"What's the problem Rhea?" he says looking right into my soul.

"This is all so fast. Where are you wanting to take us?"

"You don't need to know the destination, just trust me," he smiles in a confident, manly way.

"But, why me? Out of all the people on this planet, why do you want me, why now?"

He puts his hand into his pocket to retrieve something, while maintaining sweet eye contact with me. I break our gaze to watch him bring a brownish, cotton ball wad out of his pocket.

"Smell this," he says putting it under my nose. I take a whiff and immediately feel an incredible sensation throughout my entire body. I am losing all sense of myself and my physicality as I meet the ground.

He kneels down to assist my fall and says, "Are you ready now?" I am feeling complete bliss and am overcome with the wonderment of a child. I ponder to myself, do I take the red pill or the blue pill? I could wander off to the SUV, not even sure where it is parked at this point, and drive to wherever, not even sure where I am, and go to where nothing else seemed to matter. OR I could go skydiving with these loving confident people and Jesus, to do whatever else they have in mind for me and just trust."

The answer is becoming quite clear as I wake up, JUST TRUST MY LIFE! As Jesus said, "I don't need to know the destination, just trust it all."

I am thrilled about my revealing dream with Jesus reminding me to just trust. I ponder this idea and realize even if I do worry about how Tatum takes the news, it won't help the situation in any way. So I choose to trust. As I acknowledge this powerful sentiment, my entire body relaxes. I take a deep breathe and I am ready to pick up sweet Tatum. And I do wonder how his little nine year old mind will interpret this very adult situation.

We make small talk about school and his friends on the way home. Tatum and I sit in our new living room on our comfy gray couch, surrounded by many boxes in various stages of being unpacked. Newspaper and padding are scattered everywhere, from moving day.

"Why did you pick me up from school today? Where's my Dad or Ada?"

I take a deep breath and attempt to tell the complex dynamic of child molestation to my ever so innocent sweet son. To add to the dynamic, the victim was his buddy. They call each other friends as they have been playing together for most of their lives.

I begin, "Tatum, your Dad is going away for awhile."

"Where to, Mom?

"Well, he has been having a difficult time."

"Where is he going?"

"Tatum, this is so difficult to tell you, Sweetie,"

I attempt to remain calm.

"Your Dad had to go to the police station last night."

"Why?" His eyes have doubled in size.

"He has to go to jail for awhile. He broke the law."

"What did he do?"

"Um, he had been drinking too much and you know how he loves his massage work, well, he was massaging Olivia to sleep last night and he went a little too far."

"What do you mean a little too far?" Tatum's radar is ever present as he looks at me with his big dark eyes. I notice his little hands are picking at the pillow next to him.

"Well Tatum," I gingerly ease into the rest of the sentence, "he touched her in her private parts."

"Oh," is all he can say as his eyes meet the couch.

I want to explain this situation and realize, I will go at his pace. If he wants to know more, I'll share more, otherwise I'm reminding myself this is so much already.

"How long will my Dad be gone?" his little voice cracks. His hands are rubbing the fabric of the couch, as if this movement is soothing him somehow.

I reach my hand across to him to run my fingers through a lock of his golden brown hair buying time to find my words very carefully, "We're not sure yet, sweetie. He has to go to a trial first and then they will decide how long."

"Will he be gone about 23 days?" he asks.

"What made you think of 23 days?"

"From a boy at school. His dad was arrested for a speeding ticket and he had to go to jail for 23 days," Tatum explains.

"Oh, I see," wondering if this is the best time to reveal it will be quite a bit longer. Yes, I need to be honest with him. I continue,

"Sweetie, we have been told it could be longer than that," I manage to say, wishing this conversation weren't even happening. I feel sick inside.

"How much longer?" he asks looking down, not really wanting to know the answer.

I pause while looking at his little body. I'm checking into my feelings inside, needing guidance right now.

"A whole year?" his fearful voice manages to muster.

"Probably more, Tatum. I want you to know this is very difficult for me to have to tell you this."

I hold his little hand as gently as I can, while looking into his sweet eyes now becoming fearful.

"We've been told it could be quite a bit longer."

I had to say it now before I couldn't handle saying it. I dropped the big bomb as gently as I could.

Tears formed in his eyes as he looked down at his nine year old feet. I watch his entire demeanor shift as he digests the meaning behind these words.

"What happened to your Dad is considered a sickness. He needs time to go away for awhile to heal and become a better man."

Pause...tick. tick. tick.

"Come here, Tatum," I say as I cuddle and rock him. I hold him for as long as he needs me. He feels so small in my arms as his tears flow so slowly.

"Tatum, please remember he loves you very much. We'll talk more as we get more details."

"OK Mama," he says.

Tatum hasn't called me Mama for quite awhile. I commit to myself to pay close attention to his words, moods and overall attitude. How will this affect my sweet boy, my mommy part wants to know?

"I Love You," I say, "so much."

"Love you, too," he whispers falling asleep in my arms.

Telling Tatum is a tragic mix of maternal protection and unbearable heartbreak. Every part of me, as a Mom, has to realize I can't protect him from his pain or his loss. I feel helpless and exhausted as I realize this situation has also brought a profound exchange of love and loss into our little family. It truly feels like a death. Will I take little Tatum to prison to see his Dad? Or will I turn my head and walk away from Harrison, as some of my friends suggested. I have some thinking to do seeing this situation from the higher perspective. One thing is blatantly clear, our lives will never be the same.

The verdict is seven years in prison. There wasn't even a trial since Harrison pleaded guilty to the charges. One day, several months after he was taken away, I told Tatum the story; the whole story. We are hiking in the red rocks and I feel the time is right as my higher self seems to be hinting to me.

"Tatum, do you have any questions about Daddy leaving?"

I've opened the space. Beyond telling him about the seven year sentencing, we haven't talked about 'the situation" since the first time. Tatum, a master sleeper even as a baby, has had challenging nights trying to sleep. This breaks my heart to witness the effect his Father's sudden disappearance has on him. Despite this, Tatum hasn't shown many signs of wanting to talk about it. I have asked him and he declines.

As Tatum walks, his head seems to be bouncing as if only attached by a string, while remaining focused on the red rock path. This time he did not look at me, as he took all this within. Tick. Tick. Tick. I want to know what his little mind is thinking, when he asks reluctantly,

"Is Olivia OK?"

"Well, yes physically she is fine, we will see how she deals with the emotional part of it."

I forget how truly young he is when we are talking. Sometimes he thinks so much like an adult.

Tick tick tick…time stops for a moment.

Then I ask, "Tatum do you and your friends ever talk about sex?"

"A little bit," he answers honestly, "Keane speaks of things his older brother has told him."

"Do you understand what sex is?" I notice his shifting eyes and body language, "Do you know what it involves between two people?"

Am I saying too much? I have no idea, all I know is that I need to be telling him some understanding of the depth and degree of what his Dad did. My concern is that he could feel fear about living, thinking that when we do certain things, we can suddenly end up in prison. As I'm pondering this, he says rather sheepishly, "Yep Mom, I know what sex is."

"Do you have any questions about it?" I ask.

"No," he says, "I'm not comfortable talking to you about it." This is a first, as we have always talked so easily about everything. And I do understand at this point, sex is even more of a loaded topic for him.

"OK. Well if you have any questions, you can always ask me, OK?"

There is a quiet moment as we continue hiking together.

"Momma, are you or Merrick going to go to jail?"

There it is, yes, one of the many possibilities I have wondered about.

"Oh Sweetie, no we are not going to go to jail." as I grabbed his little hand and squeezed it.

I look at him with compassion for clearly he had been carrying this fear around since Harrison's abrupt disappearing act. This is the moment I commit to staying on this crazy planet for Tatum. All for sweet Tatum.

"Tatum, please realize we are not leaving you. Not ever. I promise you."

I look into his eyes; clearly this realization has changed his demeanor. He seems a bit more relaxed. Already I am glad we are having this conversation, as difficult as it is. Beyond the pain of losing his Father, this question must have been lurking within him. We walk a few more yards in silence feeling the Arizona sunshine on our backs.

"Are there any other questions you have about Daddy?" I ask wanting to protect him from this crazy world.

After some reflection Tatum continues, "Did he do sex to her?"

"No, he did not do this with her, but he touched her in private places, that's why he needs some time away to heal and become a better man."

"Yes, become a better man," Tatum says lightening his load a bit. He smiles at this thought.

"We can imagine he is away at an ashram finding time for himself and becoming a better person."

"OK, a better man and I'm done talking about him that way. I feel sorry for him."

"Sure thing, Tatum. Thanks for your honesty."

I so appreciate his clear sense of boundaries and his honest way of taking care of himself and his needs. I so appreciate Tatum in this moment. These are the only words he says about his Dad, that he feels sorry for him. Despite this challenging situation, we are doing our best to keep it in the higher perspective.

> *CHECK-IN: 'Tatum is indeed a shining beacon for many and he inspires people around him that there truly is still good on this planet. He is shining his light and sharing his goodness in a way that is not invasive yet is available for people to witness and see, even on an unconscious level. His friends also sense there is something very special about Tatum. However, they cannot quite put a finger on what that means*

nor do they really need to understand. This allows opening within their families of which they have no clear indication of. There is a space he brings to the table with them that can provide more realness and integrity, for they wish to be their best around him as he does for the two of you. He watches what you drink, what you eat and how you do your lives for he really does carry the integrity of Christ within him. Tatum is truly your teacher. This is what he shares and what he brings more and more into the lives of everyone he meets.'

We are doing our best to find some sense of normalcy for Tatum and the sudden loss of Harrison. Beyond his sleeping being affected, he seems to be handling things quite well.

Our Art studio, with windows on all four walls is open and yet private with many large pine trees gracing our yard. The room has been set up with easels, paints and all my art supplies and is ready for my exploration at any time, day or night. I so appreciate having the freedom to create freely and in a beautiful space. Promptly, the paintings seem to be pouring out of me.

In my dreamworld,

'I am in a quaint, old house with little rooms and tall thin wooden doorways. In one particular bedroom hangs a special painting of a woman in blue. Everyone in the family thinks Cameron painted it. He receives all the praise for the lovely painting's depth and beauty. I excitedly tell myself in the dream, my family would finally realize my brilliance, for you see, I had painted this piece.

I am so proud, my family would soon realize my worth through the unveiling of my creation. I walk into the bedroom one last time, before

I reveal to my brothers and sisters the truth of this masterpiece.

It is gone; the painting is gone! The wall is blank besides a little nail from which the painting had hung. I blink my eyes to make sure I'm seeing correctly. I feel deep fear crawling up from the pit of my stomach.

"What?" I grasp searching for air.

Slowly, I turn to Cameron who appears out of nowhere.

"Where's my 'Magical Realms' painting?"

"I gave it to Mrs. Conner at Goodwill."

I am not sure I've heard him correctly.

I swallow, "Come again?"

"I gave your painting to Goodwill," he says laughing.

In the dream, I wondered about the reality of my life. Does Cameron downplay my light? I despise him. I find the depths of a scream forming within me. The first attempt to move it out of me only brings a little noise from my throat. The next try is a futile attempt from my gut. The last attempt, ah yes, the last attempt to scream let out all my anger to this man. It came bursting from somewhere deep, deep within me; a place I had never touched before.'

My scream pierces the quiet night air. As it bellowed out of me, Merrick awakens trying to grasp what is happening.

"What is it honey? You're shaking all over? he asks as he reaches out to touch me.

When I could find my breath again, I slowly tell him the details of the dream.

"My frustrations with Cameron. Finally some of my anger has been released."

— *Magical Realms*

Well, who would have seen this coming? Merrick and I are taking dear, sweet, ten year old Tatum to prison, to visit his Dad's new Home/Ashram. I'm learning the difference between jail and prison? Jail is the temporary place of confinement until the appropriate sentencing and placement is chosen. Prison is the long term version, as Harrison will be in prison for a very long time, basically until Tatum is almost an adult.

We arrived at 8:00am when visitation for Harrison's unit begins. Little did we know we are overdressed, I had brought a little purse for my identification photo which is mandatory. Consequently, my little purse has to go back to the car. We fill out the necessary paper work and then after the long walk to the car and back, we attempt to go through the scanners and again. NO, I couldn't take my sunglasses. This is sunny Tucson for goodness sake. No sunglasses allowed, so back to the car again.

Sitting outside on benches, waiting for our names to be called again, I am pleased that at least we are able to be outside enjoying the pleasant weather. We watch with interest as other people go through the scanning system much like our airports. Basically, this place echoes the unmistakable thought, "we trust nobody here."

Two black women are sitting across from us and they could

tell we are newbies to this game, as one of them mentions,

"Do you realize you can only take coins inside, paper money is not allowed. There are no food or drinks available, except what you buy at the vending machines. There's a gas station down the road if you need to get change."

"Thanks," I say smiling in appreciation of their extension of kindness.

Clearly, we need to return to our car yet again, where I find a grand total of $1.75 in coins. And we aren't allowed to take any water bottles inside. So get this, one of the many ironies of this system is we are allowed to take a pack of cigarettes inside, but not a water bottle. What?

Back at base again, we await our admission to the show.

A young woman attempts to go through the scanner after taking off her shoes and putting her plastic bag of coins and I.D. and something on her body sets off the beeper. Everyone looks and she is faced with the realization she may not be able to enter the doors of doom. It's obvious she is there to see a loved one, as tears quickly find their way down her cheeks. The army-like female guard asks her several questions as to any of the many possibilities for setting off the scanners. No, she answers to all of the questions.

"Are you wearing a bra with an underwire in it?"

"Yes," she admits.

"Well, you have two options if you want to enter today, take off the bra or cut the sides of your bra and bring the wire back to me?"

"I suppose I'll go to the bathroom and take out the wires," she surrenders.

We watch with fascination at this drama. I'm attempting to digest this as a new part of our lives now that Harrison is here for many years. The young lady returns and hands over the wire from her brazier like it is a weapon. Apparently, in their eyes anything can be considered dangerous.

Finally, our name is called again, and the woman is looking at my t-shirt and she says I can't wear it in because my collar bones are showing. What? Really? I look at Merrick and he looks at me with his "what the heck do we do now look." I'm not feeling comfortable with Tatum going in without me, when Merrick remembers he has a t-shirt in the car that just might fit. At this point, I really don't care what I am wearing; I just want to get this visit over and leave this bizarre world. Back to the car...again. Hi Sophie. My car loves all the attention, I suppose.

Fortunately, Merrick's t-shirt covers my collar bones and I am able to enter. All three of us make it through the scanner success-fully. Next, as we are standing in the open hallway awaiting the door to open, a guard shouts at us, "Stand with your backs to the fence on your left."

We all jump and press our backs to the chain link fence. I hear commotion and scuffling so I turn slightly to look behind me and on the other side of the fence is a large german shepherd sniffing our butts. I am ready for anything at this point.

Having passed the multitude of 'tests', we are now allowed to enter through the huge metal doors. We cautiously move through the first massive door and the next door doesn't open until the one behind us has fully closed. There's a moment of awkward silence until the next door opens. Ah, fresh air again. We emerge to await our prison bus which will take us to the appropriate unit.

Within five minutes, a shiny new shuttle pulls up and the doors open automatically. The young driver smiles broadly and asks, "Your destination?" Merrick and I exchange glances. It eerily feels as if we stepped into an airport and the shuttle driver is asking what airline we want.

The giveaway is that the driver is dressed in all orange prison wear and he wants to know what correctional unit to drop us off at.

"Lowchester, please." I find my mouth to speak but my voice

inside is saying, "OMG, we are being driven by one of the inmates."

We scurry aboard, moving toward the back of the shuttle. As the doors close, I look around to see we are the only ones on this vehicle. Curiously, I watch this man with tattoos all over his arms, as he drives happily along. As I pull Tatum close to me in the vinyl seat, I need to justify this decision to bring Tatum here, by telling myself, "Of course the driver must have proven himself to be driving around this complex with innocent people."

I take another deep breathe to calm myself remembering my anxious feelings can affect Tatum as well. As we move through the complex, I am able to view the entire area, which is a huge open field with one story tan buildings surrounding it. There are actually a few cacti in the courtyard. Yes, we need to bring some cheer to Harrison. Besides being visually bland, my eyes take me to the twenty foot tall fences surrounding us with curled razor wire at the top. This prison reality sinks in again on a deeper level.

The ride is short and soon we see his Unit written largely on the building front. It follows the rest of the complex design, a tan one story building. We walk up to the huge doors trying to determine where to enter. As we are looking for the correct entrance, the door buzzes and Merrick reaches for the handle. It opens easily considering it is huge and about eight inches thick. We are greeted by a man in a tan uniform and he asks for our photo ID's. This is the third time we've had to show them this morning.

"I'll keep these until you leave today," he says.

I'm about to object when my inner voice advises me differently. Of course, they will be in safe hands until we leave; we are in a guarded prison. I am constantly reminding myself to trust.

We can visit Harrison for two hours. In this area, where all the sex offenders are kept, I am already wanting to leave before we even enter. The guard ushers us toward the opposite entrance way. Again, we wait for the doors behind us to close before the doors in front of us open and allow us into the final hallway.

A new guard says,

"Harrison is waiting for you through the doorway on your right."

The man I shared a history with, greets us wearing his orange outfit and smiling face. He appears somewhat anxious, despite his ample grin. He is clearly moved to see Tatum, his beautiful son. Tears well in his eyes, as he gives him a quick hug. As we find out later, he is only allowed to touch Tatum briefly.

"I am so happy to see you, Tatum."

Harrison doesn't seem to be able to take his eyes off his son, as if a blind man being able to see again. His smile is plastered on his face as he directs us to one of the many square tables with four chairs, although there are some larger round tables. As I scan the long rectangular room, there is a pleasant aura of appreciation as each table has a single orange outfit with all eyes of their family and friends on them. To the right is a long row of vending machines with a variety of drinks, snacks and sandwiches.

"How are you?" Harrison asks looking at Tatum then to me.

"I am good," Tatum offers. I notice a bit of apprehension in him.

I take a deep breathe and let my shoulders relax a bit, as I am surprised how comfortable I'm now feeling even though we're in a prison. There's a steady stream of conversation amongst the fifty or so people in the room. I look out the side wall of glass doors and see a covered patio with many picnic tables. Harrison notices me looking outside and says we can go outside if we want, after we've had a chance to talk.

"How are you really doing Harrison?" I get the conversation going.

Harrison has always had an opinion on things and is clearly ready to talk.

"I was concerned you weren't coming when you were so late."

"Yeah, sorry about that, we had to go back to our car four times; the

last trip to change my shirt because my collar bones were showing,"
I giggle.

"Welcome to my reality," he says matching my laughing. "Is that why you are wearing a Deathly Hallows tshirt?"

We all have a needed laugh.

"Yes, tell us about your new life," I say.

"I'm working in the bakery and I'm teaching Tai Chi classes."

"Really?"

"A bakery?" Merrick says surprised.

He nods his head, "Yeah, it's one of the few jobs in here."

"What is your cell like?" I ask.

"Well, it isn't actually a cell, I am in a large room with about forty men and only three bathrooms."

"Really?" I shudder.

"What's your bed like?" Tatum chimes in.

"Well, Tatum, if you want to call it a bed but it's more like a cot."

"Is the food good?" he asks again.

"Pretty bland and all out of cans, but it's edible. I sure miss my fresh organic meals from Sedona."

Harrison changes the subject, "How's school Tatum?"

"I'm liking Math and art. Hey, I see a table of games and cards, can we play something?"

"Sure," we all say in unison as we're all fidgeting at this point.

I watch Tatum go to the game table and look back at Harrison.

Taking advantage of Tatum's absent ears—for he misses nothing—I whisper, "How is it really?"

"Crazy, Rhea. I have had to prove myself; that I would stand up for myself. If you let your guard down in here or show any weakness, they take advantage of you, in every way," he says while rolling his eyes.

"But I've made connections in here. I mean, once I've proven myself, we all support each other. You learn to find your place and what works and what doesn't. Like I said, I offer Tai Chi classes to some of the guys. I'm thinking of a meditation group next. I checked out some buddhism books from the prison library."

Merrick's eyes are wide open, "You know, Harrison, this sounds like more of an Ashram than a prison."

There is a smile growing on Harrison's face as that thought clicks in his mind as well.

Tatum has returned to our little table with a deck of cards. Through our written letters, Harrison and I had agreed we would not speak of the full reality of prison life in front of Tatum. The conversation moves back into the safe zone once again.

We play a card game and for a few moments it feels semi-normal, like we could be playing Hearts in some hotel lobby. Tatum does very well and seems to enjoy winning. Afterwards we spend time outside, walking the small courtyard and sitting at the picnic tables; us on one bench and Harrison on the opposite one. This arrangement is not by choice but by law.

When the guards announce closing time we all migrate back inside and say our goodbyes.

I had walked into this prison expecting to find a bunch of criminals, instead I found a community of men.

We promise to return.

It seems every effort has a purpose in the overall scheme of things. When I was introduced to Hypnotherapy, I had no idea it would change my life so drastically. This is why I am thrilled to share it with my Clients. I work in the People Industry, assisting people to become healthier, emotionally clearer and finding more of their authentic self. In my many years of doing trance work, I certainly have seen a lot happen in my office. And I've had the pleasure of meeting most of our historical Guides, such as Buddha, Jesus, Archangel Michael, Mother Mary, and many loved ones from the other side. Even deceased relatives and pets come and visit my clients in their inner world.

I have created a powerful and unique style of working with my clients, called Nouveau Hypnotherapy, which allows them to gently crack open their hearts, minds and souls. This is not necessarily glamorous work, rather it is a sacred service, which I have been guided to do.

I've experienced so many modalities from working with five different Spiritual Retreat companies in Sedona, and I still find the Inner Journey to be the most insightful and powerful of them all. From all my own soul searching and changing, I'm pleased to share these spiritual sessions with others.

My Clients are guided to their inner world, to the part of their brain where memories and imagination work together and waking consciousness is reduced so intuition can become available. They genuinely feel emotional because any unresolved situations can be met and ideally released. I joke with my friends that my job is making people cry. Symbolically, my job is to scrape caked-on-grime off the pots and pans in the sink of the subconscious mind. As it is released, any of the buried feelings come to the surface, often in the form of tears.

This process introduces my Clients to their own inner world where they can meet the magical, archetypal part of themselves, their Guides and any shadow part that needs to be released. Once we shine the light on their old beliefs, they lose their power and new beliefs can be created.

I love my office with its high ceiling and loft on the left side, adorned with lush plants overlooking the natural light bouncing off the white cotton curtains and spanish tile floor. My client, Jon, who is from Brazil, sits in the white leather chair across from me. His dark piercing eyes appear to be hungry for something he may not even be aware of.

"How are you?" I begin.

"Fine. And you?"

His hands, with perfectly trimmed finger nails, have a movement suggesting a nervousness within.

"I am great. As my son Tatum says, it's the kind of day where you can throw water on your head and it's OK."

"Yeah, I saw your husband and Tatum leaving as I arrived. You have some nice looking men in your life."

"Thanks," with a slight grin, I continue, "what brings you to Sedona right now? What are you seeking?"

"I'm visiting with my wife. We've been married for 31 years. The main reason, I am here is because I don't feel she loves me. My wife just doesn't love me," Jon says sadly.

"What makes you feel this way?" I ask as I reach for my note pad.

"By the way she treats me, she criticizes me and bosses me around," Jon responds.

"How does that make you feel?" I ask.

"Lonely and sad, well, I feel unloved. See...she really doesn't love me," he reveals as tears fill his eyes.

"I understand this situation must be confusing and it would seem she doesn't love you, however, let's look at this dynamic from a different angle, shall we?"

"I am here, I am committed," he says a bit defensively.

"Here's a question for you; are you ready?"

"Sure," he says easily.

"Do you love yourself? I mean really love yourself?" I ask.

"Well, I don't know," he pauses and looks up to this left side.

"Sounds a bit cliche doesn't it? I mean, loving yourself," I prod.

"Well yes, that does sound a bit, as you say, cliche," he replies.

"Imagine this? You're wanting her to love you, correct?"

"Yep."

"Then you're asking your wife to do something you may not be doing yourself," I reply.

Jon's demeanor has lost some of its strength as he says slowly, "Good. Point."

He remains cute despite his turned up nose. In fact his action compliments his boyish face with his perfect tan.

"Yes, I'm beginning to understand. I think I get it," his body seems to relax a bit. "If I want my wife to love me, I need to love myself first. But how? How do I love myself."

He shifts in his chair leaning forward with a clear desire to engage more, "That's...hmm...interesting. How can I expect her to love me when I don't even love myself!"

"From my perspective, I believe we teach others how to treat us by how we treat ourselves. So treat yourself with the kindness, love and acceptance you want from others."

"I never thought of it that way."

"I suggest you consider becoming your new best friend," I reply.

"This is an 'ah ha' moment for me," Jon pauses then asks, "Do you practice this idea?"

"Absolutely, I'm practicing loving myself each day as much as I can. Some days are easier than others. As I turn my focus inward, I'm seeing more and more of my outer world change around me."

"Could you give me an example?" he asks.

"Sure, I've been a victim in this life and the best way I found to move beyond this was to change the way I think of myself. I am changing my reality a little more each day, by committing to looking within and loving myself. Then my world shows me this. It's quantum physics at play."

"Change my thinking? But how?" he asks excitedly.

"I am going to guide you within to meet more of your guidance, wisdom and truth," I say.

"I think I am ready. And this will help me to love myself as well?"

"What do you think?"

"Well, if I have everything I need within me, then I can learn more about my Authentic Self. Is this correct?"

"Yes."

"And," Jon excitedly continues, "if I learn more about myself, then I can appreciate more of who I really am?"

"Go on."

"Then this can lead to loving myself."

"You got it! Ideally, you will witness how amazingly complex you are within, then the process of loving yourself will be natural. You see, when you're feeling your truth, you can find the love within you," I assure him.

Lying in my reclined chair, Jon is gently guided to his inner Circle to meet his archetypal parts. His sixteen year old self appears, then his nine year old self moves into the Circle, then his five year old self shyly comes into the circle. Jon welcomes all of them and gives each a warm hug.

Going deeper into hypnosis, Jon's mother had left his one year old self in a crib. Jon's focus is taken to the baby who is crying hysterically. Jon reveals to me that his mom had left him alone for days in the crib. Sadly, adult Jon is watching little baby Jon crying and screaming for attention, wanting to be loved. As he got in touch with his little child's anguish and pain, adult Jon cried and cried.

I have him make an agreement to this little boy that he, as the adult, will take care of and nurture this little boy. He readily agrees as he holds him and rocks him for almost an hour. They form a bond together and adult Jon agrees to always be there for little Jon. His tears of joy flow as a wonderful reuniting occurs.

Jon's 59 year old body has been carrying this need for love and attention a very long time. Now the healing can begin.

After coming back into the room and feeling lighter, I ask, "How are you feeling?" while handing him some water.

"Exhausted, yet relieved," he says slowly.

"May I share my interpretation?" I ask making sure he is feeling present enough to listen.

"Yes, please," he signals with a thumbs up sign.

"Jon, this could have been the beginning of the belief you are unlovable. It really has nothing to do with your wife. And you have been carrying this idea around that you are unlovable your entire life. It is time to let this belief go, would you agree?"

"Oh my, yes," Jon says with heightened energy coming back into his body. "That was truly amazing!"

"Just be aware where any of these feelings come up for you. Honoring your agreement to love your little boy that so needs you.

My experience has shown me that if you commit to greet this part of yourself each and every day, this little baby boy can grow up emotionally and be the man you are physically. Does that make sense?"

"I think I get it," he says. "I really had no idea all that was in there. I was surprised how aware I was of everything that was going on. And I agree to love myself each and every day as much as I can."

Merrick and I have been invited to explore the sailing world of Belize. This possibility is beyond enticing as neither of us have been on the open sea for an entire week! We've been dancing around the kitchen while we cook dinner and sip on a cold beer. Even though its October, the Arizona weather still hits the 90's during the day with lots of bright sunshine.

Our eclectic home is very comfortable, with our personal art pieces embellishing the walls and ornate masks collected from around the world expressing their ethnicity. People comment how they appreciate the feel of our home. The previous owner of our house traveled around the world and collected diverse multi-colored rocks from the various places. These powerful rocks decorate the land, giving our home a nice grounded feeling.

As we are discussing our upcoming trip, we need to determine where Tatum can stay while we are gone. Thank Goodness, Tatum is dearly loved by his buddies and many of their Moms ask him to hang out at their house. One friend of Tatum's said, "Thanks for letting us have Tatum this whole time." This is a common sentiment. In fact, one day when Tatum was about 12 years old, he asked me why everyone likes him? This was a wonderful heartfelt moment for me as his Mommy. Having his Dad taken out of his life at such a vital age, Tatum could have gone in many directions, becoming the obnoxious teenager or the rebellious one like me. Instead he chose the higher perspective. Still the only thing Tatum has ever said about his father's disappearing act is, he feels sorry for him.

Finding a cat sitter for our two cats, a brother and a sister, Ninja and Segway, is important. I'm convinced Ninja is a transanimal, he is in a cat body, but he wants to be a dog. Ninja comes when I call him, chases objects, follows us around the house and wants a lot of attention, just like a puppy dog. While talking about the trip, I threw a wine cork for Ninja to chase and hopefully wear him out, just like a dog. The last one I tossed sent the wine cork out of my hand and right into Merrick's forehead, bopping off to the far end of the room with Ninja in pursuit. Merrick didn't move a muscle; he just looked at me. His lack of reaction made me laugh, as I found it even more humorous than the actual 'bonk on the head.'

"I opened your third eye!" I say, still laughing.

"That's not all you opened, look at Ninja." I turn my head to look and Ninja is literally smiling at us, with the wine cork in his mouth, as if proud of the shot as well.

I am excited to experience this new adventure on the sea. We'll be sailing with eight other people on a 60 foot sailboat and the captain, a private cook, Alex and his girlfriend. The other three young women are already waiting for us as we show up in Belize.

Before our journey begins on the vast ocean, a few of us decide on some sightseeing. We take a long tour into the jungle to the remote Mayan archaeological site, Lubaantun. This is an impressive rock city of temples and ball courts made with black stone. It has an unusual feeling to it and we push our Mayan guide to tell us more beyond his usual tourist spiel. He tempts us by saying the infamous Crystal Skull was believed to have been found here by the adventurer, Mitchell-Hedges. We ask for more information about how this city could have been built upon a plateau when the black stones originated near the river far below. He looks at us through different eyes and his scripted tour ends as he realizes we are open to hear more.

The ancient Maya of this community were made up of priests of different types. Some held rites for communicating with the Gods while others had duties involving more practical matters, like the building of the city. He explained the builder-priests had the ability to clear vast areas of jungle overnight. They also had the inner guidance to move massive stones from one location to another via levitation, even as high as this plateau. Some of these intuitive abilities were secretly passed down over generations through family members who had inner gifts. Other abilities were lost to time.

Apparently, 'this magical' gift was passed onto his grandmother. Her way of punishing the grandchildren was to have them line up facing her and she would put her hand above the head of the ones in trouble and actually move their bodies off the ground, levitating them for a brief moment. He said it scared them into behaving better. Wow. We are reminded of the big magic in this world when we choose to open our minds and look fully.

Our guide takes us to lunch at his family's little house. After a drive along dirt roads, we stop at a small adobe-like home with chickens and dogs wandering freely about. We walk into the first room, with barren walls and little open windows with no screens. Then my eyes meet a wooden table set beautifully with fresh flowers and all the accoutrements needed for fine dining. It was quite a contrast to the dusty dirt floor below, as chickens run in and out of the house. Their five children are all sitting on a wooden bench across the room, staring at us, as if they have never seen white folk before. The meal that follows surprises and delights our taste buds equally. Everything was grown or raised on the land surrounding us. Delicious chicken soup, hot bread dripping with butter, freshly squeezed orange juice, and papaya and star fruit are served for dessert. What a delightful day.

With our curiosity about the tropical land surrounding us pacified, we are ready to explore the great ocean. Excitedly, we board our sailboat at Caye Caulker to head out to the barrier reefs. As we step down into the cabin to put our bags in our sleeping quarters, I am amazed that everything is a small version of itself. A teeny kitchen which only holds two people, with a little sink and stove and a few tiny cabinets. Our cozy sleeping quarter is in the bow of the sailboat. Merrick and I try out the small size of our bed, and realize our feet will be touching as they meet at the bow. Lying on my back, I can touch the roof of the cabin by stretching my arm upward; it's that close. Appreciatively, Merrick and I do have our own head which accommodates only one person at a time.

Soon we cast off from the pier and head out to open waters. Riding the wind and waves is an amazing experience from growing up with traditional motorboats. There is no other sound than the rippling of wind on the sails and the lapping of waves on the bow. With only water everywhere the eye can see, we are thrilled when dolphins appear, racing alongside our boat in a dance of playful energy toward our first destination, the uninhabited tropical islands.

Snorkeling is a great lesson in trusting. While anchored in the waters, I ask one of the other woman, how to put on my goggles, mouthpiece and flippers. After she dove off the stern into the mysterious water below, she comes up and says, "It's easy, just put them on." I plummet into the glassy, fresh salt water and begin fumbling with all my gear. It becomes comical, as I am treading water trying to put on my new costume of the moment. My mask is on upside down which means my snorkel is cockeyed and keeps popping out of my mouth. By the time I have on all my gear, I am exhausted. This doesn't affect my enthusiasm of snorkeling, as beauty enhances my view in every direction. After fixing my gear, I enjoy the many colorful fish and the mystery of this underwater world.

We sailed onward for many days. Wanting to feel some earth beneath our feet, we stop at an island in the middle of the Caribbean. All we could see is water surrounding us in every direction. This is an eerie feeling not seeing anything, not even any people on the island. We splash in the water, play in the surf and make sand hills while basking in the privacy of all this beauty.

One starry night, appreciating the ocean breezes, a discussion leads to memorable dreams. I begin telling them about my flying dream,

"In my dream, I could feel myself flying through the sky, above the clouds, without any fear, just delight. Suddenly I see this very bright white light coming toward me and then passes by me ever so quickly. I turn my head to follow its glow and the light is gone out of sight within seconds. It seemed I was supposed to see it for some reason?" my voice raises with the wondering of the mysterious light?

"Rhea, could this have been your brother Cameron's spirit, as he had just passed over; is that possible?" one of the women asks.

"Honey, I was wondering the same thing when you first mentioned this dream," Merrick offers, "Was this Cameron's spirit? How cool is that idea!"

"My Clients have told me on numerous occasions how they see birds, dragonflies and other flying creatures after their loved one has passed over. They are convinced its them," I interjected.

"There's so much more to this life than we can even imagine!"

Oh my goodness! My body is covered with goosebumps as I ponder this possibility. Did I really see Cameron's spirit leave this planet as he was dying? I'll never truly know the answer to this question, however, its sure intriguing to wonder about it. I go to my dream world with this mysterious possibility.

Reflecting back to other trips Merrick and I have shared, there seems to be a common theme. Some kind of processing occurs for me, like facing my death in Hawaii or seeing a past life in Paris. On this boat are several lovely women and I realize I haven't been triggered by their running around in their teeny swim suits in front of Merrick. This truly is a wonderful change for me. I am open to relax and enjoy myself this whole trip!

Merrick looks at me and smiles, "You've come a long way baby. Let's enjoy the motion of the ocean. Let me help you take off your invisibility cloak, for Good!"

I had my infamous dream again. The 'frightening feeling of' the dark corner and the walk around the block was still present, however, this was a bit different.

The dream begins with me in some unknown living room on the third floor of a strange building. Through the front door walks the same tall, mysterious man from my childhood dreams, and he is clearly after me. Fear envelops my body and I realize I have to get away from this man or he may kill me. I run to the closest window and realize I'll have to jump out of it to the hard concrete street below to escape him. I take the plunge, even though I am barefooted and continue running through the streets with him close behind me. He continues chasing me for what feels like a very long time. I am exhausted and am pleased to see some friends parked on the street in a station wagon. I hop in for safety.

The man walks up to the station wagon and I begin breathing deeply not knowing what he wants from me. He gets in the car with us and interacts in a friendly way with everyone in the car. I am the last person he speaks with. He looks deeply into my eyes and I realize there is nothing to fear of this man. I am surprised by the amount of love I feel for him! This is the same man I have met within my nightmare dream so many times before. Ironically, I came to realize this tall mysterious man only wanted to LOVE me!

After awakening from the dream, I realize I have been running from LOVE my entire life. I have been afraid to love fully because I had learned that love was painful and secretive. I learned that love meant rejection as well. I've been running from my family, running from love relationships, running from friendships, running from jobs before I could get hurt again!

This tall mysterious man of my dreamworld simply represented love. I believed love had the power to actually kill me. I can now fully surrender to loving myself and anyone who wishes to dance in my loving reality. Just. Wow!

With this idea of trusting love, my mom and I were talking on the phone and after a sweet conversation she said, "Rhea, I love you! I love you very much!" I am beaming from this conversation. This reminds me how I feel inside is what is created outside. My outer world simply matches what I'm feeling within!

I have lived two lives. The first one, I learned. The second one, I chose how I live. I've made a conscious effort to live my second life; my life of choice!

Finally, I understand I am the one who created my self-made prison and I am the only one who can break free of its bars. It's time. This is where the true beauty lies; it's all within me. The culmination has my mind spinning with possibilities and is a beautiful reminder of me claiming my world and focusing on myself. It is all about Me, as I proclaim I will be vigilant to own my unique personality. Finding my own center and being able to see both sides of any situation; allowing for more compassion in myself. I will not allow others to affect me or for me to take on their remarks, ideas, and misunderstandings of me, personally. Not any longer, as I own my inner Beauty and appreciate I'm doing my best.

After doing my meditation and yoga, which helps me to find my higher vibration within, I am ready to start my day. I am greeted by the warm Arizona sunshine as I walk, feeling something foreign clinging to my skin, something without a name; something new. I walk slowly through the tree-lined streets, trying to find an accurate term for this feeling; not worrying about whether there's anyone looking at me and indifferent to the chance of bumping into someone who can trigger me whenever I approach the next corner. There is no external signs on me to suggest I'm a different woman then the one who'd walked this pavement many times before, perhaps in the same clothes and my feet in the same funky shoes. No one who saw me going then and returning now would have been able to detect any change, except I AM NO LONGER CARRYING THE HEFTY BURDEN OF NEEDING TO PROVE MYSELF! FINALLY I FEEL I AM ENOUGH.

I know in my heart what has changed, as each lingering step has a new, subtle confidence. What I feel in my bones, as the final rays of sunlight accompany my return home, isn't what I would term happiness, either. Or emotion. Or excitement. Perhaps the words that best align with this feeling accompanying me is compassionate pride. For the first time in a long while, perhaps for the first time in my life, I feel proud of myself. Proud of what I'm capable of and what I have moved through; proud of taking space to find ME. I'm proud of forgiving myself. Proud to know I'm capable of making this mad world an easier place for myself, my family and my Beloved Clients. I'm proud of the brilliant woman I'm becoming and finding the courage to love Myself.

Yes, it's true that Jade had helped me grow into my adult self. Eli had spurred me on to move to many new places, ultimately introducing me to lovely Sedona, while teetering me on the very edge at times. Just as it is true that Harrison had created a life with me to bring lovely Tatum into my world. Without Tatum, I may not have lived to tell this story. Yes, all that is true. But it is Merrick who mirrors both my dysfunctions and possibilities to me, more than I could have even imagined, and introduced me to my higher guidance. It's also true that I'd made my own contributions, with my courage and my endless determination, to bring the mission I'd been spiritually assigned to a successful ending/beginning. All my fears, all the sleepless nights, and the flying leaps without a safety net had been worth something after all: not only to reveal beliefs that would assist in putting an end to my inner war, but especially, to show myself and those around me what I am truly capable of: real success in being my true self!

As I became aware of this possible reality, I know the time has come for me to stop going down the paths other people have made for me; putting an end to the "victim" ancestral lineage I'd inherited. It will stop with me!

It had been Eli's idea to go to Sedona, Harrison's presence that solidified the idea to have a baby and Merrick's presence that allowed me to trust my heart with love. And a special thanks to Grey for showing me the dysfunction of trying to control others. I'd passed between them from hand to hand, like a child looking for love. For the glory of heaven or the flames of hell, they had all made decisions for me.

These men, probably without any of them being aware of it, were helping me to mature in different ways. Each of them taught me how to trust, not necessarily to trust in them, but for me to trust in myself. I probably wouldn't see Eli or Jade again. As for Merrick, I'm sure I'll be seeing him for quite some time. I'm eager to keep him exactly as close as he'd been in the early hours of this morning: a closeness of affection and bodies; the recollection of which still makes me delightfully squirm.

It is now time for me to create some personal enlightenment. Time for me to take the reins of my own existence, to choose my path, to decide who I truly am. I'd tumbled along the way, encountered sharp edges, accidents, and shadows of darkness. I trust I'm facing an easier future as I continue to listen and trust my Guidance. Will I continue to stumble? Yes, of course, however now I choose to "get back up" with grace, integrity and freedom. I no longer have to prove myself to anyone. That's my idea of real freedom!

But, most important of all, I will define my new terrain like Tatum drawing a line on the ground with a colorful piece of chalk. This is my crazy life and I am grateful for it. It guides me to soar like the Phoenix from the ashes. And even though it feels as if I have a rebel spirit at times, at least I'm courageous enough to be me.

— *Honoring the Feminine*

Imagine Getaways Retreats

I have been a hypnotherapist for over 25 years, working with five different retreat companies in Sedona, Arizona.

Imagine Getaways Retreat Company was created from this experience paired with my own creative twist. I have had the pleasure of guiding a variety of sessions for people where traditional therapy was not enough. **Nouveau Sessions** invoke self-exploration and insight of 'old ways of thinking and being' that no longer apply. The goal being to transform and become more of your Authentic Self.

Beyond guiding my clients to the freedom of being their true self, I live this freedom in my personal life.

Imagine Getaways is a lovely dance between depth, wisdom, truth, creativity and fun! Are you ready for a Personalized Solo retreat with me?

I will design the perfect Retreat just for You.

Call for a free consultation today: 928.204.0878
or visit www.imaginegetaways.com

Imagine Getaways Testimonials

"Opening up with you feels right; a safe place where fear, intimidation, judgment and shame hold no power, exploration is welcome and trust can grow. You guided me with such kindness, gentleness and compassion into places I never dreamed of going, never wanted to go and yet so needed to go. You respectfully and honestly answered my many questions. Having you as my spiritual guide, life coach, teacher, confidante and friend...no amount of money is enough. Your gifts are that huge!"
— Jen, Colorado

"An orchestrated and truly remarkable four-day retreat awaited me. On our first call, she listened and understood my needs. She worked in concert with me and my personality. When I resisted, she used alternative angles until I was able to break through the blocks — no small feat for me! My personalized retreat was well-balanced between deep-dive intensity and fun. She is truly gifted and I am beyond grateful she was my guide through to the openings I achieved."
— India, Connecticut

"She is amazing! I came to her with a sad spirit soul – one full of shame and in need of inspiration, motivation and the ability to forgive. With her inner and outer journeys, she guided me to restore my spirit soul, my joie de vivre, my spark. She saved me from myself. She is exceptional in her abilities to sort through a person's chaos so they can heal themselves and move forward. I will be eternally grateful that our paths crossed.'
—Laura, Canada

"The art sessions I experienced with Rhea changed my life! By tapping into the flow of my creativity, I was able to let go of my mind and sink fully into my heart. It allowed me to open to new ideas, as I literally felt like my imagination had dried up and gone away forever. The joy and freedom of being able to express myself fully in a safe place is a gift beyond words. I'm grateful."
— Lise, Sedona

Thanks for reading **Rebel Spirit**. Please pass it on to someone who could benefit from my story of feeling invisible to becoming a courageous person with a powerful voice.